Studies in Jewish and Christian Literature

Messiah and the Throne, Timo Eskola
Father, Son, and Spirit in Romans 8, Ron C. Fay
Defilement and Purgation in the Book of Hebrews, William G. Johnsson

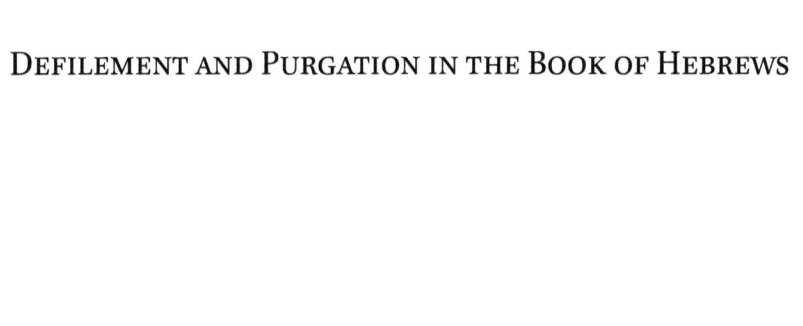

Defilement and Purgation in the Book of Hebrews

William G. Johnsson

Fontes

Defilement and Purgation in the Book of Hebrews

Copyright © 2020 by William G. Johnsson

ISBN-13: 978-1-948048-29-3 (hardback)
ISBN-13: 978-1-948048-30-9 (paperback)

All rights reserved. No part of this publication may be reproduced, stored in a retrieval system, or transmitted in any form or by any means—electronic, mechanical, photocopy, recording, or any other—except for brief quotations in printed reviews, without the prior permission of the publisher.

FONTES PRESS
DALLAS, TX
www.fontespress.com

Contents

1. An Enigma and Its Significance.. 1

2. The Cultus of Hebrews in Modern Investigation......................... 13
   The Issue of Continuity/Discontinuity of the Old Cultus and Christianity.....29
   The Question of the "Spiritualizing" of the Cultus 31
   The *Religionsgeschichtliche* Approach to the Cultus of Hebrews 35
   The Issue of the Canons of Interpretation of the Cultus of Hebrews 37
   The Issue Regarding the Significance of the Cultus in the Study of Hebrews...39
   The Possibility of Employing General Patterns of Religion
     to Illumine the Cultus 41

3. Towards a Methodology Appropriate to the
   Cultic Language of Hebrews 45
   Formal Questions of Methodology.. 46
   The Nature and Interrelations of Defilement, Blood and Purgation 53
     A Phenomenology of Defilement 53
     A Phenomenology of Blood 66
     A Phenomenology of Purgation 74
     Defilement, Blood, and Purgation in Dynamic Relation 84
   Conclusion 94

4. Defilement, Blood, and Purgation in the Book of Hebrews:
   An Exegesis of Hebrews 9–10 97
   Contextual Considerations.. 99
   The Leitmotif(s) of the Passage 9.1–10.39................................... 103
   The Nature and Interrelations of Blood, Defilement, and Purgation.......... 106
     Defilement and Purgation 116
     Defilement, Blood, and Purgation in Dynamic Relation 123
   The Progress of the Argument in Hebrews 9–10 127
   Blood, Defilement, and Purgation Elsewhere in Hebrews..................... 164
   Conclusion 169

5. Cultus and Pareneses—Defilement and Purgation in Relation
   to the Total Argument of Hebrews 173

6. Conclusions and Implications.. 193
   Implications of the Study 198
     Methodological 198
     The Historical Situation of Hebrews 201

Bibliography... 203
   Books and Reference Works... 203
   Articles 209

Chapter 1

An Enigma and Its Significance

The book of Hebrews confronts the modern Western mind much like Otto's *das Heilige*—[1] it at once stupefies and attracts. On one hand, it sets out its convoluted argument in terms of priests, sacrifices, and holy places reserved for the initiates. Moffatt[2] was correct: we today have no true concept of the ancient office of priesthood, which was similar to that of consecrated butcher. Even farther away is the thought of bloody offerings—a repulsive suggestion to the "enlightened" occidental conscience. And where in the secular city is to be found a place where one may feel a numinous dread upon entering? New York has no burning bushes! In short, the *auctor ad Hebraeos* selected categories of argumentation that are singularly unhelpful to us.[3] And yet—Hebrews continues to attract: there is the puzzle. If in some places the reasoning leaves the exegete groping, in others it appears to be devastatingly simple.[4] The masterly language, the broad sweep of ideas, above all, the impression that here is a brilliantly creative writer who is in no doubt as to the course of his argument even if we are—all serve not only to fascinate but to elicit a wholehearted grappling with the text.

---

1 Rudolf Otto, *The Idea of the Holy. An Inquiry into the Non-Rational Factor in the Idea of the Divine and Its Relation to the Rational*, 2nd ed., trans. John W. Harvey (Oxford University Press, 1950).

2 James Moffatt, *A Critical and Exegetical Commentary on the Epistle to the Hebrews*, ICC (T&T Clark, 1924), xlvi.

3 Hermann Strathmann, *Der Brief an die Hebräer*, Das Neue Testament Deutsch (Vandenhoeck & Ruprecht, 1963), 73, states that Hebrews, because of the cultus, is the most foreign to us of all the New Testament writings.

4 But T. H. Robinson, *The Epistle to the Hebrews*, Moffatt Commentary (Harper, 1933), ix—"its thought is simple and usually obvious"—has surely overstated the matter.

Indubitably it is the cultus that presents the leading difficulty to the student of Hebrews. By "cultus" we understand that which pertains to corporate *worship*, especially as such worship is considered in terms of priesthood and sacrifice.[5] The passage 7.1–10.18 is therefore at the heart of the enigma of Hebrews. Yet the scope of the cultus is certainly broader, encompassing in addition at least 4.14–5.10, 12.18–24, 13.10–16 and possibly 1.1–14.[6] Indeed, Hebrews presents such a "seamless robe" that the often made assignations of its material as "parenetic" or "cultic"[7] disguise the interwoven texture of the letter.

Cult: the very word has unfortunate associations in modern thought. It conjures up snake handlers in the mountains of Tennessee, voodoo rites in Haiti or Melanesian devotees of the wildly "enthusiastic" "cargo cults." It signifies "primitive," "magical," "superstitious," "mysterious," "uncritical."[8] Small wonder, then, that commentators of Hebrews over and over are found to express their bafflement at the "foreign," "primitive" ideas that the writing embodies.[9] It follows that remarkably little attention has been given to the cultus *in its own right*.[10]

We may conveniently bring together the principal obstacles to understanding the writer's argument thrown up by the cultic roadblock: they are three. We have already referred to the first—the "outmoded" ideas of priest-

---

5 Cf. the definition of "cultus" in Philip Babcock Gove (ed. in chief), *Webster's Third New International Dictionary of the English Language, Unabridged* (1961): "organized religious practice or system of worship: the practical aspect of a religion embodying the aggregate of its ritual forms, sacred ceremonies, liturgies, rites, and all acts expressive of veneration or worship."

6 This does not include scattered references such as 2.17; 3.1; 4.9–10; 6.6; 11.4, 28; 13.20.

7 E.g., John H. Davies, *A Letter to Hebrews*, Cambridge Bible Commentary (University Press, 1967), 15, sets out in parallel columns labelled "Doctrine" and "Exhortation" the material of the letter.

8 Thus, Gove, ed. in chief, *Webster's Dictionary*, includes under "cult": "a religion regarded as unorthodox or spurious ... a system for the cure of disease based on the dogma, tenets or principles set forth by its promulgator to the exclusion of scientific experience or demonstration."

9 A very extensive list might be drawn up. We shall confine ourselves to three writers: Spicq, Cody and Purdy. C. Spicq, *L'Épître aux Hébreux* (J. Gabalda, 1952), I, 1: "De toute la collection des écrits néotestamentaires, en effet, cette lettre est, avec l'Apocalypse, la plus éloignée au point de vue littéraire de notre mentalité occidentale et moderne." Aelred Cody, *Heavenly Sanctuary and Liturgy in the Epistle to the Hebrews* (Grail Publications, 1960), 1: "The depth of meaning in his ideas of heavenly sanctuary and heavenly liturgy is not so plain for those of us who live separated by a whole world of thought patterns from the religious and philosophical climate in which the Epistle was written." Alexander C. Purdy, *The Epistle to the Hebrews*, The Interpreter's Bible (Abingdon Press, 1955), 693, sees "primitive ideas of placating an angry deity, or of the magical efficacy of blood as averting penalty" behind the imagery of Heb 9.15.

10 This will become apparent in the follow chapter.

hood, sacrifice and holy place. Yet it is to be stressed that it is the Western, technological mind which finds insuperable difficulty at this point. After all, the Brahmin and the priest of Shinto still jealously watch over the most sacred rites of their respective religions; goats are yet slaughtered in the great temple to Kali in Calcutta; while no person may enter the Jainist, Buddhist, or Hindu temple or the mosque without removing his shoes. Beyond this immediate conceptual difficulty, however, is the fact that the *auctor ad Hebraeos* has *saturated* his writing with cultic terminology.[11] That is, we cannot suppose that we have done with the cult when we move away from the passages listed above. For instance, when we are told about "drawing near" to God (προσέρχομαι), in an apparently "parenetic" passage,[12] the metaphor is that of the priest entering the temple;[13] likewise, the famous eleventh chapter, with its roll call of "heroes," makes several references to the cultus.[14] In this light, clear cut distinctions of cultic-parenetic appear increasingly dubious.

Finally, we should make mention of the cultic presuppositions that undergird the argumentation. The best known of these occurs at 9.22—"without blood shedding there is no ἄφεσις." The modern mind immediately raises the question, Why? But no answer is forthcoming: for the writer, and presumably for his readers, the statement is axiomatic.[15] Likewise, 8.4 baldly states that a priest must have something to offer, 9.13–14 that the blood of animals avails to purge the flesh but Christ's blood extends to the cleansing of the conscience, 10.4 that it is impossible (ἀδύνατος) for animal blood to "take away" (ἀφαιρέω) sins and—most startling of all—9.23 that the "heavenly things" must be purified with better sacrifices than animals. If the painstaking exegete, tortuously following the writer's argument, has managed to overcome the first (conceptual) and second (linguistic) roadblocks, at this point (presuppositional) he apparently must admit defeat.

But, after all, how *significant* for the book of Hebrews is the cultus? If, as pointed out above, the cultus does pose considerable problems to the exegete, is not the writer's real purpose to be seen in the pareneses (granting, as is widely held, that the letter is primarily pastoral in its thrust)?[16] That is, may

---

11 Spicq especially has brought out this point; see e.g., his *L'Épître aux Hébreux*, I, 281–83.
12 Heb 4.16. The same term likewise occurs in a "parenetic" context at 10.22.
13 With A. Nairne, *The Epistle to the Hebrews*, Cambridge Bible for Schools and Colleges (University Press, 1957), 16. Nairne refers to Lev 21.17–23 and Ezek 44.1–16.
14 Vv. 4, 17, 28.
15 Cf. Moffatt, *Epistle to the Hebrews*, xlii: "We ask, why? But the ancient world never dreamt of asking, why? What puzzles a modern was an axiom to the ancient."
16 Kuss in particular has emphasized this point. O. Kuss, *Der Brief an die Hebräer*, Regensburger Neues Testament (Friedrich Pustet, 1953).

we not with Käsemann[17] (chapters 3–4 of Hebrews) or Dibelius[18] (chapters 12–13) find the focus of the writing outside the cultus?[19]

We shall treat at some length the previous investigation of Hebrews in the following chapter; however, it is necessary to deal here with the substance of the question raised above, inasmuch as it highlights the relative significance of the cultus in Hebrews. Surely it is the author himself who must give the verdict in this matter. We hold that, quite apart from our earlier remarks about the frequency of his cultic terminology, that verdict is made explicit at 1.3b and 8.1 and is implicit in his *dependence* upon the language of the cult in the course of his argument. Let us examine more closely each of these points.

Hebrews 1.3b contains one of the most frequently overlooked phrases of the letter. That the proem 1.1–4 is programmatic for the entire work is generally held; consequently, most commentators devote minute attention to each detail, that is, with the exception of 1.3b—καθαρισμὸν τῶν ἁμαρτιῶν ποιησάμενος—"having made purification for sins." Discussion of this phrase has confined itself to the textual problems,[20] to the sense of the genitive,[21] to the remarkable fact that this bare statement is the only reference to the earthly life of Jesus in the proem.[22] What has *not* been sufficiently recognized is that Christ's work is from the outset described by the *auctor ad Hebraeos* in cultic terms; nor has the nature of ἁμαρτία so designated—as a defilement requiring purgation—been adequately discerned. Were this the only mention of καθαρίζειν in the letter, 1.3b might not be significant;[23] yet, as we shall see in the course of the Käsemann, καθαρίζειν and its antithesis κοινός (defilement) are crucial to the argumentation of the work.[24]

---

17 Ernst Käsemann, *Das wandernde Gottesvolk*, 4 Aufl. (Vandenhoeck & Ruprecht, 1961).
18 M. Dibelius, "Der himmlische Kultus nach dem Hebräerbrief," *ThB*, XXI (1942), 1–11.
19 More recently, Bertold Klappert, *Die Eschatologie des Hebräerbriefs* (C. Kaiser, 1969), has drawn attention to the situation of the community addressed (weary, anticipating persecution) as the way to understand the document.
20 The sense of the aorist middle participle ποιησάμενος which is defectively conveyed by the Old Latin and Vulgate; also, the textual variant which includes δι' αὐτοῦ.
21 Cleansing of sins or from sins.
22 A capsule history of the earthly life is clearly not intended, however; it has been seen that this brief reference to the human Jesus is slanted in the direction of the later discussion of his high priesthood.
23 The exegesis of Heb 9–10 (Ch. 4 of this study) will show the importance of "defilement" and "purgation" for the argumentation.
24 Michel's contention that in 1.3 we have a hymn in no wise lessens the force of our point. The fact remains that the *auctor ad Hebraeos* has incorporated the hymn at this point—granting Michel's contention, and that he later returns to the motifs of defilement and purgation. See O. Michel, *Der Brief an die Hebräer*, Meyer Kommentar, 12 Aufl. (Vandenhoeck & Ruprecht, 1966), 96–104.

An Enigma and Its Significance

In 8.1, the writer reaches what is avowedly the "pith"[25] or "chief point" (κεφάλαιον) of his discussion: "We have such a high priest, one who is seated at the right hand of the throne of the Majesty in heaven...." Surely, we need not belabor his underlining of the cultus in this passage!

Not less convincing is the author's *dependence* on cultic terminology in the course of his argument. We have in mind the manner in which he refuses, as it were, to divest himself of the language of the cult at key points in the development of his work. His use of the term "blood" provides a striking illustration of this. In chapter 9, αἷμα occurs twelve times: it is undoubtedly a key word. In 10.5–10, the accent appears to move away from "blood" in favor of σῶμα ("body") and thence to θυσία ("sacrifice") at 10.12. Yet, in 10.19 as the writer begins his exhortation at the conclusion of the long argument of 8.1–10.18, he reverts to αἷμα.[26] Indeed, wherever he wishes to make his most emphatic assertions concerning the work of Christ, he without hesitation speaks in terms of "blood."[27] In view of such usage, it seems impossible to escape the conclusion that the cultic language of Hebrews was not merely some momentary illustration to be picked up and cast aside quickly in favor of the "real" meaning. No: the cult furnishes the vehicle for the most profound reflections of the writer. That is, the *auctor ad Hebraeos* apparently thought in cultic categories.

If the cultus of Hebrews is an enigma, it is therefore an enigma of the greatest significance to the overall work. The exegete cannot be justified in concentrating upon the parenetic sections: what if it should turn out that the paraenesis in fact arises in view of the author's cultic predilection? Then he will have been found putting the cart before the horse. Likewise, attempts to lay out a "structure" of Hebrews from purely external criteria[28] (chiasm, catchwords, and so on) without proof of corresponding content strike one as incredible exercises which serve to convince very few apart from the structural architects themselves.[29]

To find a way to "get inside" the cultus of Hebrews: this then is the object of this current study. I propose that it is by a study of the cultus from its human side—that is, its view of the human "problem" and "solution"—that such a path may be found. Specifically, I intend to give serious attention to

---

25 Following Coverdale's translation.
26 Αἷμα in fact occurs three times in ch. 10.
27 See e.g., 9.12, 14; 10.19, 29; 12.24; 13.12, 20.
28 The most important of these is provided by Albert Vanhoye, *La structure littéraire de l'Épître aux Hébreux* (Descleé de Brouwer, 1963).
29 A point made also by Hugh Montefiore, *A Commentary on the Epistle to the Hebrews*, Harper New Testament Commentaries (Harper & Row, 1964), 32.

the concepts and interrelations of the term "defilement" (humanity's "problem" according to the cultus) and its cultic correlate—"purgation." Inasmuch as the term "blood" plays, as we have seen, a dominant role in the cultic argumentation, it will be advantageous to consider the complex of ideas associated with the defilement-purgation in view of the understanding of "blood."

In fine, the study to be undertaken concerns itself with the anthropology revealed by the cultus. Previous studies of the cultus of Hebrews, such as there have been, have been interested primarily in the christological implications of cultus, thereby having their focus in the concept of priesthood.[30] While some of these studies have tentatively looked toward anthropology, as we shall see in the following chapter, there has been no work devoted exclusively to this topic. To this extent my study will break new ground.

That the anthropological concentration is well suited to the task of gaining entry to the cultus will be readily apparent. In the cultus we see humanity's efforts to find a way to approach God.[31] That such efforts reflect the understanding of deity is obvious, but just as clearly do they mirror the self-understanding of the devotees. If the sacrifice is in some way the *via media* for the "drawing near" to deity, it is also a reflection of the existential concerns of the one who presents it: it mirrors his religious unease, his sense of falling short, and his desire for the religious "solution" or "answer" to his "problem." There is a deep truth in Feuerbach's dictum[32] that theology is ultimately anthropology. We do not need to subscribe to Feuerbach's denial of the *extra nos* of religion to recognize that, simply because it is a *human* enterprise, it will inevitably tell as much about the self-understanding of the theologian as it does about God. Thus, the concentration of this Käsemann upon the ideas of "defilement," "blood," and "purgation" points us to the very heart of the cultus.

By now a presupposition of this study will have become clear: we regard Hebrews as, first of all, a *religious* document. Grässer[33] has placed the *auctor ad Hebraeos* along with Paul and "John" in the "Big Three" of New Testament theologians; less happily—indeed, quite mistakenly—has Schierse called him "an accomplished philosopher."[34] No one seems so far to have mentioned that he is a religious man; yet this is what he is, first and foremost, and first

---

30 See Ch. 2.

31 E. F. Scott, *The Epistle to the Hebrews* (T&T Clark, 1922), 129, argues that it is the author's "primary conception of religion as consisting, above all, in access to God" which gave rise to the cultic language.

32 L. A. Feuerbach, *Lectures on the Essence of Religion*, trans. Ralph Manheim (1851; repr., Harper & Row, 1967), 17.

33 Erich Grässer, "Der Hebräerbrief 1938–1963," *ThRu*, XXX (1964), 138–236.

34 F. J. Schierse, *The Epistle to the Hebrews*, trans. B. Fahy (Burns & Oates, 1969), xiii.

of all his letter is a religious document. It is a presupposition which very few are likely to challenge; indeed, it is taken for granted by commentators of Hebrews. Perhaps it is time, however, for someone to give the assumption its full valence. With all that has been written about the theology of Hebrews, almost nothing has been said about the religion of Hebrews.[35] We hope to make a beginning by the work of this Käsemann.

Since this study will constantly underscore the *religious* nature of the cultic language of Hebrews, we need to clarify our use of "religious" vis-à-vis "theological" language. We recognize that it can be argued that theological language is also religious language, so the proposed contrast is unreal. Yet the distinction of "religious" from "theological" is one that is made by other writers,[36] so it seems preferable to maintain the terminology and set out clearly the way in which we are to use the terms.

Joachim Wach's differentiation of "*endeictic*" from "*discursive*" expressions of religious experience provides a convenient beginning. "Endeictic" signifies that "by which something is pointed at, hinted at, or expressed in veiled form"[37]—and this describes "religious" language as we understand it. Religious language is seen most clearly in worship: anciently and today, it is the language of liturgy, hymns, and prayers. It is mythopoetic in form,[38] and tends to be spontaneous, emotive, and personalized. This language is the language of experience rather than of reflection: it struggles to express humanity's encounter with the Holy[39] and his questions of ultimate concern.[40] The

---

35 An exception is provided by E. W. Parsons, *The Religion of the New Testament* (Harper & Brothers, 1939), 140–58. Parsons' treatment, however, is brief and generalized: it lacks the thoroughgoing study of the cultus of Hebrews which we are attempting in this study.

36 E.g., ibid., 4–5; more recently, Clifford Geertz, "Religion as a Cultural System," *Anthropological Approaches to the Study of Religion*, ed. Michael Banton (Frederick A. Praeger, 1966), 2: "Nor is it necessary to be theologically self-conscious to be religiously sophisticated."

37 *The Comparative Study of Religions*, ed. Joseph M. Kitagawa (Columbia University Press, 1958), 60. Wach himself does not set out the contrast between religion and theology in terms of "endeictic" and "discursive" language; his employment of these terms for the overall expression of religious experience is in harmony with the use to which we put them here, however.

38 A point made powerfully by Paul Tillich. e.g., "The Nature of Religious Language," in *Theology of Culture*, ed. Robert C. Kimball (Oxford University Press, 1959), 53–67; "Theology and Symbolism," in *Religious Symbolism*, ed. F. Ernest Johnson (Kennikat Press, 1969), 107–16; "The Religious Symbol," in *Symbolism in Religion and Literature*, ed. Rollo May (George Braziller, 1960), 75–98.

39 Cf. Otto, *The Idea of the Holy*, passim. Eliade prefers to speak of the Sacred: cf. his various works, especially *Patterns in Comparative Religion*, trans. Rosemary Sheed, Meridian Books (World Publishing Co., 1970), and *The Sacred and the Profane*, trans. Willard R. Trask (Harcourt, Brace & World, 1959). G. van der Leeuw, however, prefers Power: cf. his *Religion in Essence and Manifestation*, trans. J. E. Turner (George Allen & Unwin, Ltd., 1938), passim.

40 Cf. Tillich, "The Problem of a Theological Method," *JR*, XXVII (1947), 23: "The presence of the demand for 'ultimacy' in the structure of our existence is the basis of religious experience."

cultic language of Hebrews clearly belongs in this category. Regardless of how structured the cultic argumentation may be, it is based on religious symbols. The very motifs which are the focus of this study—"defilement," "blood," and "purgation"—manifestly are religious symbols. It follows that they will only come to understanding if they are recognized as symbols and investigated in a manner appropriate to their nature.

The nature of "theological" language now will be clear. Whereas "religious" language expresses religious experience inductively, "theological" language expresses it discursively. Whereas "religious" language proceeds via myths and symbols, "theological" language seeks to articulate the "meaning" of the myths and symbols. So, while theological language also is concerned with religious experience, it is more reflective, systematic, definitive, and critical, and less emotive and personal than religious language. If religious language seeks to *express* the faith, theological language is faith seeking to *understand* itself.[41]

This distinction calls for two caveats. First, religious language is not "inferior" to theological language. To the contrary: religious language is indispensable, opening up a level of reality accessible by no other means.[42] Symbols such as defilement, blood, and purgation point to humanity's *Existenz* with a directness and power which no amount of discursive "explanation" can ever replace. Second, religious language is not exhausted by the investigations of the historian, the psychologist, the sociologist, or the linguist. Every religious datum is at once a historical datum (and therefore is amenable to investigation), but religion is not to be collapsed into history.[43] Consider "blood," for instance: a mere study of the history of its interpretations in a particular religion cannot engage the *religious* nature of the symbol. Only *as* the symbol is dealt with as religious—that is in terms of the demand for ultimacy and the encounter with the Holy—will it disclose its "meaning."

It follows that our attempt to grapple with the cultic argumentation centering in defilement-blood-purgation must neither take these symbols literally nor treat them as a code directly decipherable into matching abstract concepts. For this reason, this study is particularly concerned with questions of method. We shall argue that a method appropriate to the task of the study

---

41 Cf. Anselm's *fides quaerens intellectum. Prosloion*, I.
42 A point made often by Tillich; e.g., "The Nature of Religious Language," 56.
43 Cf. Eliade, *Patterns in Comparative Religion*, xiii: "A religious phenomenon will only be recognized as such if it is grasped at its own level, that is to say, if it is studied as something religious"; again in *Shamanism: Archaic Techniques of Ecstasy*, trans. Willard R. Trask (Pantheon Books for Bollingen Foundation, 1964), xiv: "Although the historical conditions are extremely important in a religious phenomenon (for every human datum is in the last analysis a historical datum), they do not wholly exhaust it."

is one which calls into its service insights from that discipline which is concerned with the religious per se—namely, *Religionswissenschaft*.[44]

While the particular topic of this study breaks new ground, our insistence that the prior question in a religious document should be raised at the religious level is not something new. Rudolf Bultmann, for instance, shares this view. He applauded the combating of the intellectualistic understanding of Christianity by the *religionsgeschichtliche Schule*.[45] Of Bousset's *Kyrios Christos* he wrote:

> In Wilhelm Bousset's brilliant *Kyrios Christos* (1913; 2nd ed., 1921) the religion of earliest Christianity appears, on the contrary, as essentially a cult-piety which sent forth as its flower: mysticism. One-sidedly but powerfully the basic idea is here carried through; and because many things are here seen in a new way, the problems which are active in New Testament theology emerge in a new light.[46]

Bultmann's own *Theology of the New Testament* shows his debt to *Religionsgeschichte*. In our endeavor to "get inside" the cultus of Hebrews by illuminating its ideas of "defilement," "blood," and "purgation," we see our task as roughly equivalent to Bousset's.[47]

That task will involve us in the following five steps:

1. Chapter 2 will examine the previous treatment of the cultus of Hebrews. We will confine ourselves to the modern period—from the time of Ferdinand Christian Baur. The investigation of the chapter is interested to see to what extent earlier students of Hebrews have

---

44 *Religionswissenschaft* is a more accurate title than the corresponding English name, "History of Religions." We discuss the methodology of *Religionswissenschaft* in the third chapter of this study.

45 Rudolf Bultmann, *Theology of the New Testament*, trans. Kendrick Grobel (2 vols.; Charles Scribner's Sons, 1954–55), II, 246.

46 Ibid., II, 246–47. Again, in his preface to the English edition of *Kyrios Christos*, trans. John E. Steely (Abingdon Press, 1970), Bultmann wrote: "Though it can be regretted above all that in his presentation, essential motifs of the New Testament, especially of Pauline theology, have not been brought into operation adequately, one must still remember that in *Kyrios Christos* Bousset did not intend to write a theology of the New Testament, but that he wrote a monograph, the theme of which to be sure can be characterized as the central theme of New Testament theology: 'the history of belief in Christ from the beginnings of Christianity down to Irenaeus.'" (p. 9).

47 The similarities lie in the common concern with the text as a *religious* document. The differences are due to the *historical* concerns which characterize Bousset's (and the *religionsgeschichtliche Schule* in general) but which are foreign to the methodology of phenomenology of religion. See *infra* on the methodology of this study (Chapter 3).

been aware of the problems which we have outlined above, and also to evaluate such treatments of them as have been hazarded.
2. In Chapter 3 we shall propose a methodology for coming to terms with the ideas of defilement, blood, and purgation. We shall argue that *Religionswissenschaft* points to a methodology appropriate to the cultic material of Hebrews.
3. Chapter 4 will afford a demonstration of the proposed method. We will show, by an exegesis of Hebrews 9–10, how the understanding of the text as a religious document may be strongly illuminated. In choosing these particular chapters for exegesis, we will be tackling some of the most difficult passages of Hebrews as well as taking up the very heart of the cultic argumentation of Hebrews.
4. This religious illumination of cultus has inevitable theological implications. They will be the concern of the fifth chapter. Specifically, we will have to come to grips with the relation of the anthropology suggested by the cultus to the understanding of the human situation as set forth in the rest of Hebrews.
5. The final chapter of this study will take up the inferences from the overall study. Here we are interested in two areas: methodology and history. That is to say, we will discuss methodological implications for New Testament research in general and the bearing of the study on the vexed question of the situation of Hebrews.

In closing out the concerns of the present chapter, it is necessary to give attention to two queries regarding the proposed study which are likely to spring to mind. They deal, first, with the questions of "introduction" for Hebrews which the study assumes, and, second, with the important caveat concerning the "seriousness" of the author in his use of cultic language.

As to the first query, the sad truth is that, despite the torrents of ink that have flowed regarding the writer and his readers, the "assured results" are practically nil. Concerning the identity of the *auctor ad Hebraeos*, Origen's verdict[48] has not been surpassed: only God knows! The situation of the readers (Gentile? Jewish-Christian? full congregation? a Jewish-Christian segment?) likewise remains in doubt. The Gentile-Christian view, which has long been favored in Germany,[49] has never found widespread acceptance

---

48 Quoted by Eusebius, *Hist. Eccl.* VI. 25. 11–14.
49 Eugéne Ménégoz, *La théologie de l'Épître aux Hébreux* (Librairie Fischbacher, 1894), traces this view from M. Koehler (1834) through M. Roeth, Schurer, Weizsaecker, Pfleiderer, and von Soden.

An Enigma and Its Significance

among British scholars, despite its espousal by Moffatt[50] and Scott.[51] Nor has a consensus emerged regarding the location of the readers (Rome? Alexandria?) or the date of writing (before or after 70 CE?). A commentary as recent as Montefiore's can posit that Hebrews is the first letter to Corinth, sent between 52 and 54 CE.[52]

We therefore approach the study of the cultus in Hebrews without commitment to any particular view of author, readers, or date. We feel that it is vital that the text be allowed to "speak," as it were, wholly on its own terms. Nor does our particular topic demand a prior decision concerning such questions of "introduction." That the study from within the letter itself, however, will suggest clues as to the historical situation is likely.

The second query raises the issue of the importance which the author of Hebrews attaches to his cultic terminology. What if the imagery of the cult is meant to be no more than extended metaphor, a theologoumenon? What if, in fact, the author uses cultic language for the purposes of an anti-cultic polemic?

We should underscore that our study in no wise begs these questions. Only after we have engaged the text in close and thorough investigation will a decision regarding them be in order. But this point is clear: even if the cultic language is a theologoumenon, it is still used "seriously"—the cultic argumentation rests upon it. It would be out of place to insist, for instance, that we must establish that the author and his readers were engaged in actual cultic acts having to do with defilement-blood-purgation before we can give serious consideration to the cultic argumentation. No; the task of this study—the unravelling of the *internal logic* of the cultic argumentation—cuts to a level deeper than both the issue of theologoumenon or the question of actual cultic acts.

We turn, then, to a consideration of the previous investigation of the cultus of Hebrews. How have earlier scholars approached this enigma? Or to what extent has the problem even been discerned? And what shall we say as to the adequacy of these past efforts? These are the issues that shall occupy us throughout Chapter 2.

---

50 Moffatt, *Epistle to the Hebrews*, xv–xvii.
51 Scott, *Epistle to the Hebrews*, 14–19.
52 *Epistle to the Hebrews*, 11–30.

Chapter 2

The Cultus of Hebrews in Modern Investigation

As we scan the horizons of research on Hebrews since F. C. Baur, one fact is immediately apparent: there has been no Protestant work devoted to the cultus during the past fifty years. This absence is all the more remarkable in view of three other observations. First, while Hebrews has not served to focus New Testament scholarship in modern times, nevertheless there has been a continuing interest in it by Protestant writers.[1] Second, a series of books,[2] commentaries[3] and articles[4] by Catholic scholars have been primarily interested in the cultus. Finally—and most significantly—the earlier investigations of

---

1 This is made apparent by Grässer's review article, "Der Hebräerbrief 1938–1963."

2 Especially Cody, *Heavenly Sanctuary*; F. J. Schierse, *Verheissung und Heilsvollendung*, Münchener theologische Studien (K. Zink, 1955); and Jerome Smith, *A Priest for Ever* (Sheed and Ward, 1969).

3 Notably those of Spicq, Kuss, Schierse, P. J. Bonsirven, *Saint Paul: Épître aux Hébreux* (2nd ed.; Beauchesne et ses Fils, 1953), and Peter Ketter, *Hebräerbrief*, Herders Bibelkommentar (Herder, 1950).

4 Grässer in the review article cited above has given a comprehensive bibliography up to 1963. As indicative of the interest of Roman Catholic writers in the cultus of Heb, we might mention the following articles published since 1963: by A. Vanhoye: "De instauratione novae Dispositionis (Heb 9, 15–23)," *VD*, XLIV (1966), 113–30; "Mundatio per sanguinem (Heb 9, 22, 23)," *VD*, XLIV (1966), 177–91; "Par latente plus grande et plus parfaite ... (Heb 9, 11)," *Bib*, XLVI (1965), 1–28; "Thema sacerdotii praeparatur in Heb 1, 1–2, 18," *VD*, XLVII (1969), 284–97; by James B. Swetnam: "The Greater and More Perfect Tent; a Contribution to the Discussion of Hebrews 9.11," *Bib*, XLVII (1966), 91–106; "Hebrews 9, 2 and the uses of Consistency," *CBQ*, XXXII (1970), 205–21; "On the Imagery and Significance of Hebrews 9, 9–10," *CBQ*, XXVIII (1966), 155–73; "Sacrifice and Revelation in the Epistle to the Hebrews: Observations and Surmises on Hebrews 9, 26," *CBQ*, XXX (1968), 227–34; "A Suggested Interpretation of Hebrews 9.15–18," *CBQ*, XXVII (1965), 373–90; by P. Andriessen, "L'Eucharistie dans l'Épître aux Hébreux," *NRT*, XCIV (1972), 269–77; "Das grössere und vollkommenere Zelt (Heb 9, 11)," *BZ*, XV (1971), 76–92; and by L. Sabourin, "'Liturgie du sanctuaire et de la tente veritable' (Heb 8.2)," *NTS*, XVIII (1971), 87–90; "Sacrificium ut liturgia in Epistula ad Hebraeos," *VD*, XLVI (1968), 235–58.

Hebrews displayed a lively concern with the cultus; thus, around the turn of the century this subject was at the center of Protestant research in Hebrews.[5]

Two implications follow for our study of this chapter. On the one hand, the recent absence of works devoted to the cultus in no way makes our task easier. We are now required to sift the modern commentaries and works ostensibly dealing with other matters in Hebrews for clues as to the treatment of the cultus. Certainly, we need not imagine that the lack of study of the cultus suggests that its problems have been satisfactorily solved: commentators continue to refer to the difficulties of understanding they have faced![6] In this search for clues, the manner in which a writer takes up Hebrews 1.3 and chapters 9–10 rather quickly reveals his hand. On the other hand, the drift of Hebrews research relative to the cultus suggests that we must look into developments from the previous century for hints concerning the surprising facts mentioned above.

Let us then take our stance at the turn of the century. We could look back on a line of scholars whose work was to set out the parameters for the twentieth-century study of the cultus. We take them up in chronological order. Baur, Delitzsch, Lünemann, Ritschl, Westcott, Robertson Smith, Davidson, Ménégoz, and A. B. Bruce.

In F. C. Baur's reconstruction of the history of the church,[7] the book of Hebrews was assigned a mediating position between Judaism and Paulinism. Such mediation, however, was "unconscious" and derived from the Alexandrinisms of the writing.[8]

So far as the cultus is concerned, Baur stressed the priesthood. Here, too, was a reconciling conception, speaking both of continuity and of discontinuity. That is, while the motif of priesthood served to link Jewish Christianity with the work of Jesus Christ, the teaching of Hebrews of a priesthood that was above the law indicated a sharp break with the past.[9]

Baur's interest was in church history, not the book of Hebrews per se. We look in vain for any attempt to explain the ideas of priesthood and sacrifice, nor does he catch the cultic "problem" of defilement.[10] But his work on

---

5 This will become apparent in the discussion of this chapter.
6 See p. 4, n. 4.
7 F. C. Baur, *The Church History of the First Three Centuries*, trans. Allan Menzies (2 vols., 3rd ed.; Williams and Norgate, 1878–1879). The first German edition appeared in 1857. Baur's treatment of Hebrews here is expanded—though keeping the same conclusions—in his posthumous *Vorlesungen über neutestamentliche Theologie* (Friedrich Andreas Berthes, 1892), II, 27–55; first pub. 1864.
8 *Church History*, 121, n. 1.
9 Ibid., 115–21.
10 This is true in spite of his employment of the language of defilement of Heb; e.g., "Der Grund und Zweck der Menschwerdung ist, die Menschen von den Sünden zu reinigen, 1, 3" (*Vorlesungen*, II, 42).

Hebrews, brief though it is, raises a problem which is to face all subsequent writers concerning the cultus of Hebrews—the question of continuity and discontinuity. With Baur, a nice balance between the two is struck. There is both continuity and discontinuity. While this achievement fitted admirably Baur's general thesis, the position was not one which later scholars would be likely to maintain.

In the commentary of Franz J. Delitzsch,[11] we encounter at once much of what is best and worst in the study of the cultus of Hebrews. On the one hand, Delitzsch is concerned to come to grips with the difficulties raised by the cultus. But on the other, his efforts at solution leave much to be desired.

Delitzsch, first of all, goes back to the Old Testament and rabbinic sources.[12] The problem with this method is that, while thematic links with the cultic material of Hebrews can clearly be established, we are brought no closer to a penetration of the hard shell of the cult. The fact is that the Old Testament, like the *auctor ad Hebraeos*, merely *assumes* the cultic outlook that we mentioned in the first chapter.

It is not surprising that Delitzsch casts his net wider in a search for explanation of the cultic argumentation of Hebrews. Here the attempt ends in disaster: he endeavors to interpret Hebrews by recourse to other parts of the New Testament and—more seriously—in the interests of a preconceived theory of atonement. Thus, for instance, he introduces Luke 22.20 to explain the rare word αἱματεκχυσία at 9.22,[13] thereby opting for "blood-*shedding*" as its meaning. In fact, Delitzsch cannot feel free to let Hebrews speak in its own terms since he has already decided that its author is Luke writing under Pauline influence![14] It comes as no surprise, therefore, when he lays great stress on the term λύτρωσις in 9.12,[15] even though this word appears as a non-cultic anomaly in the midst of the cultic reasoning of Hebrews 9–10. Furthermore, Delitzsch sees "wrath" as the defiling element in the heavenly sanctuary[16]—a category which he has wholly to import into the line of argument. His reason for doing so begins to become apparent as he discusses 9.27–28 in terms of penal suffering and vicarious representation[17] and emerges full-blown in the excursus at the close of his commentary: "On the Sure Scriptural Basis of the

---

11 *Commentary on the Epistle to the Hebrews*, trans. Thomas L. Kingsbury (2 vols.; T&T Clark, 1868–1872).
12 Ibid., I, x–xi.
13 Ibid., II, 122.
14 Ibid., I, 4; II, 409–17.
15 Ibid., II, 82–84, 139–40. Apparently Delitzsch did not see that it is Luke who omits Mark 10.45 and has no real doctrine of atonement!
16 Ibid., II, 125.
17 Ibid., II, 136–38.

Ecclesiastical Doctrine of Vicarious Satisfaction."[18] Now it becomes clear that Delitzsch has used his commentary as the medium for an attack against the atonement theories espoused by von Hofmann, who denied that the death of Jesus was the vicarious punishment of humanity's sin.[19]

In short, Delitzsch's attempt to grapple with the cultus of Hebrews is a failure. The waters are so muddied by outside influences that the text is never allowed its due hearing. It follows that in this commentary "defilement" and "purification" pass by almost unnoticed: the writer is too busy with his own interests to discern them.

One other issue of major concern for students of the cultus of Hebrews comes to sharp expression in Delitzsch's work. This has to do with the extent to which the heavenly liturgy of Christ is an *actual* one. Against von Hofmann, Delitzsch opposes an actual heaven of the blessed as the σκηνή ("tent") of 9.11 to the former's "spiritual view";[20] likewise, he sees Christ's heavenly "offering" as that of "glorified blood."[21] The point at issue between the two scholars—the question of literal versus metaphorical or "spiritual" use of language in the cultic terminology of Hebrews, particularly as pertaining to "blood"—is one which would be continued long beyond their era.

Lünemann's commentary,[22] which ran through four editions in the Meyer series, sharpened the issue raised by F. C. Baur. It was not merely that Lünemann expressed himself clearly in favor of the discontinuity between the old cultus and the work of Christ; the question was now posed as a decision for ritual vis-à-vis the ethical. Thus, Lünemann could write in his comments on Hebrews 9.14.

> The Levitical act of sacrifice is then an external one wrought in accordance with ordinance, a sensuous one; Christ's act of sacrifice, on the other hand, one arising out of the disposition of the heart, thus a moral one.[23]

And again concerning 10.4: "By a rudely sensuous means we cannot attain to a high spiritual good."[24]

---

18 Ibid., II, 418–63.
19 Delitzsch in his preface indicates that he considers von Hofmann's *Der Schriftbeweis: ein theologischer Versuch* to be in error concerning the doctrine of the atonement and that it is his duty as a "professional interpreter of holy Scripture" to refute it. See ibid., I, xi.
20 Ibid., II, 20ff., 75–89.
21 Ibid., II, 88.
22 Göttlieb Lünemann, *The Epistle to the Hebrews*, Meyer Commentary (Funk & Wagnalls, 1885). The first German edition appeared in 1855.
23 Ibid., 614.
24 Ibid., 641.

While Lünemann's commentary is generally marked by splendid scholarship, it is a disappointment to the student of the cultus of Hebrews. We look in vain for an alertness to the presuppositions undergirding the cult, for an awareness of the *religious* dimension of the interlinked ideas of defilement, blood, and purification. Lünemann either failed to discern these matters or chose to ignore them in his denigration of the cultus.

What is the origin of this anti-cultic prejudice—"a rudely sensuous means"? Is it a child of the Enlightenment, or do its roots extend even to that upheaval in the life of Christendom which saw the emergence of Protestantism? The question is tantalizing, but one which we are not at liberty to pursue further in this study.

It is obvious, however, that we are to hear more from later detractors of the cultus of Hebrews. But over and over they will come back to the basic argument of Lünemann: that the cultus stands for that which is external, non-ethical and "rudely sensuous."

No study of later nineteenth-century theology would be complete without due consideration of the teachings of Albrecht Ritschl. It is not merely that his is "the most prominent name in German theology at the close of the nineteenth century,"[25] but it is clear that the book of Hebrews played a major role in the expression of his views. The study of Hebrews influenced him in his consideration of dogmatic questions;[26] he lectured on Hebrews;[27] finally, his theology may be considered to be an attempt to bring Pauline teachings under the umbrella of the categories of Hebrews.[28]

We cannot here take up Ritschl's central concern with justification and reconciliation.[29] Limiting ourselves to that which is significant for the topic at hand, we notice three aspects of his work which warrant comment: his theory of sacrifice as "covering," his view of humanity's "problem," and his understanding of the work of Christ relative to that "problem."

---

25 J. H. W. Stuckenberg, "The Theology of Albrecht Ritschl," *AJT*, II, (1898), 268.
26 Albert Temple Swing, *The Theology of Albrecht Ritschl* (Longmans, Green, & Co., 1901), 12.
27 Ibid., 18.
28 Ménégoz, *La Théologie de l'Épitre aux Hébreux*, 245–46: "M. Ritschl a fait l'inverse. Il a essayé, par des tours de force exégétiques vraiment extraordinaires, de ramener la doctrine de l'expiation substitutive de Paul à la doctrine du sacrifice de l'Épître aux Hébreux."
29 This is developed in his three great volumes, the first of which is historical in nature: *A Critical History of the Christian Doctrine of Justification and Reconciliation*, trans. John S. Black (Edmonston & Douglas, 1872); the second exegetical: *Die christliche Lehre von der Rechtfertigung und Versöhnung: Der biblische Stoff der Lehre* (Adolph Marcus, 1882); and the third systematic: *The Christian Doctrine of Justification and Reconciliation*, trans. H. R. Mackintosh and A. B. Macaulay (T&T Clark, 1900). The first German editions appeared 1870–74.

Ritschl saw the idea of sacrifice in the New Testament as taken over from that of the Old. He makes explicit his understanding of its function:

> The symbolism of all animal sacrifice in the Old Testament has the following content: The ministering priest, who is authorized, in the place of the people or of the individual Israelites, to bring their gifts (*corban*, that which is brought near) into God's presence, fulfils this purpose in sprinkling the blood, in which is the life of the animal, upon the altar where God meets with the people (Exod 20.24), and in burning the animal, or certain parts of it, in the fire, which signifies God's presence (Lev 9.24). By these actions, which present the gift to God, the priest "shields" the people or the individuals from God there present. This is according to the presupposition that no living being can come *uncalled* into the presence of God without being destroyed. But the gift, brought according to the divine order, is the covering or protection under which those in covenant with God are in thought brought into His presence. In the sin-offering there is no rite prescribed which would signify any different conception from that of the burnt-offering and the peace-offering.[30]

Whatever may be the correctness of this view relative to the Old Testament, it is to be underlined that it finds no basis in Hebrews. There the "blood" does not "*cover*"—an idea not at all brought into the cultic argumentation—but instead "purifies."

We note two points concerning Ritschl's understanding of humanity's "problem" (sin): it is "any action contrary to the divine-human end of the kingdom,"[31] and it is not of major weight.[32] That is, Ritschl sees the corresponding "solution" under the category of *forgiveness*, which is the overcoming of humanity's feelings of guilt. Thus, his major exegetical treatment of this topic bears the title: "Die Bedeutung des Todes Christi als Opfer zum Zwecke der Sündenvergebung."[33] Again we must emphasize that such ideas cannot be made to comport with Hebrews 1.3 and chapters 9–10, where humanity's "problem," set forth as "defilement" requiring "purgation," carries with it the extreme consequence of exclusion from the presence of God.

---

30 Albrecht Ritschl, *Instruction in the Christian Religion*, trans. Alice Mead Swing, in Swing, *The Theology of Albrecht Ritschl*, 222.

31 Earle Fowler Gossett, "The Doctrine of Justification in the Theology of John Calvin, Albrecht Ritschl, and Reinhold Niebuhr" (unpublished Ph.D. dissertation, Vanderbilt University, 1961), 280.

32 Ibid., 205, 221, 279.

33 *Die christliche Lehre*, 157–263.

Ritschl rules out all theories of "sanctification" or "substitution" relative to the work of Christ. Christ's vocation is to establish the kingdom[34] and in fulfilling that vocation his death is merely an "accident of His positive fidelity."[35] The significance of the death, then, is that it manifests Christ's unity of will with God and thus his right to forgive. Thus, the death of Christ is of the nature of a self-sacrifice, an act of devotion.[36] But does such teaching in fact harmonize with the heavy weight given to the "blood" of Christ in Hebrews 9–10? Quite obviously not—as we shall establish in our fourth chapter.

We conclude that, despite the brilliant theological work of Ritschl, we cannot consider his theories to be of aid in our grappling with the cultus of Hebrews. Rather, the contrary! The use of sacrificial language, the frequent references to Hebrews—these serve only to confuse the exegete since in the final analysis they are being put to a dogmatic, not an exegetical, purpose. Let us state the matter plainly: Ritschl is not really interested in the cultic argumentation of Hebrews *in its own right*, and such exposition of it as he does give is a distortion.[37]

But it was inevitable that his theology would be felt among subsequent students of Hebrews. Just how far-reaching was his sphere of influence will become apparent throughout the remainder of the current chapter.

In 1889, two works appeared from British scholars which are of profound significance for the study of the cultus of Hebrews. Although the nature of each is very different, their initial and continuing influence demands that we give them careful consideration. We refer to Westcott's commentary and to W. Robertson Smith's *Lectures on the Religion of the Semites*.

In the work of Westcott,[38] we discern a happy blend of linguistic acumen with concern for the religious level of the cultus. In fine, there is a determined effort to have the *auctor ad Hebraeos* speak to us in his own way, with sedulous guarding against importing "explanations" from other parts of the New Testament or from dogma.

Particularly interesting is the way in which Westcott is led to seek for religious understanding by recourse to comparative religion. The material available was, of course, quite limited in those days; yet we see him making use

---

34 *The Christian Doctrine of Justification and Reconciliation*, 449.
35 Ibid., 566.
36 *Instruction*, 219–25.
37 A devastating criticism of Ritschl's exegesis was given by Otto Pfleiderer, "Die Theologie Ritschl's nach ihrer biblischen Grundlage," *JPT*, XVI (1890), 42–83.
38 Brooke Foss Westcott, *The Epistle to the Hebrews* (2nd ed., reprinted; Eerdmans, 1950).

of the pioneers in the field such as Tylor.[39] Westcott's work is fascinating to watch: unlike some later researchers such as Sir James Frazer,[40] who sought to find specific parallels to the biblical text by drawing out willy-nilly from the hat of religious data, as it were, he clearly is seeking after *general* religious structures. His essays on the universal priesthood[41] and universal sacrifice[42] make this point quite clearly. In this, Westcott is ahead of his time: he is anticipating the "structures" sought after by modern exponents of the phenomenology of religion.[43]

Thus, Westcott feels the deep religious currents associated with the term "blood":

> It is the power of a pure life which purifies. Under this aspect the Blood becomes, as it were, the enveloping medium *in* which (ἐν), and not simply the means or instrument *through* or *by* which, the complete purification is effected.[44]

And again:

> The Blood poured out is the energy of present human life made available for others.[45]

Likewise, he discerns that "defilement" and "purification" are terms which are to be given due valence in their own right, and not merely subsumed under imported categories such as "atonement" or "forgiveness."[46] So he sees that the *auctor ad Hebraeos* presents sin "as a defilement which clings to man, a force which separates him from God,"[47] and that 9.23 calls for a "cleansing" of the heavenly order—he will not permit a watering-down of the text so that καθαρίζειν ("to cleanse") becomes "to inaugurate."[48] As to how such purgation

---

39 Ibid., 137.
40 As in Frazer's *Folk-lore in the Old Testament: Studies in Comparative Religion, Legend and Law* (3 vols.; Macmillan, 1919).
41 Westcott, *Epistle to the Hebrews*, 137–41.
42 Ibid., 281–92.
43 E.g., ibid., 137, after listing characteristics of the general idea of priesthood: "These thoughts are of universal application, and find manifold embodiments in the experience of mankind." Again (p. 237): "Sacrifice, in fact, in the most general form, belongs to the life of man, and, in the truest sense, expresses the life of man."
44 Ibid., 268.
45 Ibid., 294.
46 He does, however, pass quickly to the talk of "the completed atonement wrought by Christ" in his discussion of Heb 1.3b! See ibid., 14.
47 Ibid., 276.
48 Ibid., 270.

is to be understood, he confesses his bafflement,[49] but he will not back away from the difficulty of the text presented by its cultic argumentation.

Yet Westcott's treatment of the cultus, laudable as it is, still leaves much to be desired. He is feeling after a method of coming to grips with the language of cultus; but because of the early stage in the study of non-Christian religions, he has comparatively little material to work with. That is, his work is at best tentative and sketchy. Second, he appears to run into considerable problems with the argument of Hebrews because his general concern to give the cultic language due place does not seem to comport with the view that the *auctor ad Hebraeos* uses this terminology in a "spiritualized" sense. For instance, having decided that the "heavenly sanctuary" equals Christ's body, which in turn equals the "spiritual" church,[50] he finds great difficulty in understanding the writer's statement relative to Christ's ministry in the "heavenly sanctuary."[51] We cannot help but wonder whether the tension would be eased if he had conceived of an actual heavenly cultus as the explanation of the "heavenly sanctuary."

Despite the caveats above, Westcott's work must continue to elicit serious attention from any student who seeks to crack the hard nut of the cultus of Hebrews. Not as a finished study, but as a pointer to the way to be followed.

In conclusion, it occurs to us that the work of Westcott relative to the religious appreciation of the cultus of Hebrews marks the high point in the history of research on Hebrews and the author's use of the cultus. Both before and after we are conscious of walking in the lowlands: his efforts are never surpassed and, sadly, often unrecognized. We would have thought, for instance, that the term "blood" would, after Westcott, be associated with life rather than with death; but such is not necessarily the case.[52]

With W. Robertson Smith's *Lectures on the Religion of the Semites*[53] we approach a classic at once claimed by two fields—biblical studies and comparative religion. It is a work which was very quickly translated into German, so that its influence became as great on the Continent as it did in England and the United States.

These lectures—the Burnett series for 1888–89—take us, of course, far beyond the confines of Hebrews. But they have the most important implica-

---

49 He sees cleansing of the heavenly order, but cannot define how this can be. See ibid., 270–71.
50 Ibid., 256–58.
51 Ibid.
52 Cf. A. B. Bruce's study of Hebrews, written within a decade of Westcott (*infra*, p. 26).
53 *Lectures on the Religion of the Semites: The Fundamental Institutions* (3rd ed.; A. & E. Black Ltd., 1927).

tions for the study of the cultus of Hebrews, as we shall see by considering questions of methodology and the views of ritual, cultus, and "defilement" which result from Smith's study.

Stanley Cook[54] sees Robertson Smith as the founder of the "Science and Theory of Religion" in this work. Hahn[55] classifies him under the "anthropological approach to the Old Testament." It would be more correct, I think, to consider his methodology as a mixture of comparative religions and latent *Religionsgeschichte*. In some chapters of his book,[56] Smith ranges far and wide in the search for religious data relevant to his purpose: here he is working along the lines of comparative religion, already begun by Tyler and others. But the concentration of the book upon *Semitic* religion—particularly Semitic institutions and sacrifices—and the emphasis he puts upon the evidence from "primitive" Arabic tribes ("primitive" in culture, but later in time than the Old Testament) point clearly to that concern to trace historical links and horizons which was to specify the work of the *Religionsgeschichte Schule*, very soon to arise.

What do these methodological details imply for our study of the cultus of Hebrews? Principally, that an attempt to understand the cultus on merely *religionsgeschichtliche* grounds may not be fruitful. Smith noted that sacrifice is not explained in the New or Old Testaments and so was led to consider other Semitic nations.[57] But for the crucial piece of evidence in his argument he was unable to establish the historical link necessary for *Religionsgeschichte*: his case rests on the dubious assumption that Saracen sacrifices of 400 CE may directly inform our understanding of biblical sacrifice. Furthermore, not infrequently he turned to data outside the Semitic field.

Of vital concern for this study is the view of ritual which emerges from Smith's study. In brief, it is this: ritual belongs to undeveloped, early religion, where concepts of morality are but dimly discerned and the material overrides the spiritual, which is still incipient. The final lines of his book make clear the point:

> The one point that comes out clear and strong is that the fundamental idea of ancient sacrifice is sacramental communion, and that all atoning rites are ultimately to be regarded as owing their efficacy to a communication of divine life to the worshippers, and to the establishment or confirmation of a living bond between them and their god. In primitive ritual

---

54 In his introduction to the third English edition.
55 Ferdinand Hahn, *The Old Testament in Modern Research* (Fortress Press, 1966), 47–53.
56 Especially chs. 5, 6, 8, 9.
57 Ibid., 3–4.

this conception is grasped in a merely physical and mechanical shape, as indeed, in primitive life, all spiritual and ethical ideas are still wrapped in the husk of a material embodiment. To free the spiritual truth from the husk was the great task that lay before the ancient religions, if they were to maintain the right to continue to rule the minds of men. That some progress in this direction was made, especially in Israel, appears from our examination. But on the whole, it is manifest that none of the ritual systems of antiquity was able by mere natural development to shake itself free from the congenital defect inherent in every attempt to embody spiritual truth in material forms. A ritual system must always remain materialistic, even if its materialism is disguised under the cloak of mysticism.[58]

Undergirding this account, we clearly discern that evolutionary theory of the development of religion which marked the late nineteenth century. Thus, "primitive" religion was not merely early but inferior. And it was in this phase that the cultus was to be placed. It was, of course, a schema which accorded splendidly with Wellhausen's reconstruction of Israelite religion,[59] particularly with regard to the denigration of the cultus vis-à-vis "prophetic religion."[60]

The implications for the study of the cultus of Hebrews are obvious. If the *auctor ad Hebraeos* thinks of Christianity in terms of actual ritual, he has employed a most unfortunate conceptual vehicle, one which takes us back to an inferior stage in religion (elsewhere,[61] Robertson Smith compared the Catholic view of the Mass to "magic"!). The alternative—that he expects the reader to "spiritualize" or allegorize his cultic terminology—is hardly more inviting to the scholar. On either view the result is likely to be this: bypass the cultic argumentation as an unfortunate intrusion and look elsewhere to find what the writer is trying to say.

Robertson Smith's estimate of ideas of defilement will now be apparent. He finds that rules of uncleanness have nothing to do with "the spirit of Hebrew religion"; he groups them with "primitive superstition" and "savage" ta-

---

58 Ibid., 439–40.
59 J. Wellhausen, *Prolegomena zur Geschichte Israels*, 5 Aufl. (George Reimer, 1899). The first edition appeared in 1878. Robertson Smith wrote the preface to the English edition.
60 Ibid., especially in chs. 1–4.
61 In his inaugural lecture: the Catholic Church "had almost from the first deserted the Apostolic tradition and set up a conception of Christianity as a mere series of formulae containing abstract and immutable principles, intellectual assent to which was sufficient to mould the lives of men who had no experience of a personal relation with Christ...." "Holy Scripture is not, as the Catholics tend to claim, 'a divine phenomenon magically endowed in every letter with saving treasures of faith and knowledge.'" J. S. Black and G. W. Chrystal, *The Life of William Robertson Smith* (A. & C. Black, 1919), 126–27. Quoted in Mary Douglas, *Purity and Danger* (Penguin Books, 1970), 29. (See also ibid., 74.)

boos; he speaks of their "irrationality."[62] Their origin, he says, is in the primitive concept of taboo, in which holiness is not differentiated from defilement: taboos relative to friendly powers signify holiness, while those relative to hostile powers signify uncleanness.[63] Such strictures are hardly designed to encourage a study of defilement and purgation in Hebrews!

We shall return to Robertson Smith in the next chapter. At this point we simply state as our estimate that, despite the many fine insights in individual details of *The Religion of the Semites*, its major conclusions are to be found wanting when weighed in the light of the evidence we now have. Because the work is founded on faulty presuppositions, it is faulty in its results. It is, therefore, a work which should be studied by biblical scholars in terms of the *history* of their discipline, not as a sourcebook of "assured results." The justification for these remarks will become apparent in the methodological discussion of the following chapter.[64]

If the great studies by Westcott and Robertson Smith are to be counted among the most influential for the study of the cultus of Hebrews, that of A. B. Davidson[65] should be seen as one of the most underrated efforts. It is a modest work, both in size and in breadth of ideas, yet it contains some extremely clear thinking concerning the cultus. Its leading virtues may be summed up in a word: balance.

Thus, Davidson is careful to balance the factors of continuity and discontinuity with the Old Testament cultus.[66] He argues strongly against a ceremonial/moral dichotomy corresponding to the two testaments: the Old Testament sacrifices could *go no further* than to purify the flesh.[67] Likewise, Christ's offering was not of value because it was one of obedience and hence spiritual, but rather because it was the sacrifice prophesied according to the divine will.[68] Again, with the question of the "heavenly sanctuary": while the relational aspect is foremost (the drawing near of the believer to God), the local sense is to be maintained.[69] In this manner Davidson strenuously opposes any effort to "spiritualize" the cultic language so that it is seen as an extend-

---

62 *Religion of the Semites*, 447, 449.
63 Ibid., 153–59.
64 Douglas, *Purity and Danger*, 21–40, has set out severe strictures of Robertson Smith's presuppositions and conclusions. She writes as an anthropologist.
65 *The Epistle to the Hebrews*, Handbooks for Bible Classes and Private Students (T&T Clark, n.d.). The British Museum General Catalogue of Printed Books, Vol. XLIX, gives 1882 as the date of publication.
66 Ibid., 35–36.
67 Ibid., 167–68.
68 Ibid., 193–94.
69 Ibid., 201–3.

ed illustration only, or to drive a sharp wedge between the old cultus and the new. It is not surprising that he displays a keen interest in the "ritual axioms" that are at the base of the argumentation. In an elementary way he seeks to discern the manner in which sin is viewed as a defilement and blood may act as a purifying medium.[70] His efforts here lack the broad sweep of Westcott, but they are nonetheless impressive.

Davidson's attempts to resist the "spiritualizing" of the cultus were running against the tide of British scholarship, however. His book now appears as the last of such efforts to come out of England. But in France a contemporary would espouse his cause.

Ménégoz's *La théologie de l'Épître aux Hébreux*, which appeared five years after Westcott's work, is most notable for its grasp of the history of interpretation of Hebrews.[71] For Ménégoz, this history centers in the conception of the sacrifice of Christ, which he sees as the original contribution of Hebrews.

The true understanding of the *auctor ad Hebraeos* was, according to Ménégoz, lost almost immediately. The Church Fathers read "sacrifice" as self-sacrifice, an act of devotion, and brought in ideas of ransom.[72] With Anselm, "satisfaction" replaced ransom; the reformers employed the cultic terminology of Hebrews (especially in terms of the "threefold office" of Christ) without grasping its peculiar teaching.[73] So the misunderstanding of Hebrews has continued to Ménégoz's day: he groups modern theologians by either how they interpret Hebrews via Pauline theology or by their attempt to reconcile Hebrews and Paul.[74]

What then is the correct understanding of Christ's "sacrifice" according to Hebrews? As a *real* sacrifice, a *cultic* sacrifice not to be collapsed into metaphor:

> C'est ici qu'il faut nous garder d'une méprise dans laquelle sont tombés de nombreux théologiens. Ils ont confondu le sens propre et le sens figuré du mot *sacrifice*. L'auteur de l'Épître aux Hébreux voit dans la mort du Christ un vrai sacrifice, un sacrifice rituel, assimilé aux sacrifices lévitiques, un holocauste offert à Dieu sous une forme spéciale, exceptionnelle, mais réalisant d'une manière parfaite le type prophétique de ceux de l'ancienne Alliance, et procurant la rémission des péchés aux fidèles qui l'offrent, par

---

70 Ibid., 204–6.
71 Ch. 7: the theology of Hebrews in the history of dogma.
72 Ibid., 230: concerning the early fathers' use of Hebrews' sacrificial language: "Mais c'est une influence purement formelle. C'est le triomphe de l'image au detriment de l'idée."
73 Ibid., 230–39.
74 Ibid., 243–52.

l'intermédiaire du Christ, devant le trône de Dieu. C'est le sacrifice au sens propre de ce mot.[75]

The work of Ménégoz, penetrating as it is, is concerned almost wholly with the concept of sacrifice. We hear little about the term "blood," which probes to a deeper level of religious intuition, and nothing at all concerning "defilement" and "purgation."

Like Davidson, Ménégoz clearly stood for the *continuity* of the cultic ideas from the Old Testament. It was a point of view which, as the nineteenth century came to a close, came under severe attack in the work of A. B. Bruce.[76]

Bruce sees Hebrews as "the first apology for Christianity."[77] The document is directed toward Jewish Christians at Jerusalem, who—contrary to often held views—are not tempted to return to Judaism but who have no real insight into the nature and worth of Christianity.[78] It is the cultic argumentation which is designed to enlighten the readers, and it is this which occupies Bruce's attention for almost the entire book.

The cultic language of Hebrews, then, serves an anti-cultic purpose. Two words sum up the relative worths of the old cult and Christianity: "flesh" and "spirit."[79] The Old Testament cultus was not different in *degree* but in *kind*: it belonged to the realm of the fleshly, the external, the unethical. If the *auctor ad Hebraeos* used the old cultic terminology, only the form of the statements is the same: the substance is changed. So, Bruce takes note of Ménégoz's statement that the ritual notion of bloody sacrifice does not vary from Leviticus to Hebrews and bitterly opposes it:

> The statement is true in form only, not in substance. Blood, as such, is not the important matter in the sacrifice of Christ, as conceived by our writer. Blood, death, has value only as revealing will, spirit. It is the eternal spirit of holy love, the righteous will fulfilling all righteousness, that gives the sacrifice of Jesus transcendent worth, and makes it differ *toto coelo* from the ritual sacrifices of Leviticalism. Till that truth is clearly seen, and firmly grasped, we have not escaped from the religion of shadows.[80]

---

75 Ibid., 229.
76 *The Epistle to the Hebrews: The First Apology for Christianity* (Charles Scribner's Sons, 1899).
77 This is the subtitle of Bruce's work and is emphasized in the preface (p. x) and throughout the book.
78 Ibid., 390–92.
79 Ibid., 337–54.
80 Ibid., 438.

In analyzing Bruce's treatment, it soon becomes apparent that Hebrews 9.14 is definitive for him. Christ offered himself "through eternal spirit" (διὰ αἰωνίου).[81] Bruce sees in this phrase an attack on the legalism and externalism of the old cultus; Christ's sacrifice is valuable because it was "an affair of the mind and spirit."[82] He avers that the argument really ends with this verse, and the reader might as well pass on to 10.19ff.[83] Accordingly, he is puzzled that the *auctor ad Hebraeos* should return at 9.17 to elementary matters.[84]

Bruce's thesis demands that we test it by the evidence of Hebrews itself. It does not require searching scrutiny to realize that the theory is one-sided (and therefore distorted) in its presentation of the argument of Hebrews. The clearest example of this, as we saw above, is in the use to which 9.14 is put. If Bruce sees the vital point in the argument there, the author of Hebrews does not—or at least is not ready to commence the exhortation of 10.19ff. In fact, as we shall see in our exegesis of Hebrews 9–10, each verse is significant for the development of the writer's skilfully-woven presentation. Bruce has chosen to disregard the cultic axioms undergirding the argument in favor of this single occurrence of πνεῦμα. It seems incredible, furthermore, that, although he acknowledges the commentary of Westcott,[85] he can equate "blood" with "death"[86] and assert, as we saw above, that "blood, as such, is not the important matter in the sacrifice of Christ, as conceived by our writer."[87] Finally, the dichotomy of flesh and spirit, which counts for so much in Bruce's reconstruction, is not one which is native to Hebrews. It is not surprising that Bruce turns to Philo for support,[88] for the cleft cannot be derived from the *auctor ad Hebraeos*, the Platonic bent of his cosmology notwithstanding.

What are the roots of this vigorous anti-cultic prejudice displayed by Bruce? We discern a strong antisacerdotal polemic in statements such as:

> But the religion of the spirit will acknowledge no other priest beside Him. Priestcraft, sacerdotalism, sacraments turned into magic sources of spiritual benefit, have no place in true Christianity. They are a lapse back to

---

81 Especially evident in ibid., 337–54: "'spirit' unfolds the implicit significance of 'Himself', and gives us the rationale of all real value in sacrifice" (pp. 343–4); he contrasts blood to spirit (pp. 342–43); "spirit" expresses the ethical element in the writer's thought (p. 348).
82 Ibid., 348.
83 Ibid., 355.
84 Ibid., 360.
85 Ibid., ix.
86 Ibid., 346–47.
87 Ibid., 438.
88 Ibid., 343.

the era of shadows, a lapse only too intelligible and explicable, nevertheless lamentable.[89]

Do we see here the epitome of the Protestant spirit? Or are we reaping the first fruits of the labors of Robertson Smith?

With the dawn of the twentieth century, students of Hebrews could look back on at least fifty years of agitation of the questions raised by the cultus of Hebrews. That the cultic language is significant for following the reasoning of the letter had not been uniformly recognized, while the efforts to comprehend it had flowed in various directions. It is obvious that the following issues had come to the fore: (1) the question whether Christianity is to be seen as basically *continuous* with the Old Testament cultus, or whether a radical break is intended by the *auctor ad Hebraeos*;[90] (2) the degree to which Christianity "spiritualizes" the cultic terminology; specifically, does Hebrews conceive of the work of Christ as an *actual* heavenly cult, or not?;[91] (3) the attempt to gain insight into the cult by a study of the genetic history of ideas;[92] (4) the question whether the cultus of Hebrews is to be interpreted in its own terms;[93] (5) the basic issue as to whether the study of the cultus needs justification: is the cultic language an unfortunate lapse into primitive, inferior religious terminology;[94] and (6) the possibility that the structures or patterns of religion in general may illumine the religious level of the cultus.[95]

These, then, are the questions and options which provided the matrix for the study of the cultus of Hebrews during the twentieth century. We say "study"—but, as we saw above, we should include "non-study" of the cultus as a lively alternative. Let us see now how the modern study of the cultus of Hebrews has developed in terms of the six categories listed above. It is not our purpose to attach labels to modern scholars, thereby thinking we have come to an understanding: for one thing, the categories mentioned are not necessarily mutually exclusive. No; our endeavor is to critically trace modern developments in the light of the previous research, and for this purpose the six groupings form a convenient springboard.

---

89 Ibid., 438.

90 For continuity: especially Delitzsch, Ménégoz and Davidson; opposing continuity: especially A. B. Bruce and Lünemann.

91 An actual cult: Delitzsch, Ménégoz, Davidson; opposing: Westcott, Lünemann, A. B. Bruce.

92 Seen especially in Delitzsch and Robertson Smith.

93 Influence of dogmatic ideas in the interpretation: Delitzsch, Ritschl, A. B. Bruce; authorship bias: Delitzsch.

94 So Robertson Smith, A. B. Bruce, Lünemann.

95 Westcott.

The Issue of Continuity/Discontinuity of the Old Cultus and Christianity

D. Bernhard Weiss's work on Hebrews[96] devotes thirty-two pages to Hebrews 12.12–13.25 but only twelve pages to the portion 8.6–10.18—and this under the heading, "Der Abschaffung des Opferkultus!"[97] Here was set forth in sharp relief an attitude to the cultus which was to mark much of twentieth-century study of Hebrews. In his argument on the heavenly cult[98], Dibelius argued, on the basis of the last two chapters of Hebrews, that the letter was opposed to *all* earthly cults, not merely to the Old Testament cultus. Spicq in his magisterial commentary found himself on the horns of a dilemma: on the one hand he saw that the argument of Hebrews 9–10 hinges on the continuity of ideas of "blood," yet he wanted to reject all materiality in terms of Christ's sacrifice, thus denigrating the old cultus.[99] On balance, he belongs among those who emphasize the discontinuity of the old cultus with Christianity. Héring, however, found himself in no doubt:

> No one who practices the Jewish religion, priest or layman, can ever obtain the essential thing, the one thing which matters, viz. the purification of his conscience.[100]

Elsewhere, Héring likewise associates ideas of "blood" and "defilement" with a "magical conception of religion."[101] Likewise Strathmann in his commentary on Hebrews in the *New Testament Deutsch* series: the Old Testament cultus merely furnishes ideas to make meaningful the death of Jesus; the cultus itself rested on a delusion.[102]

Two additional works serve to bring this view of discontinuity to focus: Michel's commentary in the Meyer Series, and Jerome Smith's *A Priest for Ever*. The former is surely a magnificent commentary on Hebrews; its treatment of the perplexing issue before us is correspondingly incisive. Michel faces squarely the dilemma which Spicq was loathed to admit: Hebrews 9 deals in cultic categories while Hebrews 10 brings in *obedience*.[103] Michel

---

96 *Der Hebräerbrief in zeitgeschichtlicher Beleuchtung* (J. C. Hinrichs, 1910).
97 Ibid., 47–58.
98 "Der himmlische Kultus."
99 *L'Épître aux Hébreux*, II, 217, 278.
100 Jean Héring, *The Epistle to the Hebrews*, trans. A. W. Heathcote and P. J. Allcock (Epworth Press, 1970), 75.
101 Ibid., 78.
102 *Der Brief an die Hebräer*, 123, 128.
103 Michel, *Der Brief an Die Hebräer*, 329.

makes his decision: the tenth chapter is to override the ninth.[104] Thus, Heb 9.22, the famous "blood rule," is not constitutive for Christian understanding of the death of Christ; rather, it is a summary judgment on the Old Testament cultus.[105] Again we see the triumphing of "prophetic religion" over the cultus. Jerome Smith's dissertation, on the other hand, seeks to draw a sharp line between the priesthood of Christ and all other cults on the basis of eschatology:

> We have reached explicitly the question implicit in this whole essay: continuity or discontinuity with the Old Testament priesthood, and through that, in a more limited way, with pagan priesthoods generally. Since the full-blown sacrificial system of Israel was in a large measure taken over from the Canaanites, though with a considerable conceptual transformation, there is a definite link between Old Testament priesthood and sacrifice and that revealed to us in the study of comparative religion.... It is when one gives full value to the eschatological element in Hebrews that the fundamental discontinuity that underlies the very real continuity is most securely grasped.[106]

In considering the arguments of those who have posited a radical break with the Old Testament cultus, a criticism common to all seems justified: they have failed to give the cultic language of Hebrews its due weight in the argumentation. That is, the passage 7.1–10.18 *is there*: it cannot simply be bypassed in favor of other portions, such as the concluding chapters. Nor is one free to pluck out an isolated non-cultic term from the midst of chapters 9–10 and frame the argument around that. Thus, while Michel's explanation that the ninth chapter stands in tension with the tenth is a bold expedient, his resting of his case on "obedience" from 10.5–10 displays the same sort of one-sided exegesis that A. B. Bruce manifested in his reliance on "spirit" at 9.14. The fact is that the cultic language does *not* end with Hebrews 9,[107] so the explanation in terms of tension falls to the ground. Smith, likewise, is so concerned to show the difference of Christianity from all other cults that he is purblind to the religious coloration of the text which comes to expression in "defilement," "blood," and "purgation."

---

104 Thus, ibid., 334. Hebrews stands not for the internalization of offerings, bur for their abrogation.
105 Ibid., 321–22.
106 Smith, *A Priest for Ever*, 192–94.
107 Nor with the tenth verse of chapter 10! We have already pointed out (Ch. 1) how the *auctor ad Hebraeos* reverts to the key term αἷμα in the important conclusion which commences at 10.19.

As we saw with our discussion of the work of F. C. Baur, the question of balancing continuity and discontinuity in Hebrews is a delicate one. The issue is whether the *auctor ad Hebraeos*, by using the language of the cult, saw fundamental axioms such as the "blood-rule" of 9.22 as continuous, or whether he intended to break the cultic presuppositions, thus employing the cultic terminology in an utterly transmogrified way. It is an issue that can only be settled by careful exegesis; we expect this to be one of the results of our detailed study of Hebrews 9–10 in Chapter 4 below.

We should note briefly that the view of discontinuity has been by no means universally held during this century.[108] Important exceptions are furnished in the works of Moffatt,[109] Windisch,[110] Purdy,[111] Kuss,[112] and Montefiore.[113] And here a correlation, interesting with regard to the subject of this study, is to be noted: those scholars who have seen a continuity of cultic presuppositions in the argument have at the same time been alert to the *religious* note of the text. It is a correlation which is to have been expected: after all, if one considers that the author's purpose is to denigrate the cultus, he is not likely to be interested to probe the cultic language in its own right.

The Question of the "Spiritualizing" of the Cultus

The very word "spiritualize" is ambiguous[114] and is used carelessly by the writers on Hebrews. In terms of the argument of Hebrews, it may refer to: (1) a

---

108 In dealing with authors who have opposed the idea of a radical discontinuity of the old cultus with Christianity, we by no means imply that *no* discontinuity at all is understood: obviously the *auctor ad Hebraeos* clearly argues for the superiority of Christianity. What is at stake is whether, in the course of his argumentation, he relies on certain cultic presuppositions and ideas as the continuous axioms of both the old cultus and Christianity.

109 The author's aim is "to discredit the Levitical priesthood of bygone days"; nevertheless Christ's work is asserted to be superior "on the ground of a presupposition which was assumed as axiomatic, namely, the impossibility of communion with God apart from bloodshed in sacrifice (9.22)," *Epistle to the Hebrews*, xxxii, xlii.

110 Hans Windisch, *Der Hebräerbrief*, Handbuch zum Neuen Testament, 2 Aufl. (J. C. B. Mohr, 1931), e.g., 79: "Dass der Verkehr zwischen Gott und den Menschen nur durch Opfer und zwar durch blutige Opfer möglich ist, ist die selbst-verständliche Voraussetzung."

111 *Epistle to the Hebrews*, 690. The axiom of Heb 9.22 "is true in the old and the new dispensation alike; the new achieved what the old foreshadowed because it presented a better priest with a better offering made in a better sanctuary."

112 Kuss's emphasis on *Heilsgeschichte* is at the foundation of his view of continuity: *Der Brief an die Hebräer*, 98, 106, 181–83.

113 Montefiore asserts that the "self-evident datum" of Heb 9.22 "forms the ground of his whole doctrinal argument"; *Epistle to the Hebrews*, 158–59.

114 This ambiguity is reflected in Gove (ed.-in-chief), *Webster's Third New International Dictionary*, where "spiritualize" means "to make spiritual: refine intellectually or morally: purify from the corrupting influences of the world: give a spiritual character or tendency ... to give a spiritual meaning to: take in a spiritual sense—opposed to *literalize* ... to endow with the

"spiritual" cult, that is, an actual heavenly cultus, in contrast to earthly ritual; or (2) a total collapsing of the cultic terminology, so that no more than the general idea of "salvation" wrought by Christ is intended. The lack of precision in the use of this term will become apparent as we consider the ebb and flow of modern discussions concerning the intent of the *auctor ad Hebraeos* in his use of the language of the cult.

Three positions are clearly discernible: a literalistic, a metaphorical, and a mediating stance. The first position takes quite literally the assignations of Hebrews relative to the offering of the "blood" of Christ. Its sole representative is Windisch: in his remarks on 5.7 he states that Christ in the ascension gives up flesh and takes only the blood heavenward![115] Again, in an important excursus on the topic of blood, he insists on the realistic character of "blood" in Hebrews—it is not to be considered as merely a

> "plastisches Wortsymbol" fur die Erlösung durch Christus, wird doch gerade die überragende kultische Wirkung des Christusblutes der rituellen Wirkung des Tierblutes entgegengesetz.[116]

At the other extreme is the metaphorical view, which denies any heavenly cultus; it is the same as the second sense of "spiritualize" above. It has found numerous exponents. One of the earliest was DuBose in his *High Priest and Sacrifice*.[117] This is in every respect a most unfortunate piece of work—a blend of homily, allegory, and "exegesis." DuBose aims to translate the ideas of Hebrews into current coin;[118] he succeeds in neither exegesis nor hermeneutic. When we find that the heavenly sanctuary equals spiritual relations equals Christ equals the Church,[119] and that its Holy Place equals the flesh and its Most Holy equals the spirit,[120] that blood equals human destiny through death,[121] and that Christ's act equals our act,[122] we see "spiritualizing" run wild. *High Priest and Sacrifice* is a flawed book, yet surprisingly Alexander Nairne refers to it favorably.[123]

---

nature and attributes of a spirit." There is a clear distinction between a *moral*, non-literalizing sense and a "spirit-ish" (having the nature of "spirit") sense here.

115   Windisch, *Der Hebräerbrief*, 47.
116   Ibid., 85.
117   William Porcher DuBose, *High Priesthood and Sacrifice: An Exposition of the Epistle to the Hebrews* (Longmans, Green, and Co., 1908).
118   Ibid., 1–4.
119   Ibid., 153–54, 184.
120   Ibid., 188.
121   Ibid., 176.
122   Ibid., 192.
123   *The Epistle to the Hebrews*, xlviii, lxxv, xci–xcii.

Both Nairne's *Epistle of Priesthood*[124] and commentary on Hebrews[125] are far more restrained, however, with careful exegesis. Yet the upshot is ultimately similar to DuBose: Hebrews teaches the "sacramental principle,"[126] the high priesthood signifies the "unity of all life,"[127] the cult merely provided the author of Hebrews with an analogy,[128] Christ's sacrifice is to be reenacted in us.[129]

F. J. Schierse, both in his *Verheissung und Heilsvollendung* and his commentary,[130] interprets Hebrews in terms of the Platonic dualism of spirit and matter. The heavenly realm of salvation is opposed to the earthly realm of perdition, to which corresponds an anthropological dualism of spirit and flesh. According to the flesh, humanity belongs to the first tent; according to his spirit and conscience, they are raised essentially to the invisible, heavenly creation.[131] Christ's body belongs to the heavenly realm; thus the heavenly sanctuary, which signifies only the nearness of God, was inaugurated in the life of Christ.[132] Thus, references to the Eucharist underlie such passages as 10.5–10 and 10.20.[133]

Jerome Smith's *A Priest for Ever* sets out to establish the thesis that the entire cult of Hebrews is an "extended metaphor":[134] terms such as defilement, blood, sacrifice, sanctuary, and even priest are no more than theologoumena without any literal significance.[135] Finally, it is to be noticed that such "spiritualizing" of the cultic language of Hebrews opens the door to detecting references to the Mass or baptism in the text: we noticed this in Schierse's work, and he is by no means an exception.[136]

An attempt to avoid both the extreme literalism of Windisch and the collapsing of the cultic language is sought by a number of modern scholars. They have understood the *auctor ad Hebraeos* as having in mind an actual heavenly cultus, yet they have sought to avoid gross materiality. It will be enlightening to see how Cody and F. F. Bruce have argued for such a mediating position.

---

124 *The Epistle of Priesthood* (2nd ed.; T&T Clark, 1915).
125 *Epistle to the Hebrews.*
126 Ibid., lxi.
127 Ibid., lxii.
128 Ibid., lv, lvii.
129 Ibid., lxvii–lxxviii.
130 Epistle to the Hebrews.
131 Schierse, *Verheissung und Heilsvollendung*, 119–20.
132 Schierse, *Epistle to the Hebrews*, 54–58.
133 Ibid., 66.
134 Smith, *A Priest for Ever*, 11. Smith's thesis, in fact, is that the entire letter is "extended metaphor."
135 Ibid., 69, 76, 112, 196.
136 See especially the articles cited *supra*, p. 13 n. 4; DuBose, *High Priest and Sacrifice*, 145, likewise.

A. Cody's *Heavenly Sanctuary and Liturgy* is a highly speculative endeavor.[137] He posits that "heaven" is viewed under three different perspectives in Hebrews—cosmological, "axiological," and eschatological.[138] Again, he sees two "sets" from the sanctuary typology: the first, in which the outer and inner apartments represent the earthly and heavenly orders of salvation respectively, and the second in which they represent the body of Christ (humanity and Godhead) and God's dwelling in glory respectively.[139] The idea of a need to "cleanse" the "heavenly" things (9.23) remains a formidable problem, however.[140] Indeed, one cannot help but wonder just how sophisticated the readers of Hebrews must have been, if they could have threaded their way through the labyrinthine argument as Cody presented it.[141] We ask, furthermore, whether Cody is not concerned with theological questions—such as when did Jesus become priest? how does he intercede in heaven?[142]—which the *auctor ad Hebraeos* had no thought for. In a word, Cody's work is too clever.

F. F. Bruce's commentary[143] is poles apart from the speculative theology of Cody. Bruce continually uses the language of Hebrews itself: his discussion of the text is impregnated with terms such as "cleansing" and "sacrifice." Yet Bruce never explains how he understands this terminology; indeed, he displays a curious ambivalence, an (apparently) unconscious effort to have the best of both literal and figurative worlds. Thus, while his comments would lead us to the conclusion that he holds to an actual heavenly cultus,[144] suddenly we read that the heavenly sanctuary is not "absolutely" local.[145] Thus, the "heavenly things" of 9.23 refer to the "spiritual" cleansing of human beings.[146] Likewise with "sacrifice": his comments leave

---

137   Cody's avowed purpose is to join textual exegesis with speculative theology, the latter to be "Thomistic in inspiration."
138   Ibid., 77–86.
139   Ibid., 46.
140   Ibid., 182–92. After discussing the various solutions which have been proposed, Cody reverts to the explanation of A. B. Davidson: there is no actual defilement of "heaven," but instead an "objective salvation" is intended by the language of Heb 9.23.
141   Consider, for instance, his note on p. 190: "I suspect that when Hebrews uses the expression τὰ ἐπουράνια as it does when speaking of purification in 9.23, the idea of the axiological center of reality is uppermost in the author's mind, whereas when the author uses the singular οὐρανός in the following verse, where he is speaking of Christ's appearance before God, the idea of heaven as the place of God's presence of which the old sanctuary was the type, has moved to the fore."
142   Ibid., 191–202.
143   *Commentary on the Epistle to the Hebrews*, New International Commentary on the New Testament (Marshall, Morgan & Scott, 1965).
144   Especially in his discussion of Heb 8.1–6; ibid., 163–68.
145   Ibid., 219.
146   Ibid., 218–20.

us in doubt as to whether the term signifies obedience per se or more than obedience.¹⁴⁷

We observe therefore, that, despite the extensive study regarding the nature of the cultus in Hebrews, no consensus has been reached with regard to the basic question as to the weight to be attached to the cultic language of the letter. The contention of this study has already been made explicit: we suggest that it is by first probing this cultic language at its fundamental level— the *religious*—that progress is to be made.

THE *RELIGIONSGESCHICHTLICHE* APPROACH TO THE CULTUS OF HEBREWS

The *religionsgeschichtliche Schule* is customarily traced from H. Gunkel;¹⁴⁸ its roots, however, go back at least as far as W. Robertson Smith, as we have seen. With regard to the cultus of Hebrews, this school is to be considered under two aspects: (1) direct concern with the cultus, and (2) indirect concern with the cultus.

There has appeared no work wholly devoted to the cultus from a *religionsgeschichtliche* perspective. A number of scholars have given some attention to the problem, however. Thus, Bousset argued strongly that in Hebrews Christianity is set forth as belonging to a heavenly cult.¹⁴⁹ He placed the letter among

> manifestations which show how strongly the worship contexts and the attitudes of cultic piety determine and dominate the whole of the Christian religion and the position of the *Kyrios Christos* in this totality.¹⁵⁰

The commentary of the *religionsgeschichtliche Schule* on Hebrews, written by Georg Hollmann, concentrated on the high priestly christology of the let-

---

147 Thus, ibid., 233, he writes: "Wholehearted obedience is the sacrifice that God really desires, the sacrifice which He received in perfection from His Servant-Son when He came into the world." We would expect from this that sacrifice equals obedience, i.e., "sacrifice" has been totally "spiritualized" in the sense of moral, non-literalist. Yet on the next page we read: "Our author's contrast is not between sacrifice and obedience, but between the involuntary sacrifice of dumb animals and sacrifice into which obedience enters, the sacrifice of a rational and spiritual being, which is not passive in death, but in dying makes the will of God its own'" (quoting J. Denney, *The Death of Christ*, 131). Here "sacrifice" retains literal significance: the point concerns a voluntary as opposed to an involuntary sacrifice. The tension between the two statements is not resolved by Bruce.

148 So Hahn, *The Old Testament in Modern Research*, 86. Cf. Werner Klatt, *Hermann Gunkel: zu seiner Theologie der Religionsgeschichte und zur Entstehung der formgeschichtlichen Methode*, FRLANT (Vandenhoeck & Ruprecht, 1969). Klatt cites Gunkel's *Schopfung und Chaos* (1895) as the first major work of the *religionsgeschichtliche Schule* (pp. 46–80).

149 *Kyrios Christos*, 358–61.

150 Ibid., 358.

ter, endeavoring to show that the concept is derived from Alexandrian Judaism.[151] The commentaries of Windisch, Moffatt, and Michel ranged wider: they sought to relate the entire cultus to Philo, Hellenistic Judaism, and the rabbinical writings. Spicq sought to show an intimate relation to Philo—the author was a Philonist converted to Christianity.[152] That question was given thorough reexamination by Williamson in his important study: he concludes that the alleged parallels with Philo have been greatly exaggerated.[153]

The results of these studies have not been helpful for illuminating the anthropology implied by the cultus. Much light, indeed, has been thrown on the cosmology of Hebrews, particularly in connection with the heavenly sanctuary and liturgy and thus the christology—but this is not our concern in the present study. It has become more and more apparent that Hebrews is drawing upon the Old Testament in its cultic argumentation. But therein lies the problem: the Old Testament itself merely accepts, never explains, the axioms of the cult which the *auctor ad Hebraeos* has employed for his discourse. Thus, while *Religionsgeschichte* has been of great value in the christological aspects of cultus, it has not been able to untie the anthropological knots.

We turn now to *religionsgeschichtliche* studies of Hebrews which have only indirectly concerned themselves with the cultus. E. Käsemann's classic *Das wandernde Gottesvolk* indubitably takes first place here. There is a dramatic shift away from interest in the cultus: since Käsemann seeks to ground the letter in the motif of the wandering people, the focus moves from the central section of Hebrews to the second, third, and fourth chapters. Indeed, since the wandering motif does not occur in 7.1–10.18, this passage is curiously de-emphasized. For the people on the move, the great sin to be avoided is unfaithfulness; thus, we hear nothing of "defilement" and its interlocking ideas of "purgation" and "blood." Observations of a similar nature apply to Grässer's *Der Glaube im Hebräerbrief*,[154] which builds on the foundation laid by Käsemann but concentrates upon the parenesis of the eleventh chapter.

We conclude that the method of *Religionsgeschichte* has not shown itself to be helpful in the task of this study. The concepts of the cult are not amenable to a tracing of the genetic history of ideas: their roots are not in the immediate milieu of the *auctor ad Hebraeos* but instead tap the springs of primordial religious perception. On the other hand, the problems of the cultus

---

151   *Der Hebräerbrief*, Die Schriften des Neuen Testaments (Vandenhoeck & Ruprecht, 1917), 169.

152   *L'Épître aux Hébreux*, I, 39–91, 197–219.

153   Ronald Williamson, *Philo and the Epistle to the Hebrews*, Arbeiten zur Literatur und Geschichte des hellenistischen Judentums (E. J. Brill, 1970), 576–80.

154   Erich Grässer, *Der Glaube im Hebräerbrief* (N. G. Elwert, 1965).

of Hebrews still remain when motifs out of the parenetic sections are related to early Gnosis; indeed, if light begins to be shed upon the non-cultic portions of the letter, the need for a methodology which is able to deal with the cultus becomes all the more pressing!

The Issue of the Canons of Interpretation of the Cultus of Hebrews

We noticed in our survey of latter nineteenthcentury research into the cultus of Hebrews that one of the weaknesses of this period was a tendency to read into Hebrews ideas from outside the letter—from other writings of the New Testament or from dogmatic theology.[155] To give the most obvious example: so long as the Pauline authorship was adhered to, it was inevitable that the teachings of Hebrews would be assimilated to those of the Pauline corpus.[156]

The issue raised here is a far-reaching one. No exegete is in fact wholly "objective," no matter what he may claim for himself: each comes to the text with a baggage of presuppositions inherited from his cultural and religious background. What seems important, therefore, is that these assumptions be brought out into the light, so that the *modus operandi* may be plain to all. It seems reasonable, furthermore, to ask of the exegete that he make a deliberate effort to "hear" the text before him, sedulously putting aside voices from other New Testament writings or his own religious tradition.

It is impossible to gauge accurately the extent to which past studies on the cultus of Hebrews have been engaged in, perhaps unconsciously, the defense of dogmatically held positions. We cannot avoid the likelihood that a good deal of the vigorous denigration of cultus has had its roots in a militant Protestantism.

It is possible, however, to see frequent evidences of the importation of ideas from outside Hebrews. How a commentator deals with 1.3b often shows this: the language of the text—"purgation" (καθαρισμός)—is first generalized

---

[155] Shown especially in the work of Delitzsch and Ritschl.

[156] Even when the Pauline authorship ostensibly was no longer held, the idea continued to influence the interpretation of Hebrews. This was seen particularly in the tendency to assimilate the cultic language of Hebrews to that of the Pauline epistles—a tendency that still pertains in the investigation of Hebrews. At the other extreme, the attempt may be made to *contrast* Hebrews with Paul—inevitably to the denigration of Hebrews (usually the "conclusion" will be that Hebrews lacks the ethical note of Paul). In either case we see an unfair juxtaposing of Hebrews and Paul without allowing Hebrews to present its argumentation in its own terms.

as "redemption"[157] and then re-interpreted, as "atonement," for instance.[158] Likewise in 9.22, the ἄφεσις is almost invariably supplied with τῶν ἁμαρτιῶν[159] and read as "forgiveness of sins,"[160] quite wrenching the meaning of the verse out of its context.[161] The strongest test, however, is 9.23, with its clearly stated proposition that the "heavenly things" require a purgation. The efforts made to avoid the obvious sense of the text are extraordinary: thus, for instance, Spicq finds the explicit meaning to be "non-sens."[162] However, on what basis does Spicq make such a claim? Certainly not on the grounds of Hebrews, but only because of Spicq's preconception of the nature of the "heavenly things." Another way in which the individual character of the text is diluted is by the listing of "parallel" passages from other parts of the Bible. We discern at work here assumptions concerning the "unity" of Scripture which are disastrous for allowing Hebrews to "speak" in its own unique view. The commentaries of Spicq[163] and F. F. Bruce[164] especially are to be faulted on this point.

If the cultic language of Hebrews has been "used" as an anti-ritualistic weapon by Protestants, Catholics have also sought to employ it for support of their positions. The interest in the priesthood has been overriding here: for instance, Spicq decides that Hebrews itself is expressly written for ex-priests of Judaism.[165] Ketter's commentary in the Herder series provides the most blatant example, however. The unique priesthood of Christ is assimilated to priesthood in general: there are references to "Christian priests" and "priests of the new covenant."[166] Here we find continual references to the Mass also; for example, in commenting on 10.1ff.:

> Man könnte also sagen. Die Opfer des Versöhnungstages waren das stete Gedächtnis der ungetilgten Schuld und Sünde; das Messopfer dagegen ist

---

[157] E.g., Thomas Hewitt, *The Epistle to the Hebrews*, Tyndale New Testament Commentaries (Eerdmans, 1960), 52: "Christ by this one sacrifice of Himself has brought about a permanent purification of sins, which the Levitical priests were unable to do. Here is to be found the essential truth that He who fully reveals God fully redeems man."

[158] E.g., D. Bernhard Weiss, *A Commentary on the New Testament*, trans. George H. Schodde and Epiphanius Wilson (Funk & Wagnalls Co., 1906), 143, speaks of "His atoning death, which brought about a cleansing from the contamination of guilt."

[159] E.g., Delitzsch, *Commentary on the Epistle to the Hebrews*, II, 121.

[160] So RSV and NEB.

[161] See the exegesis of this verse in Ch. 4 of this study.

[162] *L'Épître aux Hébreux*, II, 266–67.

[163] We cite but one instance: Spicq sees the author's theology of blood as the result of contemplation on the (disputed!) cup-word of Luke 22.20; ibid, II, 283.

[164] *Epistle to the Hebrews*: among numerous examples might be mentioned Bruce's treatment of Heb 7.26–28 (pp. 156–60) and 9.11–14 (pp. 199–206).

[165] *L'Épître aux Hébreux*, I, 226–31.

[166] *Hebräerbrief*, 9, 37–42, 56, 58.

als unblutige Gegenwärtigsetzung des Kreuzesopfers das stete Gedächtnis der durch Christus getilgten Sündenschuld.[167]

Such distortion of the text cannot pass for exegesis.

It would be folly for one to suggest that his method of approaching the text has overcome all tendencies to "read in" ideas from without. We do propose, however, that the purpose of the present book is to study the cultic language *in its own right*, while also striving to avoid some of the theological roadblocks that have become evident in light of the discussion above.

The Issue Regarding the Significance of the Cultus in the Study of Hebrews

What is at stake here is the intrinsic value of the cultic terminology of Hebrews. Specifically, does it represent an unfortunate use of archaic, "primitive" (used derogatively), "foreign," religious language?

A sharp attack on those who would assign value to the cultus of Hebrews was launched in the early part of the twentieth century by E. F. Scott. He sees that the argument of the *auctor ad Hebraeos* proceeds in terms of ritual sacrifice, but he refuses to allow any hidden "meaning" in such rites: their only "value" is that they were commanded by God.[168] The author of Hebrews had not reflected concerning the cultus, so any labor expended toward "explaining" it is wasted effort.[169] Indeed, Scott contends that the cultic form of the argument of Hebrews leads to a deficient presentation of the Gospel by the writer.[170] A similar point is made by Wenschkewitz:[171] not only does the cultic concept present difficulties in its carrying through, but it lacks the ethical note.[172] Wenschkewitz sees the cultic language of Hebrews—notably the Old Testament ideas of priesthood and the Day of Atonement—as of no significance in themselves, but of use only as a foil to the author's interest in Jesus as high priest.[173] Other commentators of Hebrews have spoken disparagingly of the "primitive" concepts which surface in the cultic argumentation.[174] Thus, for instance, W. Neil

---

167 Ibid., 75.
168 *Epistle to the Hebrews*, 73–75.
169 Ibid., 131.
170 Ibid., 97, 131–42.
171 Hans Wenschkewitz, *Die Spiritualisierung der Kultusbegriffe* (Eduard Pfeiffer, 1932). Originally presented in *Ang*, IV (1932), 71–230.
172 Ibid., 131–49.
173 Ibid.
174 "Primitive" as used by commentators of Hebrews seems invariably to carry the pejorative accent. At times the language is stronger: "magic" or "superstition!"

in his commentary asserts that a "superstitious belief that the blood of an animal consecrated at the altar derives supernatural power from its contact with deity" is the basis of the idea of the cleansing power of blood.[175]

Accompanying this denigration of the cultus, we observe a marked trend away from any beneficial study of it altogether. The late nineteenth and early twentieth centuries witnessed a succession of works, particularly by British and American scholars, produced in quick order and concerned at least in part with the cultus.[176] However, detailed studies from the pens of Protestants have since cooled off. Käsemann's focus, as we saw, was on parenesis. Other studies[177] have concerned themselves with the old issue of the historical situation of the readers (thus, for instance, W. Manson's[178] and Theissen's[179]), with the place of Hebrews in the New Testament canon (so Renner[180]), with the *religionsgeschichtliche* horizons of Hebrews (thus Hofius,[181] apart from Käsemann,[182] Grässer,[183] and Williamson[184]), or with the method of interpreting the Old Testament employed by the *auctor ad Hebraeos* (so Kistemaker[185] and Schröger[186]).

---

175 *The Epistle to the Hebrews*, Torch Bible Commentaries (SCM Press Ltd., 1955), 94.

176 To the works of Davidson (1882), Westcott (1889), A. B. Bruce (1899), DuBose (1908), Nairne (1913, 1921), and Scott (1922), which we have already had occasion to mention, might be added the following. R. Govett, *Christ Superior to Angels, Moses and Aaron: A Comment on the Epistle to the Hebrews* (J. Nisbet & Co., 1884); Frederic Rendall, *The Epistle to the Hebrews* (Macmillan & Co., 1888); Thomas Charles Edwards, *The Epistle to the Hebrews* (Hodder & Stoughton, 1888); A. C. Kendrick, *Commentary on the Epistle to the Hebrews* (American Baptist Society, 1889); C. J. Vaughan, Πρὸς Ἑβραίους: *The Epistle to the Hebrews* (Macmillan & Co., 1890); F. B. Meyer, *The Way Into the Holiest* (Fleming H. Revell, 1893); F. W. Farrar, *The Epistle of Paul the Apostle to the Hebrews* (Cambridge University Press, 1894); George Milligan, *The Theology of the Epistle to the Hebrews* (T&T Clark, 1899); Adolph Saphir, *The Epistle to the Hebrews* (Gospel Publishing House, 1902); William Kelly, *An Exposition of the Epistle to the Hebrews* (T. Weston, 1905); E. C. Wickham, *The Epistle to the Hebrews* (Methuen & Co., Ltd.; 1910); R. Anderson, *The Hebrews Epistle in the Light of the Types* (J. Nisbet & Co., 1911); H. R. Macneill, *The Christology of the Epistle to the Hebrews, Including its Relation to the Developing Christology of the Primitive Church* (University of Chicago Press, 1914).

177 We have made no attempt at completeness in the following list; we are concerned merely to illustrate our point regarding the shift in the direction of Hebrews research in our century.

178 William Manson, *The Epistle to the Hebrews: An Historical and Theological Reconsideration* (Hodder & Stoughton, 1951).

179 Gerd Thiessen, *Untersuchungen zum Hebräerbrief* (Gütersloh Verlaghaus Gerd Mohn, 1969).

180 Frumentius Renner, *"An die Hebraer"—ein pseudepigraphischer Brief*, Münsterschwarsacher Studien (Münsterschwarzach. Vier-Tdrme Verlag, 1970).

181 O. Hofius, *Katapausis: die Vorstellung vom endzeitlichen Ruheort im Hebräerbrief*, Wissenschaftliche Untersuchungen zum Neuen Testament (J. C. B. Mohr, 1970).

182 Käsemann, *Das wandernde Gottesvolk*.

183 Grässer, *Der Glaube im Hebräerbrief*.

184 Williamson, *Philo and the Epistle to the Hebrews*.

185 S. Kistemaker, *The Psalm Citations in the Epistle to the Hebrews* (Wed. G. van Soest, 1961).

186 Friedrich Schröger, *Der Verfasser des Hebraerbriefes als Schriftausleger* (F. Pustet, 1968).

In view of the denigration of the significance of the cultus of Hebrews and the concomitant trend away from it in scholarly endeavors, we need simply to refer to two points which we have already made in this essay. First, the very structure of Hebrews—the manner in which the author goes about setting out his argument—forces us to give serious consideration to his cultic terminology. And second, it is only when this terminology is recognized for what it is, namely, *religious* language, that the cultic argumentation will yield to comprehension.

THE POSSIBILITY OF EMPLOYING GENERAL PATTERNS OF RELIGION TO ILLUMINE THE CULTUS

We saw earlier in this chapter that it was Westcott's work toward understanding the cultus of Hebrews which dominated the latter nineteenth-century study of this topic. We noticed that the success which he attained was accompanied by efforts to set forth rudimentary "patterns" or "structures" drawn from religious experience in general and not on a *religionsgeschichtliche* basis. To what extent, then, has this methodological suggestion been taken up?

It was observed earlier that those writers who saw the argumentation of Hebrews founded on the *continuity* of cultic presuppositions tended to be concerned to probe the inner religious meaning of the cult. Among these, Moffatt, Windisch, and Spicq[187] are the most thoroughgoing. Yet, as we scrutinize their work, we find that surprisingly little advance is made over the positions attained by Westcott. Indeed, there is a continual *going back* to Westcott, occasionally an enlargement of conceptions by reference to more recent studies in comparative religion.[188] What we see, in effect, is a searching for parallels—either in the Middle East or remote—which will illumine the text. But Westcott's method of seeking understanding by way of general religious structures is nowhere taken up.

---

187 Spicq's position, as we already noticed, is ambivalent (*supra*, p. 29). While his juxtaposing of a "spiritual" cult to a material one led us to classify him with those writers who have underlined the discontinuity of the NT with the OT, he nevertheless is sensitive to the way in which the author argues on the basis of blood. Cf. his excursus "La théologie et la liturgie du précieux sang," *L'Épître aux Hébreux*, II, 271–85.

188 George B. Caird, "Underestimated Theological Books. Alexander Nairne's 'The Epistle of Priesthood,'" *ExpT*, LXXII (1961), 204–6, claims that Nairne says four things concerning sacrifice which are "not only profound but original": (1) sacrifice has to do with defilement; (2) sacrifice has to do with access to God; (3) blood equals life; and (4) sacrifice is the opposite of asceticism. In fact, the first three clearly go back to Westcott. It is amazing that Caird could suggest the third point when Nairne himself has spoken of his dependence on Westcott! See e.g., Nairne's *Epistle to the Hebrews*, xlix.

In short, the possibilities for penetrating the language of the cult implicit in the work of Westcott have not been explored. His commentary has remained singularly apart: often quoted, less often understood, its lead has found no real follower. Why was this? Was its direction in fundamental opposition to the views of the great work of Robertson Smith produced the same year, and so attuned to the spirit of the times? We must leave all such questions, inviting as they are, to others. Our concern is with Hebrews and its cultus. In that concern, however, we see ourselves as the direct descendant—both in *religious* interest and in methodology—of Brooke Foss Westcott.

We began this chapter by calling attention to the remarkable absence of recent Protestant works devoted to the cultus of Hebrews. The roots of this phenomenon extend, as we have seen, at least into the previous century. Indeed, it is only by inquiring into the study of Hebrews before 1900 that the questions and issues which have shaped the study of the cultus of Hebrews become intelligible. We may bring together the work of the chapter in the following summary conclusions.

First, the study of the cultus of Hebrews is to be seen against the backdrop of the rise of the discipline of comparative religions. So long as an evolutionary schema of religion, in which cultus is denigrated vis-à-vis prophetic religion, was adhered to, it was inevitable that the cultus should not evoke serious study in its own right.

Second, the attempt to understand the cultic terminology employed by the *auctor ad Hebraeos* has been hampered, and still is impeded, by various attempts to "read into" the text. While the Pauline authorship of Hebrews has been generally discarded, the Pauline corpus has continued to act as a bias in the interpretation of Hebrews. Understanding of the text of Hebrews is still sought by assimilating it to apparent "parallels" from other parts of the Bible. Dogmatic presuppositions, of either an anti-ritualistic or sacerdotal character, have exerted a marked influence on the quest for meaning of the author's language. Only rarely has the cultic language been allowed a hearing on its own terms.

Third, important questions of interpretation, carried over from the last century, even today divide students of the cultus of Hebrews. These center around two issues: a) Are the cultic presuppositions of the argument thought of by the *auctor ad Hebraeos* as continuous from the Old Testament to Christianity, or is Christianity regarded as marking their radical severance? and b) How is the cultic language to be understood with regard to Christianity—is it to be taken literally, as an extended metaphor, or in some other sense? The term "blood of Christ" serves to focus this latter issue.

Fourth, certain passages in Hebrews 9–10 have continued to evoke confusion and widespread disagreement. What is the "tent" through which Christ entered in 9.11? What is meant by his offering διὰ πνεύματος αἰωνίου in 9.14? What weight shall we give to the "blood rule" of 9.22, and what is its precise meaning in context? Especially difficult: what is meant by the statement that the "things in heaven" must be purified in 9.23? And how does the argument proceed from Hebrews 9 to 10.1–10—are we to see a tension of ideas, or is there an inner consistency after all?

And finally, methodologically, *Religionsgeschichte* has not been found to be helpful in the quest to unlock the cultic argumentation of Hebrews. The problem is that the author does not seem to be drawing on immediate historical parallels but rather employing ancient axioms derived from the Old Testament. The problem is grounded at the religious level, so historical studies are unfruitful. Indeed, with all the study of Hebrews that has been undertaken over the past centuries, commentators today still confess their lack of comprehension when they seek to deal with the inner relations and logic of the cultus. So far, no methodology has proven itself capable of grappling with the problems of the cultic language of Hebrews. The most promising indication for fruitful dealing with this difficulty is seen in the work of Westcott, who experimented in a tentative fashion with general "structures" drawn from universal religious experience. But his efforts have remained essentially an isolated phenomenon.

In the next chapter, we shall give full attention to the question of methodology. We shall propose a method by means of which the cultus may be made understandable on its own presuppositions and inner relations as we give attention to the cultic terms "defilement," "blood," and "purgation." It is a method which, as we shall see, is a lineal descendant of the approach made by Westcott over a century ago.

CHAPTER 3

TOWARDS A METHODOLOGY APPROPRIATE TO THE CULTIC LANGUAGE OF HEBREWS

In this chapter we intend to make explicit the methodology for approaching the cultus of Hebrews which was implied in the work of Westcott. We propose that it is as the exegete takes into account insights from phenomenology of religion[1] that his efforts to comprehend the language of the cult will bear fruit.

The material of the chapter falls into two clearly distinguishable parts. In the first, we shall be engaged in formal questions of methodology, explaining what we mean by "phenomenology of religion" and showing how it is to be incorporated in the work of the exegete of the cultus of Hebrews. In the second, we shall apply the method of phenomenology of religion, using general "structures" to show the nature and interrelations of the religious terms "defilement," "blood," and "purgation." These "structures" will be drawn up from the general data of religious experience, without any reference to Hebrews. Thus, the chapter will provide the methodological and religious basis upon which the exegesis of Hebrews 9–10 is to proceed in the following chapter.

---

1   By "phenomenology of religion" we signify the characteristic methodology of *Religionswissenschaft*. Cf. Eliade, *Sacred and Profane*, 232: "At present, historians of religions are divided between two divergent but complementary methodological orientations. One group concentrate primarily on the characteristic *structures* of religious phenomena, the other choose to investigate their *historical context*. The former seeks to understand the *essence of religion*, the latter to discover and communicate its *history*." "Phenomenology of religion" has reference to the former task in each case. We recognize that often the terms "history of religion" and "phenomenology of religion" are used imprecisely and so interchangeably. But in this study, we shall be concerned with "structures" rather than with history, hence our preference for "phenomenology of religion" throughout this study.

Formal Questions of Methodology

The leading exponents of phenomenology of religion agree that the method has two principal characteristics: the "epoche" and the "eidetic vision."[2] The former refers to the *attitude* of the phenomenologist—a deliberate mental "bracketing" of the data under consideration so that questions of reality or truth are put aside.[3] No datum is to be dismissed or denigrated on the grounds of its implausibility or fantastic character. For instance: suppose the phenomenologist reads of a people who believe in fire-spewing dragons which devour children. Instead of dismissing such ideas as childish or superstitious or at best smiling indulgently, he will take them with all seriousness, as he endeavors to discern what function the dragons have in the total view of humanity, deity, and cosmos. The second mark of phenomenology—the "eidetic vision"—has to do with the search for *essences* or "structures" which emerge from the data of religion.[4] The mass of religious data from ancient to modern times is enormous. It is not, however, a shapeless mass: on careful examination under the attitude of epoche it yields coherent patterns.[5] These are not scientific "laws," even as they are not philosophical systems. Instead, they are religious patterns: they are existential, showing how humanity in its existential concerns sees itself in relation to its fellows, to deity, and to the

---

2 The procedures of phenomenology of religion are set out clearly in the following works: G. van der Leeuw, *Religion in Essence and Manifestation*, 671–78; Joachim Wach, *Religionswissenschaft: Prolegomena zu ihren wissenschaftstheoretischen Grundlegung* (J. C. Hinrichs, 1924); Wach, *The Comparative Study of Religions*, 3–26; Mircea Eliade and Joseph M. Kitagawa, eds., *The History of Religions: Essays in Methodology* (University of Chicago Press, 1959); C. J. Bleeker, "The Relation of the History of Religions to Kindred Religious Sciences, particularly Theology, Sociology of Religion, Psychology of Religion and Phenomenology of Religion," *Num*, I (1954), 142–52; C. J. Bleeker, "Comparing the Religio-Historical and the Theological Method," *Num*, XVIII (1971), 9–29; Mircea Eliade, "Crisis and Renewal in History of Religions," *HR*, V (1965), 1–17; and Charles H. Long, "Prolegomenon to a Religious Hermeneutic," *HR*, VI (1967), 254–64. For examples of the methodology in practice, see the volume of van der Leeuw cited above and the numerous works of Eliade, particularly *The Sacred and the Profane*, *Patterns in Comparative Religion*.

3 Cf. Bleeker, "The Relation of the History of Religions to Kindred Religious Sciences," 148: "In using the epoche, one puts oneself into the position of a listener, who does not judge according to preconceived notions. Applied to phenomenology of religion, this means, that this science cannot concern itself with the question of truth of religion. Phenomenology must begin by accepting as proper objects of study all phenomena that are professed to be religious; subsequently may come the attempt to distinguish what is genuinely religious from what is spurious."

4 Ibid.: "Eidetic is derived from the Greek word 'eidos', which means 'essence.' The eidetic principle has as its aim the search for the eidos, that is, the essentials of religious phenomena."

5 Bleeker, "The Relation of the History of Religions to Kindred Religious Sciences," 149, identifies four elements in "structure": constant forms, irreducible factors, points of crystallization, and types.

cosmos. It is utterly wrong to enter into judgment of such patterns on a scientific or philosophical basis: they have their own internal validity and justification.[6] In their own way they lay out that which is behind and before both the scientific and the philosophical: the primordial.[7] To discern, then, such primordial "patterns" or "structures"—this is the quest of the "eidetic vision."

It will be readily apparent that these two characteristics of phenomenology of religion—the epoche and the eidetic vision—may be profitably employed by the exegete of the cultus of Hebrews. Corresponding to the characteristics themselves, the advantages are twofold: in terms of *attitude* to the cultic language and in *content* from outside Hebrews to shed light on the cult in Hebrews. Let us look more closely at each of these gains.

So long as the exegete associates the language of the cult with that which is "primitive," "magical," and archaic, he is handicapped in the search for understanding. We noticed in the last chapter how the early studies of comparative religion influenced biblical scholarship in accordance with the theories of the evolution of religion then current.[8] But the wheel has come full circle: modern phenomenologists have long since discarded such theories and in fact often give that which is "primitive" (meaning *basic* rather than inferior) pride of place in the study of religious data.[9] It is time for biblical scholarship to take note of this development, to eliminate from its vocabulary and its thinking the denigration of the so-called "primitive" and to begin to discern the significance of language which is first of all religious and only derivatively theological.[10]

We may, therefore, summarize the advantages to the exegete of the cultus of Hebrews as he imbibes the attitude of epoche: (1) he sees the text as religious at its most basic level; (2) he overcomes the reflex denigration of material merely on the grounds that it is cultic equals "primitive" equals foreign, archaic, inferior; and (3) the internal logic of the argument from cult is not obfuscated by the wilderness of theological debate.

---

6 Cf. Eliade, *Patterns in Comparative Religion*, xii: "To try to grasp the essence of such phenomena by means of physiology, psychology, sociology, economics, linguistics, art or any other study is false; it misses the one unique and irreducible element in it—the element of the sacred."

7 By "primordial" we intend not mere chronological priority but that which is "basic," "essential," "fundamental," "deep."

8 Especially evident in Robertson Smith's *Lectures on the Religion of the Semites*.

9 This is certainly true in the work of Eliade, a leading exponent of phenomenology of religion.

10 Some of the most searching strictures of biblical scholarship at this point have come from an anthropologist. Mary Douglas, *Purity and Danger*, 37–39, has shown how the denigration of ritual has lingered on in Old Testament studies. She makes specific reference to the work of Eichrodt.

Furthermore, the *content* from phenomenology of religion, namely, the "structures" or "patterns" drawn from religious experience in general, may be brought to bear on the individual difficulties presented by the cult of Hebrews. That is, at first reading the ideas of defilement, blood, and purgation strike the exegete as indeed strange and evocative of a type of thinking long since superseded. Yet phenomenology shows the exegete that these ideas are not at all isolated; rather, that they are universal. It points, furthermore, to their *continuing* significance, even in the life of the technological person.[11] In other words, that which once seemed "foreign" was so only because of the narrow world of the exegete's thinking.

In fine, the "structures" from phenomenology offer this advantage to the student of Hebrews: they enable one to see the cultus in its own religious genus, as it were—as a particular example of a ubiquitous religious phenomenon.

It thus becomes apparent how the methodology we propose is to function in the task of understanding the cultic language of Hebrews. We conceive of phenomenology of religion as being one more tool in the exegete's bag. By no means is it a tool which is designed to *replace* all others: it is to be used *with* rather than *instead of* traditional approaches to the text.[12] Nor should it be feared that the methodology proposed will dissolve the particularity of the text in a general potpourri of "religion." No; the individuality of the text is to be sedulously guarded: it is the *text* which is the object of our concern and to which we always return. That is, the historical concern—the recognition of the text as historically conditioned—is never to be put aside. The "structures" from phenomenology of religion can never be anything but *general* in their nature, seeking as they do to point to religious commonalities which cut across barriers of culture or time.[13] But these "patterns," when held up to the text, serve to illuminate it both positively and negatively: positively, they help to "explain" the text as it is seen to comport to the general "patterns"; negatively, they show the *individual* character of the text by showing wherein it diverges from the general "structures." From both sides, then, the task of

---

11 The data presented in the latter part of this chapter will bear out this point.

12 We might draw an illustration from the field of art. A student of, say, Renaissance art might be expected not only to immerse himself in the art of that period but also to have an overall acquaintance of the "principles" of art. Even so should the biblical scholar, while not diminishing one whit his concentration on the biblical text, seek to place it in its general context as a religious document by making himself aware of the "structures" of religion in general.

13 The approach of Eliade in a work such as *Patterns in Comparative Religions* is illustrative. Each chapter consists for the most part of an array of data whose links are wholly religious (i.e., not cultural or historical), with the final few pages specifically designating the "patterns" to which the data have pointed.

exegesis is more fruitfully approached: we not only come to grasp the cultic argumentation, but we discern with radical newness the individual beauty of the text as a religious creation.

The methodology we propose—the putting to the service of exegesis of insights from the phenomenology of religion—is not entirely new. Westcott had anticipated it in rudimentary fashion. Again, Kaiser[14] in his handbook of Old Testament exegesis admits—somewhat grudgingly, to be sure—that the "structures" from the study of religion may at times be helpful for "concept exegesis." So far as we know, his suggestion has never been carried out in any more than a cursory manner; certainly, there has been no thoroughgoing application of it to the cultus of Hebrews, as we are undertaking.

The presupposition underlying this methodology is apparent: it is that the cultic language of Hebrews finds its place only when considered in light of the universal experience of *homo religiosus*. It is a presupposition which in no way negates the particularity of the text of Hebrews nor that of Judeo-Christian "revelation"; rather, it is a call for a study of the text in *religious perspective*.[15] As for phenomenology of religion itself, there is no need for us to attempt a justification of its methodology or integrity: it has long since found its place under the scholarly sun.

The methodology proposed may be clarified by considering in turn its relation to "pure" phenomenology, *Religionsgeschichte*, and "structuralist" approaches to biblical exegesis.

We conceive our use of "phenomenology of religion" to follow that of the best-known exponents of the modern study of religion, notably Mircea Eliade, Joachim Wach, Joseph Kitagawa, C. J. Bleeker, and G. van der Leeuw. That the two distinguishing marks of the discipline—the "epoche" and the "eidetic vision"—have their roots in Husserlian phenomenology is obvious; however, they have assumed a distinct character as they have been developed in phenomenology of religion. That is, in this study we are not concerned with how "pure" phenomenology may understand "epoche" or "eidetic vision": we use them wholly within the parameters of the discipline of the phenomenology of religion.[16]

---

14 Otto Kaiser and Werner Georg Kimmel, *Exegetical Method: A Student's Handbook*, trans. E. V. N. Goetchius (Seabury Press, 1967), 30–31.

15 More than twenty years ago, Joachim Wach registered a plea for a Christian theology which would take account of the religious expressions of non-Western, non-Christian people. He suggested that it might be a theology of the Spirit which would provide the necessary focus: "The Place of the History of Religions in the Study of Theology," *JR*, XXVII (1947), 157–77. So far as we know, his plea and his suggestion have remained largely unfulfilled.

16 Bleeker in particular in the two articles cited in note 2 above has drawn attention to the difference between Husserlian phenomenology and phenomenology of religion, e.g.,

Both *Religionsgeschichte* and phenomenology of religion deal in religious data and in history, but the thrust of each is markedly different. *Religionsgeschichte*[17] is concerned to trace the genetic history of religious ideas, consequently its horizons are bounded by the Middle East milieu of the biblical text. Phenomenology of religion, however, has no bounds: the world is its field. Nor is it confined to any one period of history: it seeks to draw all religious data, from "primitive" to modern, into its ken. It is not unmindful of the particularity of history and culture (for example, it would not blandly lump together Aztec lustrations with New Testament baptism), but ultimately, in its quest for "patterns" of *homo religiosus*, it is trans-cultural, trans-historical, transtemporal.[18]

The recently developed "structuralist" methodology is being applied in more and more fields. It seeks to discover the underlying "language" of human social phenomena. As Michael Lane[19] has described it, it emphasizes wholes, totalities; it is concerned with "structures" below the level of empirical reality; it deals in synchronic as opposed to diachronic structures; and it reduces relations to binary oppositions. The work of Claude Levi-Strauss in the field of anthropology is probably the best-known example of the application of the method.[20]

In very recent years, attempts have been made to bring the structuralist method to bear upon the Christian Scriptures. E. R. Leach, following closely

---

"The Relation of the History of Religions to Kindred Religious Sciences," 157—"Today the idea of phenomenology is current. It can be found in literature of many different kinds. It is unfortunately used in different senses; hence confusion of tongues and misunderstandings. In order to clear the air, let us first explain that when in what follows we speak of phenomenology, we have a science in view, which differs totally from the well-known philosophy of Husserl and his disciples, which bears the same name. Phenomenology in the sense of Husserl is a theory of the validity of human knowledge. A phenomenology of religion, however, intends to be an investigation into the structure and significance of facts drawn from the vast field of the history of religions and arranged in systematic order."

17 Cf. Hahn, *Old Testament in Modern Research*, 83: "It [*Religionsgeschichte*] was the application of the historical method to the study of religion under the influence of Positivist principles of investigation, combined with the use of the comparative method as a valuable tool of research." Cf. Carsten Colpe *Die religionsgeschichtliche Schule: Darstellunq and Kritik ihres Bildes vom qnostischen Erlösermythus*, FRLANT (Vandenhoeck & Ruprecht, 1961), *passim*, esp. 9–68.

18 Cf. Bleeker, "The Relation of the History of Religions to Kindred Religious Sciences," 148: "A phenomenology of religion is not a philosophy, but a historic science with a systematizing tendency. It is entitled to take its material from all ages and all parts of the world. The reverse of this liberty is, that some students of the phenomenology of religion bring together such heterogenous facts and draw such hurried conclusions that the science is lost in the night that makes all cats grey."

19 Michael Lane, ed., *Introduction to Structuralism* (Basic Books, Inc., 1970), 11–39.

20 In works such as the following: *Anthropoloqie structurale* (Plon, 1958); *Le cru et le cuit* (Plon, 1964); *The Elementary Structures of Kinship*, trans. J. H. Bell, J. R. von Sturmer, and R. Needham (rev. ed.; Beacon Press, 1969).

in the path of Lévi-Strauss, has worked on Genesis 1–3[21] and the legitimacy of Solomon,[22] in both cases with suggestive results. It is in France, however, that the most widespread efforts have been made, with studies by scholars such as P. Ricoeur, R. Barthes, M. Carrez, E. Floris, P. Beauchamp, H. Bouillard, J. Courtès, E. Haulotte, X. Léon-Dufour, L. Marin, and A. Vergotte.[23] The thrust of these studies has been closely tied to the vexed problem of the relation of exegesis and hermeneutic.[24] That biblical scholarship has displayed a strong interest in the possibilities of structural exegesis is evident from a past program the international congress of learned societies in religion.[25]

It seems apparent that "structuralism" as it is currently being used in the field of biblical scholarship is somewhat of an umbrella term[26]—it is used to denote literary "structure" and linguistic "structure"[27] as well as the sociological "structure" which was the original[28] thrust of the method as set forth by Lane and exemplified by the work of Lévi-Strauss. It would perhaps be more accurate to refer to "synchronic" methods of exegesis (that is, "non-historical" exegesis) in contrast to conventional "diachronic" (that is, "historical") exegesis.[29]

---

21 "Lévi-Strauss in the Garden of Eden: An Examination of Some Recent Developments in the Analysis of Myth," *TNYAS*, XXIII (1961), 386–96.

22 Lane, *Introduction to Structuralism*, 248–92.

23 See the studies in Roland Barthes, *et al.*, *Exégèse et herméneutique* (Editions du Seuil, (1971), and the special number: "Nouvelles Theologies" of *CPED*, CXLVIII (1970).

24 Roland Barthes in *Exégèse et herméneutique*, 188, describes structural analysis of the text as follows: "L'Analyse structurale du Récit (du moins telle que je la conçois) ne cherche pas à établir 'le' sens du texte, elle ne cherche même pas à établir 'un' sens du texte; elle diffère fondamentalement de l'analyse philologique, car elle vise à tracer ce que j'appellerai le lieu géométrique, le lieu des sens, le lieu des possibles du texte. De même qu'une langue est un possible de paroles (une langue est le lieu possible d'une certain nombre de paroles, à vrai dire infini), de même ce que l'analyste veut établir en cherchant la langue du récit, c'est le lieu possible des sens, ou encore le pluriel du sens ou le sens comme pluriel."

25 From the 1972 meeting in Los Angeles we note the following: Dan O. Via, "Structuralism and Literary Criticism of the Bible," and "A Structuralist Approach to Some Pauline Texts"; Robert C. Culley, "Studies in the Structure of Biblical Narrative"; Antonio Gaboury, "The Christological Implications of 'Strukturgeschichte'"; Peter Richardson, "Social and Theological Tensions in Early Christian Groups in Luke/Acts"; John C. Hurd, Jr., "The Structure and Function of First Thessalonians."

26 A useful summary of the ways in which "structuralism" is currently used is provided by R. Lapointe, "Hermeneutics Today," *BTB*, II (1972), 120–27. He includes Vanhoye's analysis of Hebrews as an example of the application of the method to biblical texts.

27 In addition to the papers of Via (note 25 above), cf. Eugene A. Nida, "Implications of Contemporary Linguistics for Biblical Scholarship," *JBL*, XCI (1972), 73–89.

28 The origins of structuralism are, of course, older than the recent interest as exemplified in Lane's *Introduction*. Lapointe, "Hermeneutics Today," 120–21, traces the term to the first international congress of linguistics in 1928.

29 The terms "diachronic" and "synchronic" derive from F. de Saussure, *Cours de linquistique generale* (Payot, 1916). Whereas the former signifies the historical approach, the

If we therefore take structuralist exegesis in the broad sense of synchronic exegesis (which is, we hold, its sense in current usage), the employment of "structures" drawn up from phenomenology of religion clearly belongs to this category. Our methodology, however, is not wholly synchronic. Rather, we are attempting to employ "structures" from phenomenology of religion as a further tool in the traditional task of exegesis: we hold that conventional diachronic exegesis will be more fruitful as it is supplemented by the synchronic approach. That is, our methodology is to be seen as an attempt to integrate synchronic and diachronic approaches to the text.

That such an integrated approach is not only legitimate but in fact necessary is argued by Daniel Patte[30] in a recent essay. He holds that exegesis can only avoid the obscurantist attitude stemming from a wholly historical methodology[31] by *adding* synchronic methods borrowed from the social sciences. Under the latter, he includes linguistics, anthropology, sociology, psychology, and history of religion.

Thus, it will be apparent that we are not proposing a totally new method per se. We are seeking to do the traditional task of exegesis and to find a way to understand the text in its own right. We suggest that it is as traditionally oriented exegesis is informed by phenomenology of religion that a breakthrough is possible. That *Religionsgeschichte*, with its concern to trace the historical antecedents and horizons of the text, has enriched biblical exegesis is beyond dispute—the *religionsgeschichtliche* task is not to be belittled or neglected. But the development of the discipline of *Religionswissenschaft* opens up the possibilities of further enrichment: the text may now be seen in the universal context of *homo religiosus* with the possibility that passages which have defied *Religionsgeschichte* may be unlocked.

While the methodology proposed finds its place under the current concerns of biblical scholarship, my work is distinct in two regards. On the one hand, it is the first attempt on a thoroughgoing scale of which I am aware to present a diversified (synchronic and diachronic) exegesis. Again, whereas other efforts in the field of structural exegesis have been concerned with a linguistic or sociological approach to the text, my methodology works from a base in phenomenology of religion.

---

latter indicates an approach which deliberately studies a phenomenon in *one* given time.

30 "The New Exegesis: An Evaluation of the Diversification in Exegetical Methods" (unpublished paper, Vanderbilt University, 1972). Patte has attempted such an integrated approach to 1 Cor 15.3–8 in "Proclamer la joyeuse nouvelle de la Resurrection," *CVC*, XXV (1972), 51–66.

31 Patte's thesis in his unpublished paper is that the modern view of man is dialectical: man is not only "creator of significations" (the historical view) but "concurrently significations are also imposed upon man." Therefore, exegesis concerned only with the historical approach to the text is obscurantist.

Granted, therefore, that the exegetes of Hebrews well may profit from the attitude of epoche as they come to the cultus, what are the "structures" or "patterns" from the general data of religion which may provide them with the necessary material background for understanding the cultic argumentation? This must provide our task for the remainder of the chapter.

THE NATURE AND INTERRELATIONS OF DEFILEMENT, BLOOD AND PURGATION

It is not our purpose to tabulate data concerning defilement, blood, and purgation. Nor does phenomenology of religion call for an exhaustive treatment of the data (which proves to be an impossible task to begin with); a comprehensive study, however, is required. Our concern must be with the patterns of religious understanding that are brought to light from a broad range of data, that is, it is questions such as the following which we seek to probe as we examine a broad crosscut of evidence:

1. What view of humanity is implied by the evidence?
2. What view of deity is implied by the evidence?
3. What view of the cosmos is implied by the evidence?
4. What are the internal dynamics of defilement, blood, and purification within this conceptual framework of humanity, deity, and cosmos?[32]

In seeking answers to these questions, we shall proceed in four stages. In the first three steps, we shall seek to lay out in turn phenomenologies of defilement, blood, and purgation. The final stage will attempt to describe the relations of defilement, blood, and purgation to each other and to the understanding of humanity, deity and the cosmos.

A Phenomenology of Defilement

The Language of Defilement

In a gripping scene from Shakespeare's Macbeth, Lady Macbeth descends the stairs in her sleep, incessantly "washing" her hands as she cries:

---

32 Cf. Martin P. Nilsson, *Religion as Man's Protest against the Meaninglessness of Events* (C. W. K. Gleerup, 1954), 26: "The business of the science and history of religion is research into the various phenomena of religion; but this science is not simply phenomenology—it also strives to discover the psychological foundation and the historical developments and interrelations of religious phenomena."

> Yet here's a spot.
> Out, damned spot! out, I say! ...
> What, will these hands ne'er be clean? ...
> Here's the smell of the blood still: all the
> perfumes of Arabia will not sweeten this little hand.
> Oh, Oh, Oh!³³

This is the language of defilement, and it is a timeless language. It is the language of Isaiah who bemoans: "Woe is me! For I am lost; for I am a man of unclean lips, and I dwell in the midst of a people of unclean lips; for my eyes have seen the King, the Lord of hosts!";³⁴ it is the language of the Egyptian "negative confession": "I have not defiled myself in the pure places of the god of my city.";³⁵ it is the language of the Aztec's confessor to the penitent: "When thou wast created and sent here, thy father and mother Quetzalcoatl made thee like a precious stone ... but by thine own will and choosing thou didst become soiled";³⁶ it is the language of the Book of Revelations in Tenrikyo: "When you have swept dust cleanly, I shall certainly bring you a miraculous salvation."³⁷

This language of defilement speaks most impressively in three particular regards—its universality, its intensity, and its astonishing durability.

Universality is manifested both in terms of the different religions of humanity and the various people or objects who have been regarded as defiled. Thus, the eleventh international congress of the International Association for the History of Religions attracted more than seventy papers drawn from the religions of "primitive" peoples, the ancient Near East, Greek, Hellenistic and Roman culture, ancient Israel and Judaism, Christianity, Islam, India, Taoism, Buddhism, and Japan—all of which were devoted to the theme of guilt or pollution and purification.³⁸ On the other hand, while it is obvious that it is primarily humanity that is defiled in these religions, very often they are not

---

33 *Macbeth*, V, 1

34 Isa 6.5 (RSV).

35 Book of the Dead, ch. 125. Quoted in Mircea Eliade, ed., *From Primitives to Zen: A Thematic Sourcebook of the History of Religions* (Harper and Row, 1967), 240.

36 Laurette Séjourné, *Burning Water*, trans. Irene Nicholson (London, 1957), 9–10, quoting from Bernadina de Sahagún, *Historia de las Cosas de la Nueva Espana* (Mexico, 1946), II, 275; cited by Eliade, *From Primitives to Zen*, 241.

37 Ofudesaki, III, 98, quoted by Hideo Nakajima, "The Basic Structure of the Idea of Salvation and Purification in Tenrikyo," in *Proceedings of the XIth International Congress of the International Association for the History of Religions*, Vol. II. *Guilt or Pollution and Rites of Purification* (E. J. Brill, 1968), 196–97. (This work is hereinafter referred to as *Guilt or Pollution*.)

38 Ibid.

alone in his problem. Defilement may extend to places,[39] to objects of secular[40] or ritualistic usage,[41] to ritual utterances,[42] to the deity,[43] or even to the cosmos itself;[44] while it may likewise embrace time.[45]

In taking note of the universality of defilement, we by no means suggest a uniformity of the phenomenon. Defilement is expressed and understood with infinite variations in the gamut of religions; nor is the understanding uniform within any one religion. What this multiform expression does show, however, is that, in dealing with defilement, we confront a *human* problem— that is, not some quirk or oddity, some flotsam thrown up sporadically by the sea of religions.

Nor has the degree of religious concern associated with defilement been constant. But it is undeniable that often the most intense religious feeling has been aroused because humanity has felt itself unclean. No one who, like this writer, has met a band of pilgrims on the Indian road will deny it. In the high fastnesses of the Himalayas or on the paved way outside the metropolis, the group is quickly recognized—not so much by the saffron or bundles of belongings slung on the back as by the sense of purpose, of religious devotion. How far have they come? Perhaps hundreds of miles. Where are they going? No matter what the place, you will be certain of one thing: there will be a sacred bathing place there; and the climax of the trek will come as the weary members of the band plunge into the sacred, snow-fed waters of Kedrinath or Badrinath, or the warm waters of Benares or Nasik. In the West, we have no sacred rivers—but baptistries are still constructed and congregations still sing:

> Whiter than snow, yes, whiter than snow—
> Now wash me and I shall be whiter than snow.[46]

The persistence of the language of defilement is astonishing. According to Ricoeur,[47] the symbol of defilement is simplest and earliest in humanity's

---

39 As in the Jewish Day of Atonement ceremony: see Lev 16.
40 As in Lev 14.33ff (a dwelling); 13.47ff (a garment); 15.4ff (a bed).
41 As in Lev 16.15ff.
42 As in purification of the *mantras* in *Kularnava Tantra*; cf. Alain Daniélou, *Hindu Polytheism* (Pantheon Books for Bollingen Foundation, 1964), 377–78.
43 Ibid.
44 E.g., the Tao: an offence against positive law is also an offence against natural and heavenly law. See Paul S. Hsiao, "Schuld als Spaltung vom Tao," *Kair*, VIII (1966), 117–24.
45 E.g., Joseph M, Kitagawa, "Gohei-Hasami: ein Ritus der 'Läuterung der Zeit' auf dem Berg Koya," *Kair*, VIII (1966), 114–17.
46 James Nicholson, "I Shall Be Whiter than Snow."
47 Paul Ricoeur, *The Symbolism of Evil*, trans. Emerson Buchanan (Beacon Press, 1969), 25–29. The methodology of Ricoeur, while in part similar to that of the phenomenology of

understanding of itself; yet, albeit transformed, the symbol retains its place with surprising power in modern society. In the history of the symbol, change has been primarily in two directions: toward a "spiritualizing" or toward a desacralization.

The prime idea of defilement is that of a physical stain or blot, that is, *dirt*. Ricoeur is no doubt correct, however, in his contention that the symbol is even here *more* than merely physical—there is a pointing beyond to an interiorized problem.[48] In many religions, the physical aspect has been almost entirely superseded: this is the "spiritualizing" or interiorizing of defilement. Such is the case in the Christian hymn quoted above; perhaps the extreme development is seen in Nāgārjuna's negation of any differentiation between defiled and undefiled:

> Thou knowest that the defilement of passion and the purification of virtue have the same taste; since no discrimination is possible in reality, thou art completely pure.[49]

Yet it seems safe to say that, just as defilement is never understood *wholly* as physical, even so it is never understood *merely* as spiritual. The same congregation that sings "whiter than snow" for "spiritual" cleansing would be horrified if a member came to sing all dirty, disheveled and unshaven: the adage "cleanliness is next to godliness" has clearly *not* been transmogrified! And even so does Buddhism show a peculiar regard for the care and cleansing of the body.

Shinto provides an excellent illustration of this dual nature of purification. The two terms associated with purgation, *misogi* and *harai*, are used for the removing of impurities from both body and mind.[50] Thus, concerning the ritual bathing in cold water:

> What is ablution? It is not merely the cleansing of one's body solely with lustral water; it means one's following the Right and Moral way. Pollution means moral evil or vice. Though a man wash off his bodily filth he will yet fail to please the Deity if he restrain not his evil desires.[51]

---

religion, is essentially a phenomenology of language—that is, of confession.

48 Ibid., 28.
49 Giuseppe Lucci, "Two Hymns of the *Catuḥ-stava* of Nāgārjuna," *JRAS*, N.S., XXVIII (1932), 313–19.
50 Jean Herbert, *Shinto: At the Fountain-head of Japan* (Stein and Day, 1967), 80.
51 Ibid., quoted from Y. Tomobe, *Shinto-shoden-kuju* (n.p.).

Accordingly, the process of spiritual discipline of the Yamakage Shinto school involves four stages: *misogi-harai* of the body, *misogi-harai* of the heart, *misogi-harai* of the environment, and *misogi-harai* of the soul.[52]

Even in a post-Freudian era, the symbol of defilement is ubiquitous—though desacralized. It surfaces in the modern idiom: we see it in expressions like "dirty money," "dirty politics," "filthy story," "dark deed." The modern cult of the bathroom is not simply a matter of our knowledge of hygiene, any more than is the preoccupation with spring-cleaning, washing machines, dishwashers and vacuum cleaners.[53] Two terms in particular show that what we have in all this is in fact a desacralized defilement ritual: "pollution" and "water." The ready acceptance of the term "pollution" by modern person in the context of the concern for the environment points up its deep-rooted associations; while the anxiety for "pure" water, coupled with the huge per capita usage of water, shows again the astonishing durability of the symbol of defilement. Howard Hughes is supposed to have a sliding scale, as it were, of the relative "dirtiness" of the people he meets, and to have admired Katharine Hepburn because she took three or four baths a day:[54] thus, even in desacralized forms does the symbol of defilement strike an answering chord in modern times.

The Nature of Defilement

The religious concern associated with defilement prompts two questions: (1) In what manner is this defilement, so significant for religious life, viewed? and (2) What is it that imparts to defilement its peculiar character?

The descriptive nature of defilement is relatively straightforward. Nilsson's remarks, although made in the context of Greek religion, provide a good summary of the universal phenomena:

> Uncleanness was conceived of as an infection, as a material substance which could be washed away with water or the blood of sacrificial victims, rubbed off or else burned away with fire, or smoked out with sulphur.[55]

---

52 Ibid., 79.
53 Hugh T. Kerr, "The Christ-Life as Mythic and Psychic Symbol," *Num*, IX (1962), 151.
54 *Time*, Jan. 24, 1972, p. 14. Whether or not this was true of Howard Hughes, the fascination of modern man with the possibility illustrates the continuing power of "defilement" patterns of thought.
55 Martin P. Nilsson, *A History of Greek Religion*, trans. F. J. Fielden (Clarendon Press, 1925), 85.

That is, defilement has as its foci the ideas of material "substance" and contagion.

The root symbol of defilement as a spot, stain, blemish, or impurity comes to expression in numerous ways. The clearest are those in which defilement is viewed as "dirt" or "dust" which is to be washed, swept, or rubbed away.[56] Particularly illuminating also are the rites of "sending away": the boat cast adrift,[57] the "sacrifices" of the Thargelia festival which absorb the impurity of the town,[58] the sin-laden bundles of grass which contain the sins of the Japanese community,[59] or the goat sent to Azazel "bearing" Israel's sins.[60] In the Jainist religion, the material view of defilement is wedded to karmic theory in a unique concept: defilement is a subtle matter which clings to the soul, making it "heavy" and so leading to metempsychosis.[61]

But this defiling "matter" is not merely a source of religious danger to the defiled individual: over and over we see that it cannot only be transmitted but in fact may act as a contagion. Thus, defilement passes naturally to the idea of "sickness"[62]—not merely in the sense that actual sickness may ensue (though this may often happen as we shall see below), but in that defilement itself spreads like a plague. Almost anything may act as a defiling agent, depending on the religion, but most generally the body issues—blood, spittle, semen, menstrual blood, feces[63]—dead bodies,[64] or sexual intercourse.[65]

Mere contact, wittingly or ignorantly, with a defiling agent (thing or person) suffices to transmit the defilement;[66] indeed, one may become defiled simply by coming near a corpse, for instance. Thus, the Mishnaic tract *Taharoth*, which deals exhaustively with uncleanness, treats at length with dwellings communicating the defilement of a corpse.[67]

---

56 Cf. Sokyo Ono, "The Way of Purification: The Shinto Case," *Guilt or Pollution*, 189: "There are three traditional forms of purification in Shinto: *Misoqi* or purification by water, *Harai* or purification by sweeping, and *Aganai* or purification by redemption."

57 E. N. Fallaize, "Purification (Introductory and Primitive)," *ERE*, V, 466.

58 Nilsson, *History*, 86–87.

59 Herbert, *Shinto*, 192.

60 Lev 16.20–22.

61 Nathmal Tatia, "Purification in Jainism," *Guilt or Pollution*, 130–32.

62 Thus, with Zwingli: sin equals *morbus*. See Paul T. Fuhrmann, "Adam's Guilt and Man's Need for Innocence, according to Zwingli," *Guilt or Pollution*, 95.

63 E.g., Edward B. Harper, "Ritual Pollution as an Integrator of Caste and Religion," *JAS*, XXIII (1964), 151–97.

64 This horror of the corpse is seen in its sharpest expression among the Parsees. The dead body can neither be burned nor buried (lest it defile fire or earth); hence it is exposed in the "towers of silence."

65 4QCD xii, 1–2: "No one should sleep with a woman in the city of the temple, defiling the city of the temple with their impurity."

66 Cf. Lev 4.1ff.: even sins of ignorance defiled the sanctuary.

67 The tractate *Oholoth* is given over to this topic.

Before we take up the matter of what it is that gives defilement its particular character, it is necessary to clarify the issue of ritual (cultic) defilement in relation to moral (or spiritual) defilement. From at least the time of Robertson Smith, it has been fashionable to draw a heavy line between the two. Ritual defilement was to be associated with "primitive"-type religious thinking, in which ideas of *tabu* and *mana* were supposedly to the fore: breach of *tabu* entailed dangerous defilement through the transference of impersonal power (*mana*).[68] Moral defilement was a product of "developed" religious thinking in which religion was personalized and internalized and wherein irrational and amoral *tabus* were discarded. In the light of more recent thought, however, the distinction appears increasingly dubious. Simon has shown how, even in the "apostolic decree" of the New Testament, it is difficult to differentiate between cultic and moral.[69] Mary Douglas, for her part, has demonstrated how often moral values are reinforced by so-called defilement rituals.[70] Schilling, however, has gone even further, arguing that the very "oughtness" which is coterminous with religious "experience" wherever manifested is the root of both morality and ritual.[71] We need hardly to add that the evolutionary schema of religious development which was the undergirding of the old distinction is now quite discarded.

It seems to us, therefore, that the distinction of "ritual" as opposed to "moral" defilement is as unreal as it is unhelpful. We are concerned with humanity as *homo religiosus*; defilement is pre-eminently a *religious* category. That there are great variations in the degree of materiality with which defilement is understood is indisputable; but we have already argued that defilement is never *wholly* material even as it is never *wholly* "spiritual" or moral.[72]

What then is it that gives defilement its *religious* character? Here, three aspects demand attention: power, death, and order. The early theories of Robertson Smith[73] and Frazer[74] were right to the extent that they saw in the con-

---

68 This approach is still followed by R. Hink, "Rein and Unrein," *RGG*, V, 940–41.

69 Marcel Simon, "Souillure morale et souillure rituelle dans le Christianisme primitif," *Guilt or Pollution*, 87–88.

70 Douglas, *Purity and Danger*, 154–65.

71 Werner Schilling, "Die psychologischen Zusammenhänge von religiösem Urerlebnis, Sühnegedanken and ethischem Handeln," *Guilt or Pollution*, 17–18.

72 We shall not attempt to get into the debate concerning the relation of religion to ethics. Our concern is to show that defilement is above all a religious concept, so that the attempts to differentiate cultic defilement from moral defilement have missed the mark. Do we see in such attempts a perpetuation of an unreal "body-spirit" dichotomy? Religion has to do with the whole person: it must take account of defilement of the mind as well as of the body.

73 *Religion of the Semites*, 152–55.

74 J. G. Frazer, *The Golden Bough: A Study in Religion and Magic*, Vol. III. *Taboo and the Perils of the Soul* (Macmillan Co., 1911), *passim*.

sciousness of defilement the outworking of power. Defilement is dangerous: it is a negative power. Defilement is conceived of in much the same way as modern people think of disease. They have not actually *seen* bacteria or viruses—they exist for them as quasi-material "substances" manifested by their functional power to be transmitted and to cause ill-effects.

Yet we must probe further the sources of this evil power; and before long we confront the existential plight of *homo religiosus* as they stand before death. In a dissertation written by Emanuel Feldman[75], Feldman set forth the thesis that the entire regulations having to do with defilement in the Old Testament and in Rabbinism are associated with death and the fear of death. It is certainly the case that in almost all religions a corpse is viewed as that which is most "unclean," that is, laden with negative power; and that bodily issues and functions are intimately associated with defilement.[76] Thus, it seems likely that humanity's religious concern over defilement is inextricably bound up with its desire to promote and prolong life and to avoid death—we see here reflected its attempts to come to grips with "this monstrous thing that is life,"[77] the mystery of life and death.

The third aspect—order—takes us beyond the individual in its existential anxiety. For dirt indicates disorder;[78] it is an offence to the organizing character of mind. Even so is death an anomaly: it marks a breach in society, a disordering of communal organization. Dirt and death are of a kind: they represent that which is out of place, disrupting the order of society and ultimately the cosmos.

This, then, is the nature of defilement: it is a quasi-material, quasi-moral, evil power which is readily transmissible. It represents the disruptive element, the force of disorder and chaos which stands over against the individual's existence, his society, and finally the cosmos.

If the question is pressed: Whence did this defilement itself arise? no clear answer is to be obtained. The explanation will be involved in myths of cosmogony; for instance, the defilement may have been brought *upon* humanity by evil spirit-beings.[79] That is to say, the origins are posited at a prior stage, rather than explained: what we face is the insoluble problem of the origins of evil. But this question of *source* of defilement is not the essential

---

75 Emanuel Feldman," Law and Theology in Biblical and Post-Biblical Defilement and Mourning Rites" (unpublished Ph.D. dissertation, Emory University, 1971).
76 Cf. Hink, "Rein and Unrein," 940–41.
77 The phrase is from Joseph Campbell in his arresting description of myth in Joseph Campbell, ed., *Myths, Dreams, and Religion* (E. P. Dutton, 1970), 139.
78 Cf. Douglas, *Purity and Danger*, 12–16.
79 As in Shinto; cf. Sokyo Ono, "The Way of Purification," 188–89.

one, even as it is not that which receives stress. The phenomenology of religion shows us *homo religiosus* as he is *now*; for it is in the "now" time that the problem of defilement impinges upon the world of his existence with compelling intensity.

The Effects of Defilement

The defiled person is both itself in danger and a source of danger to its society and the cosmos. For the polluted is a potential polluter; furthermore, he is inimical to ordered relationships.[80]

Subjectively, defilement is marked by feelings of *dread*.[81] This is the feeling of the one who stands alone, utterly alone, cut off from one's society and from a hostile cosmos. Such and individual feel the dread of the anomaly; they have become a "non-person." There are degrees of pollution; thus, there are degrees of dread. Certainly, many cases of transgression of defilement laws will be treated lightly; but if the defilement is of such a nature that the very cosmos is endangered, no way of purification may be possible. So arises the case of the inexpiable offence: the defiled one has ceased to be a person, has no access to the cult where alone the prescribed ritual is available, and can only be removed from a place in the cosmos.[82]

This subjective feeling of dread may or may not be accompanied by external manifestations of the power of defilement. For instance, the defiled person may become sick or lose their skill in hunting. Therefore, the occurrence of such ill-fortune may be often construed as evidence of a defilement contracted, perhaps unwittingly.[83]

The negative power of defilement reaches beyond one's own person, however. For instance, among the Nuer the man whose wife has committed adultery may suffer a backache when he next has intercourse with her.[84] More than this, the whole society is endangered by the presence of one who is "infected" by defilement; they are the "Achan" in the camp.[85] Sophocles' play *King Oedipus* strikingly portrays the miseries which befell Thebes due to the

---

80 Cf. Douglas, *Purity and Danger*, 165: "The polluter becomes a doubly wicked object of reprobation, first because he crossed the line and second because he endangered others."

81 Ricoeur, *Symbolism of Evil*, 29–33. Cf. Martin P. Nilsson, *Greek Piety*, trans. Herbert J. Rose (Clarendon Press, 1951), 42.

82 Cf. Victor Maag, "Nicht sühnbare Schuld," *Kair*, VIII (1966), 90–106.

83 Lauri Honko, "Breach of Taboo as a Primitive Concept of Disease," *Guilt or Pollution*, 31–32.

84 E. E. Evans-Pritchard, *Kinship and Marriage among the Nuer* (Clarendon Press, 1960), 120–21.

85 Josh 7.1–26.

hidden crime of Oedipus himself;[86] on a more "spiritual" level, the instruction from Paul displays a similar concern:

> Therefore come out from them,
> and be separate from them, says the Lord,
> and touch nothing unclean;
> then I will welcome you....
>
> Drive out the wicked person from among you.[87]

The polluted person, therefore, is a source of *danger* to the society in two respects: not only may they contaminate others with their religious "infection" but, because of their anomalous status, they are a divisive force in the ordering of the society.

This second aspect points to the way in which humanity, society, and cosmos are bound up in the ordering of existence. The starkest expression of this interdependence is seen in the idea that defilement has *cosmological* ramifications. By no means is this a concept confined to non-literate societies. Over and again we find the thought expressed: defiled people defile their city, their country, their cosmos. "The earth is defiled under the inhabitants thereof," cries Isaiah.[88] In the Apocalypse, God will destroy those that destroy the earth; there issues at last a new heaven and a new earth; while the saved ones are described as "virgins ... not defiled with women."[89] H. D. Betz has shown how widespread are the roots of such apocalyptic motifs of the defilement of "the elements."[90] In Shinto, on the other hand, humanity's defilement may be of two kinds: it may be no more than terrestrial or it may extend even to "the heavens."[91] Accordingly, the requisite purification is to be efficacious on either the terrestrial or the "heavenly" level.[92]

What is the religious rationale of such thought? Two indications seem to be undeniable: the material transmissibility of defilement and the organic

---

86 Nilsson, *Religion as Man's Protest*, 57–58.
87 2 Cor 6.17–18; 1 Cor 5.13 (RSV).
88 Isa 24.5.
89 Rev 11.18; 21.1ff; 14.3.
90 "Schöpfung und Erlösung im hermetischen Fragment, 'Kore Kosmu,'" *ZTK*, LXIII (1966), 160–87; "Zum Problem des religionsgeschichtlichen Verständnisses der Apokalyptik," ibid., 391–409.
91 *Kunitsu-tsumi* equals terrestrial sins; *amatsu-tsumi* equals heavenly sins. See Jun-ichi Kamata, "Pollution and Sin in Shinto," *Guilt or Pollution*, 183; Herbert, *Shinto*, 77–78.
92 Cf. Naofusa Hirai, "Shinto Purification and the Concept of Man," *Guilt or Pollution*, 185–87; Sokyo Ono, "The Way of Purification: The Shinto Case," ibid., 188–89; and Seigo Tani, "The Meaning of 'Harae' in Shintoism," ibid., 190–91.

relatedness of humanity and cosmos. If humanity's defilement can defile the land and even the heavens and the earth, this can only be because defilement is an "infection" which can pass from person to non-person. Just as a defiled object (non-person) can defile a person, so can a person defile its environment. This conception of defilement, of course, is in accord with our earlier remarks as to its nature. We must note, however, how integral to the conceptual structure is the idea of the oneness of humanity and "nature." The modern mind is quite at home with the thought of the transmissibility of "infection" from one person to another, or from animals to persons. But the idea of an "infected" ("leprous") house[93] boggles the mind—how much more an "infected" cosmos! Yet this is just the sort of thinking that we have here: the organic interrelatedness of humanity and cosmos demands that defilement of the inhabitants of a city defiles the city, defilement of the people of the land defiles the land, defilement of the peoples of the world calls for a new heaven and a new earth.

The relation of the defiled person to the cultus is a two-edged one. On one side, the fact of defilement debars from participation in the common ritual: one who is defiled cannot approach the Holy. In this sense, the polluted person is a religious outcast and defilement entails an inevitable separation.[94] On the other side, it is the cultus that provides the way back to the place in society, as it prescribes purification rituals. There is the possibility, however, that, as we have already noticed, the defilement will be considered to be of such dire cosmic consequences that no purification ritual can suffice. The defiled person in this case has become a permanent "non-person." It is the participation in the cultus that marks people from the beast; hence, if that participation is forever denied, the individual has fallen to animal status. Extinction of the "non-person" is then the only course of action.

Implications of the Religious View of Defilement

What does this phenomenology of defilement point to concerning the *human* condition (that is, the "nature of humanity"), the understanding of deity, and the view of the cosmos in which defilement comes to expression?

We have already observed how the symbol of defilement is related to ideas of death and disorder: it points to humanity's vulnerability (they are not immune in a world of powers) and the dangerous character of existence.

---

93 Lev 14.33ff.
94 Cf. the idea of the defiled person remaining "outside the camp" of the Israelites; e.g., Num 5.2–4.

It is necessary, however, to probe further behind these ideas. The problem is: why is defilement so much bound up with the *self*-reference? Granted that, as we have seen, finally the cosmos is involved in defilement, yet it is the *personal* anxiety arising from the *individual* self-consciousness of defilement that gives to defilement its peculiar religious intensity. That is to say, humankind is subject to intense feelings that *it* is out of order with the cosmos. Here the explanation of life-death anxiety is insufficient, since the cosmos as humanity sees it is subject to analogous cycles of life and death. What we find, in fact, when we probe the phenomenology of defilement to its limits, is humanity's feelings of "numinous uneasiness" (to use Bouquet's happy term),[95] that is, one's "guilt." *Why* should humankind be subject to such "numinous uneasiness"; that is, *why* should it continually feel itself to be the anomaly, the case of "dirt" disordering the cosmos? At this point, psychology of religion or theology may have answers to suggest, but phenomenology has no further word to add; as van der Leeuw has well said:

> The state of being "laden with guilt" originates in the circle of celebrations and cares; but guilt itself has no specific origin whatever: rather it pertains to the very being of man.... Guilt therefore, with faith, falls quite outside the realm of Phenomenology.[96]

The discussion of defilement which we have undertaken, it will have been noticed, has been carried on with scant reference to ideas of deity. Deity comes to the fore only in this matter: that deity is "pure," that is, undefiled, so that humanity as defiled is debarred from the approach to the deity.[97] That is to say, defilement represents the separation from deity (the ideal of purity) felt by humanity in its "'numinous uneasiness."

The very nature of the symbol of defilement, however, militates against a strong interrelatedness to deity. Defilement is not so much an act of defiance of the will of deity as it is a description of a state: what humanity *has become* rather than what it does. While deity is involved as the norm of purity and to the extent that humanity's impurity reaches the "heavens," the essential thrust is impersonal rather than personal.

---

95 A. C. Bouquet, "Numinous Uneasiness," *Guilt or Pollution*, 1–8.
96 *Religion in Essence and Manifestation*, 518.
97 Cf. Rokusaburo Nieda, "The Significance of Pollution and Purification in Japanese Religious Consciousness: A Comparative Study," *Guilt or Pollution*, 181: "Human beings, however, are thought to have many pollutions, and therefore those who enter the sacred region of the temple are requested to purify themselves. Otherwise, they would pollute the purity and holiness of nature in which the gods and Buddhas dwell."

This receding from prominence of the idea of deity corresponds to the view of the cosmos associated with ideas of defilement. In fine, this is the relationship: humanity and "nature" are seen in organic unity (and "nature," as we have seen, may extend throughout the cosmological perspective to embrace the "heavens"). Thus, humanity's problem of defilement is ultimately a cosmological problem. This is not at all to suggest that where defilement thought patterns are in vogue humanity does not make differentiations between itself and "nature." Quite the contrary, in fact, obtains: humanity is very much alert to the distinction between what is "humanity," that is, the person who has the cultus (which is to say, the one who worships), and the "non-person" who does not have the cultus.[98] But such a person feels a closeness to, and unity with, the cosmos that modern urban life has largely obliterated.[99] The ancient text from the Qumran community epitomizes this interrelationship of people and "world":

All wood and stones and dust defiled by the impurity of a man shall be reckoned like men with regard to conveying defilement; whoever touches them shall be defiled by their defilement.[100]

The cosmos, in such patterns of thought, is viewed essentially as a material, physical, organic whole. Even the "heavens" are not to be set apart in any essential contrast.[101] Certainly, there can be no dichotomy within the cosmos; for instance, no Platonic-type world of the Ideal set off against, and having no contact with, the mundane world of the material.

Humanity's concern over defilement obviously points beyond itself to a solution congruent with the problem; and the phenomena associated with purification immediately suggest themselves. Before turning to these data, however, we must pause to consider the religious significance of blood.

---

98 Cf. Maag, "Nicht sühnbare Schuld," 90–106.

99 In particular Mircea Eliade in works such as *Patterns in Comparative Religion*, and *The Sacred and Profane*, has brought out this loss of a sense of "unity" with the cosmos as the impoverishment of the religious life of modern man.

100 4QCD xii, 15–17.

101 Two attempts to relate the ideas of pollution to the view of humanity and cosmos should be noticed. Philip Wheelwright, "Hamartia and its Resolution in Three Religious Perspectives," *Guilt or Pollution*, 15–16, argues that "pollution" is viewed as humanity's problem in a "chthonic" perspective (but not in "ouranian" or "metaphysical" perspectives). K. A. H. Hidding, "Schuld and Reinigungsriten im Javanischen Islam," *Guilt or Pollution*, 111–12, contends that pollution ideas prevail where humankind views itself corporeally rather than spiritually. Both of these writers agree with our point here that pollution is viewed against a background of organic unity of humanity and cosmos.

A Phenomenology of Blood

Implications of the Religious View of Defilement

The symbol of blood immediately impresses us by its evocative potency. Whereas defilement works as a quasi-material, perhaps invisible, insidious infection, blood displays itself in stark contrast as the manifestation of blatant religious power.[102]

Consider, for instance, Prudentius's account of the taurobolium:

> The high priest who is to be consecrated is brought down under ground in a pit dug deep, marvelously adorned with a fillet, binding his festive temples with chaplets, his hair combed back under a golden crown, and wearing a silken toga caught up with Gabine girding.
>
> Over this they make a wooden floor with wide spaces, woven of planks with an open mesh; they then divide or bore the area and repeatedly pierce the wood with a pointed tool that it may appear full of small holes.
>
> Hither a huge bull, fierce and shaggy in appearance, is led, bound with flowery garlands about its flanks, and with its horns sheathed; yea, the forehead of the victim sparkles with gold, and the flash of metal plates colors its hair.
>
> Here, as is ordained, the beast is to be slain, and they pierce its breast with a sacred spear; the gaping wound emits a wave of hot blood, and the smoking river flows into the woven structure beneath it and surges wide.
>
> Then by the many paths of the thousand openings in the lattice the falling shower rains down a foul dew, which the priest buried within catches putting his shameful head under all the drops, defiled both in his clothing and in all his body.
>
> Yea, he throws back his face, he puts his cheeks in the way of the blood, he puts under it his ears and lips, he interposes his nostrils, he washes his very eyes with the fluid, nor does he even spare his throat but moistens his tongue, until he actually drinks the dark gore.
>
> Afterwards, the flamens draw the corpse, stiffening now that the blood has gone forth, off the lattice and the pontiff, horrible in appearance, comes forth, and shows his wet head, his beard heavy with blood, his dripping fillets and sodden garments.

---

102 Cf. Eliade: "Throughout the world, blood is a symbol of strength and fertility"; *Rites and Symbols of Initiation: The Mysteries of Birth and Rebirth*, trans. Willard R. Trask (Harper Torchbooks, 1965), 26.

This man, defiled with such contagions and foul with the gore of the recent sacrifice, all hail and worship at a distance, because profane blood and a dead ox have washed him while concealed in a filthy cave.[103]

No reader can take up this account without the stirrings of emotion, perhaps of deep revulsion or disgust, at least of fascination. Why is this? Certainly, we sense immediately that if the ceremony had been carried out using, for example, water, milk, wine, or oil instead of blood it would be bereft of its evocative spell.

In this gripping scene we see ideas of initiation, consecration, and divinization (note the worship accorded the initiate). On the other hand, we see two very different interpretations of the ritual: what for the devotees of Cybele is a substance of consecrating and divinizing potency is for the Christian Prudentius a defiling contagion.[104] With this multiform symbology of blood we shall be concerned below; what is to be emphasized at the outset and constantly kept in view, however, is that blood represents *potency* of the greatest religious magnitude. As a Ndembu informant expressed to V. Turner, "blood is power."[105]

The Multivalent Character of Blood

If blood stands for power, naked and immediate, the particular character of that power is manifested with what appears to be a bewildering multivalence. It is not merely that some societies may understand blood as a purifying agent of supreme power while their neighbors may see it as that which is of the greatest potency to defile (contrast the Aztecs with the North American Indians[106]); within the *same* society blood may be viewed as either defiling or purifying, depending on the ritual context. For instance, among both the ancient Greeks and the Hebrews homicide entailed severe defilement of the slayer and the land,[107] yet the supreme agent for cleansing efficacy was an-

---

103 *Peristephanon*, X, 1011–50. Quoted in C. K. Barrett, ed., *The New Testament Background: Selected Documents* (rev. ed.; S.P.C.K., 1987), 126.

104 Note the pejorative language: "foul dew," "shameful head," "defiled," "dark gore," "horrible in appearance," "contagions," "profane blood," "filthy cave."

105 V. W. Turner, *The Forest of Symbols: Aspects of Ndembu Ritual* (Cornell University Press, 1967), 70.

106 For the Aztecs, human blood was "the precious liquid," but to the North American Indians it was dirty and impure. See Yolotl C. de Lesur, "The Concept of Pollution, of Guilt, and the Rites of Purification among the Aztecs," *Guilt or Pollution*, 40.

107 Nilsson, *Greek Piety*, 43: even the sight of the homicide was polluting; Num 35.33—"blood" defiles the land.

imal blood.[108] This ambivalent character of the power of blood was highlighted by the Hebrew ritual of the red heifer:[109] while the ceremony was used to provide a means of purification, all those who were associated with the death of the heifer were themselves defiled by it.[110]

Indeed, we find the symbology of blood extending to a wide range of meanings beyond those of purity/impurity. V. Turner found that for the Ndembu blood signifies huntsmanship or meat, parturition, menstrual blood, homicide, and witchcraft or sorcery.[111] His suggestive essay, "Color Classification in Ndembu Ritual: A Problem in Primitive Classification,"[112] eventually goes beyond the bounds of the Ndembu and gives examples from other parts of Africa, the Malay Peninsula, North America, Australia, and even the Indo-European religions. Its conclusion is as follows:

> Red = bloodshed is connected with war, feud, conflict, social discontinuities; red = obtaining and preparation of animal food = status of hunter or herder, male productive role in the sexual division of labor, etc.; red = transmission of blood from generation to generation = an index of membership in a corporate group.[113]

This multivalence of blood, that is, its "capacity to express simultaneously a number of meanings whose continuity is not evident on the plane of immediate experience,"[114] is not in itself a unique thing in symbology.[115] In our search for the religious understanding of blood, however, we must seek to find the underlying structure which gives rise to these multiform manifestations. As a Ndembu observer had noticed, "red things belong to two categories; they act for both good and ill; (these) are combined."[116] We would further

---

108 In Greek religion, pig's blood (Nilsson, *History*, 86; *Greek Piety*, 15); the Thargelia, however, used a human "sacrifice." Cf. Lev 17.11—"It is the blood that makes an atonement for the soul."

109 Num 19.1–22.

110 This religious ambivalence of the red heifer ritual was a continuing source of rabbinic debate. See Joseph L. Blau, "The Red Heifer: A Biblical Purification Rite in Rabbinic Literature," *Num*, XIV (1967), 70–80. We examine the red heifer in more detail in our exegesis of Heb 9.13–14 in the following chapter.

111 Turner, *Forest of Symbols*, 70.

112 Ibid., 59–92.

113 Ibid., 89.

114 Mircea Eliade, "Methodological Remarks on the Study of Religious Symbolism," in Eliade and Kitagawa, *Essays in Methodology*, 99.

115 What Eliade terms "multivalence" is called "polysemy" or "multi-vocality" by V. Turner. See his *Forest of Symbols*, 50.

116 Ibid., 70.

clarify this categorization: the various expressions of the symbology of blood involve either an extension or a diminution of life.

Where blood is concerned with the extension of life, it is a positive power; where it is concerned with the denial of life, it is a negative potency. Thus, homicide is clearly defiling, while menstrual blood, representing as it does the denial of a new life, is likewise a negative power.[117] Again, in the circumcision ritual of the Ndembu novices, those who perform the operation are considered shedders of blood, and thus are defiled by their actions.[118] Inversely, the blood of parturition may be viewed positively, since it is involved in new life;[119] blood "makes atonement"[120] and thus restores to the full life of humankind (the life of the cultus); blood is a medium of initiation at the crises of life;[121] and—most directly stated of all—blood is life.[122]

These two "powers" of blood—the positive and the negative—in fact are aspects of a fundamental unity in the religious understanding: *the affirmation of life*. When that which diminishes life is accorded a negative potency we have as much an affirmation of life as when that which extends or preserves life is accorded a positive potency. If the extension or preservation of life itself involves the diminution of life, as in war, we see the "defiling" and "positive" aspects of blood placed in juxtaposition. That such "contradictions" are a continuing source of religious unease is evidenced by recent debate concerning "moral" and "immoral" wars.

Before we attempt to see the implications of this understanding of blood for the concepts of person, deity, and cosmos, it is necessary to consider the data provided by the practice, widespread among the religions of the world, of bloody sacrifices. Here we meet again the taking of life for the purpose of extending life.

The Religious Motivation of Bloody Sacrifices

When we ask *why* people offer bloody sacrifices, the immediate answer is that deity has so commanded.[123] If, however, we reframe the question so as to

---

117 Menstrual blood is regarded with widespread aversion; cf. Hink, "Rein and Unrein," 940–41.

118 Turner, *Forest of Symbols*, 151–279. Likewise, the Ndembu make a sharp distinction between the "blood of huntsmanship" and the "blood of procreation": "Hunters shed blood and cause it to gush and flow. Again, women give life, while hunters take it. The two functions are antithetical" (p. 363).

119 Ibid., 70, 363. (But in some religions a *woman* is unclean because of childbirth; e.g., Lev 12.1–8).

120 Lev 17.11.

121 Ellade, *Rites and Symbols of Initiation*, passim.

122 Lev 17.14; Gen 9.4.

123 With Th. P. van Baaren, "Theoretical Speculations on Sacrifice," *Num*, XI (1964), 1–12.

enquire what *benefits* the one who sacrifices hopes to obtain, we find a great variety of answers. The considerable amount of data relative to bloody sacrifices has evoked a plethora of scholarly writings on the topic;[124] yet no consensus among students of religion has been forthcoming.

It seems evident that the diversity of motivation arises from a series of factors: factors having to do with history, with the group, and with the individual. In terms of history, it is manifest that the motivation for sacrifice may alter and even be transformed within a cultus with the passage of a sufficient number of years.[125] In terms of the group, there are diversities of types of sacrifice, hence diversities of sacrificial motivation;[126] it is also likely that the same sacrifice may be viewed differently from one participant to another. Finally, when we consider the individual itself, it is reasonable to suppose that its motivation is seldom single: there may be several reasons—some dominant, some less prominent—for its offering of sacrifice. The ceremony has come to the individual laden with the hallowed traditions of the past generations; further, while the individual may offer the sacrifice as an individual, that individuality is never absolute: this one is always in some sense a part of the group.

Any list of benefits hoped for by those who offer sacrifices, as evidenced by the data of religion, would therefore necessarily be long. It would include propitiation, expiation, communion with deity, and countless "material" expectations such as fertility, healing, productivity of field and beast, success in the hunt, victory in battle, protection from danger, and safe travel.[127]

With van Baaren,[128] however, we would see that in actuality there are but three main categories operative in all this. In these, sacrifice is viewed respectively in terms of communion, gift, and cosmic rhythm.

The "communion" theory springs from the work of Robertson Smith.[129] Here the sacred meal is to the fore: as people and god partake of the sacred

---

124 Among the more significant treatments might be mentioned the following: Robertson Smith, *The Religion of the Semites*; Emile Durkheim, *The Elementary Forms of the Religious Life*, trans. J. W. Swain (Free Press, 1954); J. G. Frazer, *Man, God and Immortality* (Macmillan Co., 1927); S. Freud, *Totem and Taboo*, trans. A. A. Brill (George Routledge & Sons, 1919); H. Hubert and M. Mauss, *Sacrifice: Its Nature and Function*, trans. W. D. Halls (University of Chicago Press, 1964); E. O. James, *Sacrifice and Sacrament* (Thames & Hudson, 1962); A. E. Jensen, *Myth and Cult among Primitive Peoples*, trans. M. T. Choldin and W. Weissleder (University of Chicago Press, 1963); P. Radin, *Primitive Religion* (Viking Press, 1937); E. B. Tylor, *Primitive Culture* (7th ed.; Bretano's, 1924); G. van der Leeuw, *Religion in Essence and Manifestation*; and R. K. Yerkes, *Sacrifice in Greek and Roman Religions and Early Judaism* (Adam & Charles Black, 1953).
125 Cf. Robertson Smith, *Religion of the Semites*, 351–87.
126 Thus, the various OT sacrifices of Leviticus.
127 Eliade, *From Primitives to Zen*, 201–28, gives a series of examples of sacrifice; these illustrate the wide variety of motivations to which we have referred.
128 Van Baaren, "Theoretical Speculations," 11.
129 Robertson Smith, *Religion of the Semites*, 240, 396, 439.

(totemic) animal, they are bound in mystic communion and the life of the community is renewed. Basic to the thinking is the kinship of humanity, god, and animal; a kinship which implies both clan and covenantal relationships. An impressive example of this theory is to be found in Kitagawa's description of the Ainu bear festival.[130] On the one hand, we notice the care lavished over the cub, as it is brought up in the hut as though one of the family; its designation as the "dear little divine thing"; the designation of the festival itself as "sending off the god"; the prayer to the bear for pardon before killing; the necessity of all to receive part of the flesh; and the concern that the entire animal be consumed. On the other hand, there is no suggestion of propitiation, nor of the *do ut des* principle.

The "gift" theory of sacrifice is championed by van der Leeuw.[131] Here, "gift" does *not* signify a bribe to the gods; rather, the very act of giving involves one in a communion, in a reciprocity of life in which the distinctions of giver and receiver are obliterated. The gift always involves part of oneself; thus, it "demands" a return of the receiver's life. Instead of *do ut des*—"I give that thou mayest give"—we have *do ut possis dare*—"I give that thou mayest be able to give."[132] On these terms, in the so-called "vicarious sacrifice" there can be no absolute substitution of sacrificial victim for the offeror. The extraordinary "self-sacrifice" of Decius, who gives himself for the victory of the Romans, clearly demonstrates van der Leeuw's theory.[133] His death is expected: "if this man is killed, it is proof that all is well"; and by the same token the gods were "moved" by this singular act.

In the work of A. E. Jensen[134] we note a sharp departure from the two theories mentioned above. His theory of sacrifice as a cosmic rhythm is marked by the absence of any "god" who is being appeased, receiving a gift, or entering into a fellowship meal. Among the root-crop cultivators, ritual killing is essentially the re-enactment of the myth of the *Dema*-deities: it at once a commemoration and a participation in the creative energy of the original death that marked the end of primal time. The energy released by the original act gradually runs down; the ritual seeks to renew it. In this myth-ritual, the act of killing is no more than an unavoidable concomitant of the acts of the drama—it is not of supreme significance in itself; nor is there a general predisposition toward killing in the culture. The essential insight into reality that the myth is portraying and which the ritual perpetuates is that there can be

---

130 Joseph M. Kitagawa, "Ainu Bear Festival," *HR*, I (1961), 95–151.
131 *Religion in Essence and Manifestation*, 350–60.
132 Ibid., 354.
133 Livy, *History of Rome*, VIII, 9.1–11; 10.3.
134 *Myth and Cult among Primitive Peoples*, 162–90.

no procreation without death. In a culture far removed from the root-crop cultivators, the Hindu myth of the cosmic sacrifice of the gods offers a striking parallel.[135]

These three theories concerning the motivation for bloody sacrifices converge to a single point: *the desire for life*. The "communion" theory seeks to restore or maintain life by participation in divine life; the "gift" theory seeks the impartation of divine life as the reciprocation of the life of the giver imparted in his gift; the cosmic rhythm theory endeavors to renew the vital forces of nature by re-enactment. Throughout, whether or not the idea of deity is prominent or even present in the conceptual scheme, we see an awareness that life is threatened, either by anti-life forces or simply by wearing down. The foundation of this structure is that life is precious: it is the supreme value.

Thus, the study of the religious motivation for bloody sacrifices brings us full circle to our earlier remarks concerning the symbology of blood: blood represents the affirmation of life. In the words of the Pentateuch: "the life is in the blood"; "the blood ... is the life."[136] The implications which follow for ideas of humanity, deity, and cosmos must now be our concern.

Implications of the Religious Understanding of Blood

So far as people are concerned, the symbology of blood points to the reality of *struggle* in their human situation. They are a part of the cosmos, yet they are continually surrounded by vindictive, dangerous forces within the cosmos. Life is good—the supreme good—but it stands in peril. That is, the symbology of blood first of all directs us to humanity's sense of frailty, of finitude.

To the extent that humanity is a prey to the negative, life-sapping forces of the cosmos, they are not free but bound. Blood then appears as the manifestation of *power*—power supreme, immediately given, life-affirming. Since it arises to vanquish the forces of decay and annihilation, it comes to humanity as a liberating power. Inversely, blood which is associated with death is anomalous; yet it retains its character of power and so represents a fiercely negative, defiling potency.

Reflection on blood further points to humanity's *fascination* with the life-forces of the cosmos: the naked power represented by blood at once evokes awe and wonder. For life is a great mystery: it surrounds humanity in the cosmos, continually obtruding itself by its manifestations as by its disappearance. Humanity stands in amazement before it, seeks to grasp it, to har-

---

135 Rig Veda, 10.90.
136 Lev 17.11, 14.

ness it to his chariot. Yet continually this life slips from between the fingers of humanity; continually, therefore, humanity seeks to re-affirm it. The evocative force of blood even in our technological, desacralized context is shown by the preoccupation with portrayals of bloody death in the entertainment world.[137]

So great is the power represented by blood and so direct its manifestations that ideas of deity tend to be dwarfed by it. Indeed, the investigations of Jensen[138] have shown that in ritual killing in certain cultures no direct deity may be at all involved: then blood becomes an autonomous religious symbol. Even where, as in the "communion" and "gift" theories of bloody sacrifice, the idea of deity is present, the accent clearly falls on the life mediated by the blood rather than on the deity. In fact, in both of these schemes there is set forth a *commonality* of humanity and deity in the "sharing" of life.[139]

It will be obvious that the relative places of blood and deity will not be the same in every religious system. We think immediately of the Judeo-Christian religion and of Islam. In the former, the God-person relation is to the fore, so that blood becomes a near-independent potency which is adapted to the will of God (or vice versa). In the latter, the idea of Allah is the over-arching principle of the system and bloody sacrifices assume a very minor role.

What then of the cosmos? Clearly, it is viewed as a place of competing *powers*.[140] The positive powers are those which are life-affirming and which reach their point of convergence and direct manifestation in the symbol of blood; they are opposed by life-denuding powers, among which anomalous blood (negative blood) stands out as a symbol of extreme danger. That is, existence in the cosmos is an existence *among* the powers; humanity is not in this sense over the cosmos but part of it and subject to it.[141] Existence is a continual struggle to re-affirm the forces of life—individual, social, cultic, and cosmic.

---

137 The symbol of blood still evokes mingled horror and fascination: cf. the popularity of "Bonny and Clyde" and "The Godfather."

138 *Myth and Cult among Primitive Peoples*, 162–90.

139 Thus, it is quite wrong to think that "blood" in religious thinking invariably suggests an *offering to* a deity, a death to "satisfy" or "placate" deity's "wrath." While there may be individual "bloodthirsty" deities occasionally manifested in the data of religion, the general structure is as we have described it.

140 Van der Leeuw has based his conception of religion in the idea of power. See his *Religion in Essence and Manifestation*, 23–42.

141 The Hebrew religion is no exception: humanity is both part of the cosmos (having been created, like it) and the one who subdues the cosmos. As a creature, subject to death, his existence partakes of the nature of the cosmos.

Before we attempt to relate these views to those which were presented by the phenomenology of defilement, we shall turn to a study of the phenomenology of purgation.

A Phenomenology of Purgation

Purgation: The Religious Counterpart of Defilement

> For us he would provide a bath
> Wherein to cleanse from sin,
> And drown the bitterness of death
> In His own blood and wounds,
> And so create new life.
>
> The eye itself sees but the water
> As man pours water forth.
> But faith in the spirit understands
> The power of Jesus Christ's blood.[142]

These words of Luther's hymn well illustrate the universal longing for purgation.[143] As there is a widespread, continuing sense of defilement, so there is a restlessness *within* the consciousness of defilement and a studied endeavor to break loose: thus, purification is the religious counterpart of defilement.

Over and over this longing comes to expression. "Purity is best for man from his birth," said Zarathustra."[144] "Mary, God has chosen and purified thee," said the angel to Mary in the Quran.[145] "Wash him and deliver him from impurities as thou knowest should be, for he is confided to thy power. Cleanse him of the contamination he hath received from his parents; let the water take away the soil and stain, and let him be freed from all taint," intoned the Aztec priest to the Goddess of the Flowing Waters at the ceremonial bathing of the newborn.[146] "Oh! please keep my body as pure as the incense-pot" and

---

142 Martin Luther, "Epiphany Hymn."
143 While we have in general used "purgation" for the religious counterpart of defilement, historians of religion commonly employ "purification." We do not intend any differentiation by our choice of "purgation."
144 Ys. 48.5.
145 11.42.
146 H. B. Alexander, *The World's Rim* (University of Nebraska Press, 1953), 177; translating de Sahagún, *Historia de la Cosas*," bk. VI, ch. XXXII. Quoted in Eliade, *From Primitives to Zen*, 239.

"Oh! please keep my soul as pure as the flame of wisdom" are recited in the opening part of the Buddhist purification rite.[147]

The phenomena of purgation thus arise from, and answer to, the phenomena of defilement. As defilement is first viewed as "dirt," "dust," a spot or stain, so purgation in its fundamental symbology stands for a washing away or wiping off, a making clean. As defilement is manifested as infectious, negative power, so purification appears as health, the vigor of wholesome potency. As there are degrees of defilement, so there are degrees of purification.[148] And as defilement is interiorized and "spiritualized," so purgation moves from rites dealing with the external body to the purifying of the inner life. But as the primary symbol of defilement as dirt, disorder, anomaly is never lost, even though an internalization has gone on, so the symbol of purification retains its essential moment of cleansing, ordering, making whole.

We saw earlier how the data of defilement point inexorably to humanity's "numinous uneasiness." Even so do the data of purification point to a longing for a return to *pristine purity*: defilement is predicated on this basis as an *intrusion*.[149] Therefore, whereas defilement implies a "pessimistic" view of the human condition, purification suggests an "optimistic" view of the cosmos. That is, and paraphrasing Paul, where defilement abounds, purification much more abounds.[150]

Yet not quite so: there is the case of the defilement for which no purgation is possible.[151] Inversely, there is the case of purification where no physical defilement is to be observed. Thus, among the Aztecs, purification ceremonies were numerous, although there was no consciousness of danger of defilement from menstrual blood, dead bodies, and so on.[152] Our interpretation of defilement as "numinous uneasiness," that is, of a consciousness of the self's personal disorder equals guilt, is able to take account of such cases of interiorized defilement, however.[153]

---

147 See Shinjo Takenaka, "The Significance of the Rite of Purification in Buddhism," *Guilt or Pollution*, 167.

148 Cf. Jun-ichi Kamata, "Pollution and Sin in Shinto," 183–84.

149 Cf. Nathmal Tatia, "Purification in Jainism," 130: "Purification is possible only of what is intrinsically pure and inherently capable of achieving it. Impurity, on the contrary, must be an outsider incapable of eternally affecting what is pure by nature." Likewise, in Shinto: *tsumi* is considered more in the nature of "an extrinsic element, a mistake, which does not affect the real person." See Herbert, *Shinto*, 77.

150 Paraphrasing Rom 5.20.

151 *Supra*, page 61.

152 De Lesur, "The Concept of Pollution," 39–43,

153 By the same token, the assertion that religions such as Buddhism and Islam are not burdened by a sense of guilt because they lack any doctrine of "original sin" is taken care of. Cf. Ian H. Douglas, "Guilt and Purification in Modern Urdu Quranic Commentary," *Guilt or Pollution*, 113–147; Robert Lawson Slater, "Buddhist Serenity and the Denial of Guilt," ibid., 145.

The Character of Purgation

Our remarks above point to the basic character of purification: it is to be conceived of in terms of *passage* (transition), *regeneration*, and *healing*.

Purification is a change of status. It is the passage from the separated to the integrated, from the "non-person" to the true person, from the profane to the holy, from the disordered to the ordered, from the state of numinous unease to the state of joy and peace. That is, whereas defilement stands for what humanity *is*, purgation points to what they may *become*. Nilsson's description of the contrast between the pure and the impure in Orphism provides a good illustration of the point:

> Purifications played a great part in Orphicism; those who were admitted into the sect were purified in the ordinary ways, which included rubbing with meal and mud. Those who had not been purified and initiated lived in their uncleanness and continued to do so in the other world. Hence comes the stock expression as to the lot of the uninitiated, that they lie in the mire (ἐν βορβόρῳ κεῖται).[154]

The idea of purgation as transition points to its character as initiation. In the general sense, every purification is an initiation in that it makes the Holy accessible to humankind. In the more restricted sense of initiation as for only the cultic elite, purgation rites play an inevitable part: the greater measure of cultic privilege calls for a corresponding degree of purification.[155] These rites come to material expression in "esoteric" religions such as Vajrayana Buddhism;[156] while in "spiritualized," interiorized accounts we find such as the following (from Mahayana Buddhism):

> The significance of this religious knowledge is not that it gives information about something, but that it purifies, it transforms human existence from the limitations of delusion to the freedom of clear apprehension about the true state of things.[157]

See the discussion later in this chapter (pp. 175–76) concerning the way of purification in the Sangha. It becomes obvious that, while ideas of guilt are not part of the theology of Buddhism or Islam, in terms of religious functionality we see them operative.

154 *History*, 218.
155 George Wechman, "Understanding Initiation," *HR*, X (1970), 62–79.
156 Hans J. Klimkeit, "Guilt, Pollution, and Purification Rites in Vajrayana Buddhism," *Guilt or Pollution*, 154–56.
157 Frederick J. Streng, "Purification through Non-Discrimination according to Nāgārjuna," *Guilt or Pollution*, 119–20.

Second, purgation signifies rebirth or regeneration. The priest of Cybele was worshipped as he emerged from the taurobolium,[158] likewise the New Testament speaks of the "washing of regeneration," of being "born of water and πνεῦμα."[159] In the religion of ancient Egypt, the purification rituals associated with the coronation of the pharaoh were set forth as giving the new ruler access to a universe of glory and eternity, even the world of the gods.[160]

That purgation should be viewed in terms of rebirth accords with the understanding of humanity mediated by the symbol of defilement. The polluted person is of anomalous status: if more than a beast, they are less than a person. In purification they *become* once more a person; thus, they are reborn.

Finally, purification signifies healing, or health. In the Yasnas, "purity" is used in the sense of wholeness or spiritual completeness;[161] while an uncircumcised Ndembu boy is known as "one who lacks purity or whiteness."[162] Turner reports that an African storekeeper accused of embezzlement expostulated, "My liver is white," just as an Englishman might say, "My conscience is clear." He asserts that to be "white" (or pure) "is to be in right relation to the living and the dead. To be in right relation to these is to be whole and well in oneself."[163]

These three marks of purgation—transition, rebirth, and wholeness—come to focus in a single conception: purification is a state of *power*. Whereas the state of defilement is marked by its negativity, its infection, its separation, the state of purification is that of the positive, the "blessing": success, health, harmony, continuity, appropriateness. An old adage affirmed:

> My strength is as the strength of ten
> Because my heart is pure;

while the Quran echoes:

> By the soul and That which shaped it
> and inspired it to lewdness and God fearing,
> prosperous is he who purifies it,
> and failed has he who seduces it.[164]

---

158 *Supra*, page 66.
159 Titus 3.5; John 3.5–6.
160 Jean Leclant, "Les rites de purification dans le cérémonial pharaonique du couronnenment," *Guilt or Pollution*, 48–51.
161 Framrose A. Bode, "Rites of Purification in the Zoroastrian Religion," *Guilt or Pollution*, 54.
162 Turner, *Forest of Symbols*, 76.
163 Ibid., 74, 130.
164 91.7–9.

It will be apparent, therefore, that purification is a positive power whose effects are felt in two directions: those of reduction and of unification.[165] Purification functions to *remove* that which is negative: the defiling, anomalous, disoriented, sick. In the same moment it is efficacious to unify the individual, the society, or the cosmos to the state of health, success, order, and continuity.

The Means of Purgation

While purgation is not to be bifurcated into "external" (physical) and "internal" (spiritual) categories, it is legitimate to distinguish the agents of purgation in such terms. That is, "external" agents will be material in nature and often applied to the physical body; "internal" agents will be non-material.

Among "external" agents, water is a universally efficacious medium.[166] Pure, clean water is called for: the *Didache* calls for baptism in running water.[167] In the same vein we read of the purifying bath as a "fountain," and "living" water.[168] As Eliade has argued, the return to the waters is a symbology of the return to the forces of chaos out of which new being emerges[169]—a point suggested fifty years ago by Ninck's classic study.[170] Thus, the purgation effected by water is far more than an external cleansing: it is a religious transition. The Qumran scrolls project such a view:

> And when his flesh is sprinkled with purifying water and sanctified by cleansing water, it shall be made clean by the humble submission of his soul to all the precepts of God.[171]

Among modern nations it is India and Japan which perpetuate the concern with purgation on a large scale; and in both we see the pre-eminent place of water as the purification medium. Rivers have a peculiar significance for the Hindus—a significance which cannot at all be accounted for by reference to the hot climate or the long, dry spell before the monsoon storms erupt.

---

165   I have taken these terms from Chang, Chung-Yuan, "Purification and Taoism," *Guilt or Pollution*, 140: "The Taoist approach to self-realization is mainly two-fold: reduction and unification."
166   Fallaize, "Purification (Introduction and Primitive)," 463–64.
167   7.1–2.
168   Zech 13.1; John 4.10ff.
169   *Patterns in Comparative Religion*, 188–215.
170   Martin Ninck, *Die Bedeutung des Wassers im Kult und Leben der Alten: eine symbolgeschichtliche Untersuchung* (Wissenschaftliche Buchgesellschaft, 1960), 1–46, 138–80; first pub. 1920.
171   1QS iii, 8–9; cf. André Dupont-Sommer, "Culpabilité et rites de purification dans le secte Juive de Qoumrân," *Guilt or Pollution*, 78–80.

No: witness the thrill of religious excitement as the devotees gather at Prayag (Allahabad) where the sacred rivers Ganga, Jamuna, and Saraswati (subterranean) meet; feel the intensity of expectation as the appointed time of the *mela* draws near;[172] behold the amazing spectacle of the surging crowd—perhaps half a million strong—rushing to take the cleansing plunge at the precise moment fixed by the pandits of the religion.[173] In Shinto, the essential element likewise is the cold bath. To be complete, the bathing "should take place successively at the mouth of a river, near the source of a river, in the sea, under a waterfall, and in a spring or well,"[174] and in a state of complete nudity.

If water is a universal means of purification, it is by no account the sole medium, nor necessarily the most potent. Indeed, we must hasten to add that the symbology of blood intrudes itself as a medium of superlative power. While the waters reflect a general sense of life leading to rebirth, with blood that sense is direct, immediate, and specific. Thus, among the Aztecs every purification ceremony involved the use of blood; it was, so it was said, "the precious liquid."[175] Even more forcefully does the power of blood relative to water come to expression in the language of confession where water itself becomes a symbol of blood. Consider, for instance, the Christian hymn:

> There is a fountain filled with blood
> Drawn from Immanuel's veins,
> And sinners plunged beneath that flood
> Lose all their guilty stains.[176]

Here the prime figure is that of water baptism: the "fountain," the "plunging." Yet the water has been transformed into blood, even the blood of Christ; it is this alone which is able to purge the defilement and to impart new life.

As powerful as the symbol of blood for purification is, it is by no means a universal medium: as we have already noticed, blood in many contexts is a defiling agent.

A great many other "external" agents of purgation might be mentioned: just as any object may be a source of defilement, so seemingly any object

---

172 The *Magh Mela* is an annual event; the *Arddha Kumbha Mela* is celebrated once in six years; the *Poorna Kumbha Mela* once in twelve years. The other places where the *Kumbha Mela* is celebrated are Hardwar, Nasik, and Ujjain.

173 A photographic description of a *mela* at Allahabad is available in *The Illustrated Weekly of India*, Jan. 16, 1972, 28–29.

174 Herbert, *Shinto*, 80.

175 *Chalchiuhatl*: de Lesur, "Pollution, Guilt, and Purification," 40.

176 William Cowper.

may lend itself for purification. We list the following, however, because of their widespread occurrence: beating,[177] fire,[178] smoke,[179] and salt.[180] Finally, we should include those practices which, while not involving an actual physical agent, are clearly concerned with the purgation of the body (though not exclusively so). Prominent among them are almsgiving,[181] pilgrimage,[182] fasting,[183] and celibacy.[184]

Some religious practices, however, have no reference to "external" cleansing: these are the "internal" agents of purgation. Prayer, meditation, concentration, control of the thoughts and the emotions, and confession are examples. Thus, the Jainist seeks to purify his "soul" of the subtle karmic matter by following the five vows: non-injury, truthfulness, non-stealing, continence, and surrender of possessions.[185] In the Sangha, purification was via confession. Such confession was either public, in the *pratimoksa* ceremony, or private, in the self-accusation. In either case, the following steps were involved: recognition of wrongdoing, change of behavior, confession to an experienced monk or to the group, acknowledgment by the person confessed to, and return of the monk to his prior status.[186]

It will be apparent that purgation which is primarily concerned with "internal" agents tends to become a *self*-purification: of the self, by the self. The clearest expression is furnished by Zen Buddhism:

> Whoever has Buddhahood, is originally pure, but must practice the rules of Purification to become purer and purer for the realization of Buddhahood.[187]

---

177 Van der Leeuw, *Religion in Essence and Manifestation*, 347.
178 Matt 3.11.
179 Fallaize, "Purification (Introductory and Primitive)," 466.
180 Cf. Herbert, *Shinto*, 81: "Salt (*shio*) is considered to be a very potent purifier, more particularly in seawater." He observes that salt is sprinkled before the gate of the home each day and after an unwelcome visitor has left; it is placed before restaurants and in bathrooms; it is used after attendance at a funeral.
181 As in Islam; cf. Helmer Ringgren, "Sin and Forgiveness in the Koran," *Guilt or Pollution*, 103.
182 Again, in Islam; cf. Mohammad Rasjidi, "Guilt, Pollution, and Rites of Purification in Islam," *Guilt or Pollution*, 109: "A well performed pilgrimage is said to purify a person from all his sins so that he becomes as sinless as when he was born."
183 Peter Gerlitz, "Fasten als Reinigungsritus," *ZRGG*, XX (1968), 212–22.
184 Cf. the strictures against sexual offences in Hinayana Buddhism.
185 Tatia, "Purification in Jainism," 130–31.
186 Heinrich Dumoulin, "Consciousness of Guilt and the Practice of Confession in Japanese Buddhism," *Guilt or Pollution*, 165–66; T. R. Havens, "Dynamics of Confession in the Early Sangha," ibid., 133; and A. Pezzali, "Santideva's Statement about Confession," ibid., 134–35.
187 Koichi Matsumoto, "Soto Zen's Idea of Purification," *Guilt or Pollution*, 172.

While we have been able to group agents of purgation as either "external" or "internal," it is to be underlined that such classification does not indicate two distinct types of purification. Purgation is always of the *whole* person, regardless of the means. Islam and Buddhism furnish illuminating examples. The Quran states that Allah provided water "so that He may make you clean by means of it."[188] The traditions record Mohammed's habits of personal cleanliness and prescribe a bath after intercourse, menstruation, and so on.[189] The point to notice, however, is that where no water is available, a symbolic bathing by throwing dust meets the requirement:[190] that is, purgation by water clearly has an internal as well as external value. Inversely, in Buddhism: although the accent appears to fall on "internal" purification, a concern for physical cleanliness remains. The Buddha himself set the example,[191] and the different forms of Buddhism have stressed the place of the body in the attainment of *nirvana*.[192]

We conclude our discussion of the means of purgation with a brief consideration of the purification of specifically non-human "objects." In general, we may say that the means of purifying secular or cultic objects, the elements of the cosmos, or time itself tend to fall under what we have termed the "external" type. Thus, blood was used to cleanse the sanctuary and all its appurtenances, as well as the congregation of Israel;[193] the fasting of the Manicheans served also to purify the "elements";[194] elaborate rituals are used for the purifying of time in the Shinto New Year and "Little New Year" ceremonies.[195] In the dramatic language of apocalyptic, it is fire which is to be the cleansing agent:

> But the day of the Lord will come like a thief and then the heavens will pass away with a loud noise, and the elements will be dissolved with fire, and the earth and the works that are upon it will be burned up....
>
> But according to his promise we wait for new heavens and a new earth in which righteousness dwells.[196]

---

188 8.11.
189 Rasjidi, "Guilt, Pollution," 108. 190.
190 Ibid., 109.
191 E.g., Sumangala Vilasini, i, 45, 10.
192 This emphasis on the body reached its zenith in the Tantra; cf. E. Conze, *Buddhism: Its Essence and Development* (Harper Torchbooks, 1959), 96, 197.
193 Lev 16.15–19.
194 Gerlitz, "Fasten als Reinigungsritus," 212–22; also L. J. R. Ort, "Guilt and Purification in Manichaeism," *Guilt or Pollution*, 69.
195 Ishiro Hori, "Rites of Purification and Orgy in Japanese Folk Religion," *Guilt or Pollution*, 192–93. See also Herbert, *Shinto*, 188–93, 396–97.
196 2 Pet 3.10, 13 (RSV).

It is now time for us to look for the implications for the understanding of humanity, deity and the cosmos which the phenomenology of purgation has brought to light.

The Religious Implications of Purification

In terms of the understanding of humanity implied by purgation, three aspects are brought into view: the desire for newness, nostalgia, and hope.

Purification implies the attaining of the "ought-to-be." It signifies a perennial restlessness, a "numinous uneasiness" seeking correction in the making new, the achieving of order out of disorder, the quest for harmony, continuity and whole-ness. What is most significant is this: humanity *wants* to be "pure." It is not merely that they are conscious of personal disorder, falling short of wholeness, or "sickness"; it is that this state of things—which is to say, their own being and existence as it comes into view—is inadequate, carrying, as it were, its own condemnation along with its disclosure. It is the *whole* which forever stands out before them as the *summum bonum*. So great is its valuation in contrast to the state of defilement that its attaining is a veritable *rite de passage*, and its character is that of a new birth, an initiation.

Purgation points to the paradisal time, *in illo tempore*. Defilement is something which has come upon humanity—it is not an essential element of their being as humankind; purgation implies a longing to return to the "original" bliss of wholeness. Here, then, is the dilemma of human existence: humanity finds itself in a cosmos in which disorder is continually manifested; at no moment can they point to total wholeness of itself, its fellows or nature; yet their mind continually posits the life of bliss: pure humanity in a pure society amid a pure nature. The cruel tricks played upon the human lot—its apparently senseless tragedy, its wastefulness of the good and its free rein allowed the ill—continually indicate: *this* is not what *ought* to be! The ideal (the whole), then, lies either in the past or in the future; thus, the continual *becoming* which is of the essence of purification is at once an attempt to re-actualize the bliss of primal time.

Purification presents us in the final analysis with an "optimistic" view of humanity. It not only looks back on the primal time of bliss, but it holds out the possibility of its recovery: humanity may become "pure" even as society, the cosmos, and time itself may once again become new. Thus, the note of purification is that of *hope*.

Ideas of deity are more to the fore than in the study of defilement. The deity represents that which is the epitome of purity; thus, humanity seeks purification in order that they may approach deity.¹⁹⁷ Further, the means of purification may be those that have been prescribed by deity: this is the grounds for their efficacy.¹⁹⁸

It will be obvious that the place of deity in purgation "structures" varies from one religion to another. In the Judeo-Christian tradition, where the God-human relationship is continually in view, the role of deity is greater than in Hinduism, Buddhism, or Shinto. The apocalyptic purifying of the cosmos in that tradition eventually assigns deity the center of the stage: humanity's defilement has corrupted the very elements and purgation must come from "without."¹⁹⁹ The purifications associated with the "mystery" religions of Egypt and Greece likewise gave great prominence to deity. Plutarch describes the ritual acts of the devotees of Isis as "an image, a representation in mimic scenes"²⁰⁰ of the sufferings of the god. Beyond this representation and re-enactment, however, was the possible *divinization* of the initiate—as Apuleius, for instance, at length was set up on a pedestal in front of Isis and worshipped by the congregation as a god.²⁰¹

We noticed above that in religions where the accent falls on the inner life (the "soul") as that which requires purgation, the movement is in the direction of a *self*-purification. But this does not imply that deity is then reduced to pure subjectivity. What happens is that the conception of deity changes concurrently with the process: one is concerned with inner relations with the Ultimately Real, as in the Vedanta, where the *Atman is* the *Brahman*. So even non-theistic Zen has an awareness of Absolute Reality.²⁰²

Where "external" means of purgation are prominent, the very "otherness" implied in the disjunction of person and cleansing agent allows for direct ideas of deity. The cleansing agent is viewed specifically under the rubric of *power*, which may readily be attached to ideas of the presence of deity. Then the agent becomes a "sacrament."²⁰³

If we turn to the implications for the view of the cosmos, it is manifest that again there is an oscillation depending on the extent of the "internalization" of defilement. At one extreme, we see defiled humanity polluting its

---

197 Cf. Lev 19.2: "You shall be holy; for I the Lord your God am holy."
198 Cf. the oft repeated "I am the Lord" as the grounds for the purgation laws of Leviticus.
199 Cf. Gen 6.5–13.
200 *De Iside et Osiride*, xxvii.
201 *Metamorphoses*, xi.
202 Cf. the following works by D. T. Suzuki: *An Introduction to Zen Buddhism* (Grove Press, 1964); *The Training of the Zen Buddhist Monk* (Eastern Buddhist Society, 1934); and *Manual of Zen Buddhism* (Eastern Buddhist Society, 1935).
203 Cf. van der Leeuw, *Religion in Essence and Manifestation*, 358: "Actually the sacrifice, as such, is always a sacrament."

society, the cultus, and the very cosmos, so that any act of purification irrevocably resonates with cosmic intensity: at the other, we see humanity in its solitariness, striving for that self-purification which will reveal to its inner eye the fact that it, like the cosmos, in fact always has been pure.

Yet we would stress that it is to the first of these poles that the phenomena of purification clearly point. That is, the tendency is toward the pessimistic-optimistic dialectic of cosmology (the cosmos *is* defiled but *is* purifiable and is *to be* purified) rather than to the solely optimistic cosmology implied in the self-purification. For we find that even in religions which tended from the beginning toward the latter view, the awareness of the Shadow has ere long asserted itself; for instance, Buddhism was beset by feelings of cosmic frustration and decay in the space of a few centuries within India itself,[204] feelings which came to full bloom in the "Mappo" thought of China and Japan.[205]

We turn now from purgation per se and seek to show its interrelationships with defilement and blood.

Defilement, Blood, and Purgation in Dynamic Relation

The first thing to be said as we look back upon the study above is that it is only as defilement, blood, and purgation are viewed from a *religious* perspective that a correct view of their nature and interrelations is possible.[206] For instance, attempts have frequently been made to derive "medical wisdom" from ancient practices of defilement and purification: they were supposed to enshrine, as it were, early intimations in the field of public health.[207] In our view, all such efforts are totally misdirected. That certain benefits toward the

---

204 This pessimism seems to stem from the Buddha's words concerning the admission of women to the Sangha (Culla-Vagga, 10, 1, 1). It comes to full expression in the Anagata-Vamsa (the "Buddhist Apocalypse").

205 Alfred Bloom, "The Sense of Sin and Guilt in the Last Age (Mappo) in Chinese and Japanese Buddhism," *Num*, XIV (1967), 144–49.

206 Cf. Douglas, *Purity and Danger*, 11: "The nineteenth century saw in primitive religions two peculiarities which separated them as a block from the great religions of the world. One was that they were inspired by fear, the other that they were inextricably confused with defilement and hygiene." For her part, Douglas has given a devastating rebuttal to those who sought to explain the "abominations of Leviticus" along these lines: pp. 54–72. On the other hand, her explanation is from the stance of social anthropology rather than phenomenology of religion.

207 A useful summary of views concerning the "abominations" of Leviticus is provided by W. H. Gispen, "The Distinction between Clean and Unclean," in P. A. H. de Boer, ed., *Oudtestamentliche Studien* (E. J. Brill, 1948), V, 190–96. Gispen himself comes out with the following view: "It is my opinion that the only satisfying explanation of the distinction between clean and unclean is this, that the Holy One by these regulations shows the necessity that His people be a holy people, a nation that is not as other nations. It ought to abstain from the dirtiness of sin. It must see the uncleanness that has come into the world and that has its

health of society may have ensued is altogether likely, but these were merely incidental and derivative—just as the person who goes to church may enjoy physical relaxation. No; until we begin to look at defilement, blood, and purgation in terms of the great existential issues of life and death, until we see them in relation to deity and for the understanding of humanity and his cosmos to which they point, we have quite missed the mark.

Correspondingly, talk of "moral" as opposed to "ritual" only serves to muddy the waters. These waters are *religious* in nature—a category that embraces and transcends distinctions of ethical/non-ethical.

It is as we come to defilement, blood, and purgation as religious terms that their true nature and dynamic relations begin to stand out in sharp relief. We begin to see the intensity of feeling, the stark existential concern that throbs beneath laws and rites so apparently wooden and formal. We see at last humanity stripped of its pride, in radical unease before deity and cosmos, and striving to attain to peace with both.

How then shall we set out the dynamic relations of defilement, blood, and purgation? Let us probe to the very foundations of the religious structure and build upon it block by block. Indubitably, it is the following transition with which we must begin:

$$\text{defilement} \longrightarrow \text{purgation}$$

Purgation is the mirror-image of defilement.[208] Whereas defilement comes to expression as a quasi-material, quasi-moral, infectious state—a state which is accompanied by feelings of dread, separateness, and "lost-ness," so purification is a quasi-material, quasi-moral state of wholeness and "blessing." Defilement is never wholly external nor wholly internalized; nor is purgation. There are degrees of defilement, likewise there are degrees of purgation.

Yet the correspondence is not absolute, very close though it be. Defilement is the state of the *is*, purgation that of the *ought-to-be*. The present continually hammers the disparity: humanity continually is defiled instead of being what he ought to be. That is, defilement looms large as the "problem" which continually confronts humanity and ever arises to dash their efforts to rest in the state of purgation. In two respects, especially, does defilement tend

---

cause in sin and in the punishment of sin, the curse of God" (p. 196). This explanation itself is "theological" rather than "religious."

208 In setting out the "structures" or "patterns" of defilement, blood, and purgation here and throughout this section, we have assumed the results attained in the previous three sections dealing with these terms individually. Our attempt here is to show how these terms flow together in dynamic relationship.

to overshadow purgation so as to destroy the full correspondence. On one hand, defilement may be of such a serious character that no purgation of it is possible. On the other, the nature of defilement as an *infectious* state does not find its counterpart with purgation.

Defilement and purgation, then, are diametrically opposed religious states. They are states with the most profound implications for humanity both "subjectively" and "objectively."

Subjectively—that is, in terms of the individual's own feelings and relationships—defilement and purgation come to sharp expression as "dread" and "confidence" respectively. The defiled person is cut off from the cultus; thus, they have become a "non-person" and is an anomaly in his society. Such a person cannot approach the deity and the very cosmos has assumed a hostile stance toward them. Their feelings are intense: fear, anxiety, alone-ness, dread of the present and dread of the future. The purified person, however, enjoys the exhilaration of religious wholeness. They join with their fellows in their cultus; they may approach deity; the very heavens seem to smile upon them. Their feelings likewise are intense: security, boldness, fellowship, confidence in the present, and hope for the future.

Objectively—that is, in terms of the individual's effects upon others—defilement and purgation are comprehended under the ideas of "curse" and "blessing" respectively. Defiled humanity is a source of danger in two respects: not only are their quasi-material pollutions infectious, but they upset the ordering of society and ultimately the cosmos. That is, the polluted person is also a polluter. Their pollution may have dire ramifications upon the immediate members of their household, less directly upon the tribe or community, and finally may extend to the very cosmos. The purified person, on the other hand, is in the state of blessing. Theirs is the state from which flow material benefits such as bountiful harvest, fertility of humankind and beast, and protection from enemies. Such "external" bounties, however, are but the manifestation of relationships in correct order as humanity, deity, and cosmos have come into harmony.

The basic structure

$$\text{defilement} \longrightarrow \text{purgation}$$

thus comes to expression in terms of *power*, *life* and *order*. Let us elaborate each of these expressions in turn.

The consideration of the states of defilement and purgation above has indicated that we have to do with a network of interlocking powers. Life in the cosmos is life *among* the powers. Humanity cannot expect to find itself apart, in a state of neutrality to power, as it were. No; the very cosmos, the cultus, as well as deity, come to them manifested as power. But this manifestation is diverse: there are degrees of power and there are differentiations of power. Defilement is a state of negative power, purgation its antithesis. That is:

defilement	⟶	purgation
negative power		positive power

We have noticed earlier the intimate connection between defilement and death. The well-nigh universal aversion to a corpse and to menstrual blood finds its origin in this connection: humanity seeks to affirm life[209] as the ultimate good and to recoil in horror from that which diminishes life. The defiled person, in fact, is in a state of semi-death: a "non-person," they are dead to the cultus, the society, and the cosmos. The state of purification, however, is the place of fulness of life: access to deity, fellowship in the society, wholeness within the cosmos. Thus, the interrelations of defilement and purgation portray in vivid outline humanity's fundamental concern with the issues of life and death:

defilement	⟶	purgation
death		life

The third manifestation of the basic structure is in terms of order. The physical, external aspect of defilement—that of dirt, a stain, a blot—is never wholly lost, no matter what transformations may occur. As dirt indicates disorder, so the defiled person stands out as a blot upon the cultus, their society, and the cosmos. That is, the relations of defilement and purgation carry with them corresponding indications of disorder and order:

defilement	⟶	purgation
disorder		order

We may now conveniently bring together these expressions of the basic structure, together with the concomitant relations we have already noticed:

---

209 Cf. Walter Kornfeld, "Reine and unreine Tiere im Alten Testament," *Kair*, VII (1965), 134–47. He argues that the OT distinctions between clean and unclean derive ultimately from the desire to affirm life.

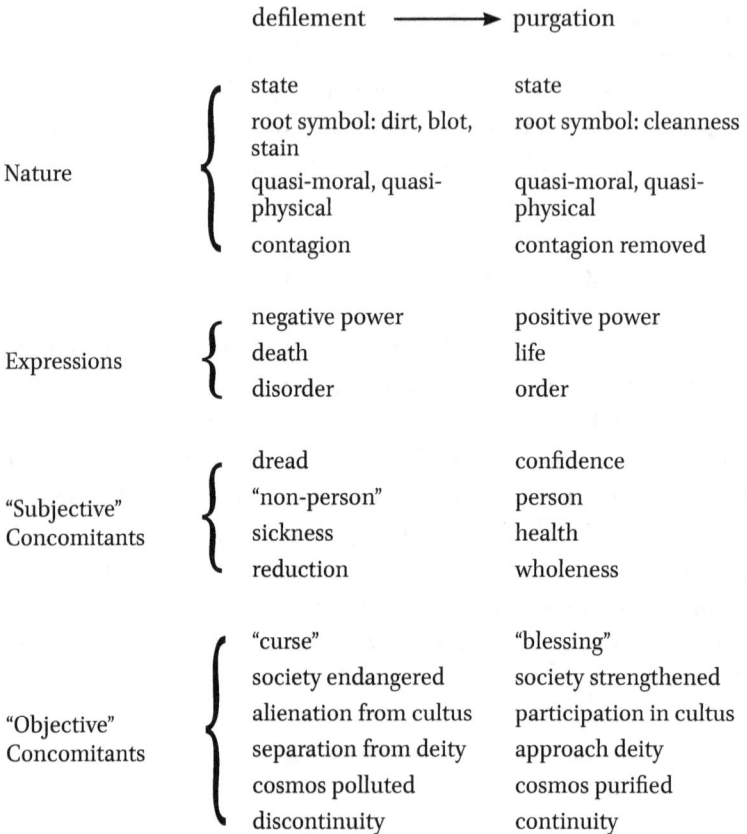

It will be apparent from this discussion that the states of defilement and purgation are not something to be taken lightly in the life of religion. Indeed, the most intense religious concern may be associated with each. Therefore, it can be no easy matter to move from one to the other. Such a transition is of the nature of a healing, or a new birth; it is veritably a *rite de passage*.[210]

How then is such a transition to be made? Obviously, only by the intervention of a new force into the network of interlocking forces; only so will a regrouping of powers be possible. While defilement and purgation are themselves states of power, the transition requires the operation of a new, strongly active power—a power which shall operate directly and vigorously as the medium of transition. Across the gamut of the world's religions, various media have been suggested; but the one which has manifested itself as having unchallenged potency is that of blood. That is:

---

210 A term made famous by the work of Arnold van Gennep, *Rites of Passage*, trans. Monika B. Vizedom and Gabrielle L. Caffee (University of Chicago Press, 1960).

Towards a Methodology Appropriate to the Cultic Language of Hebrews

$$\text{defilement} \xrightarrow{\text{(blood)}} \text{purgation}$$

With the term "blood" we encounter a religious category of pure force (power). "Blood" manifests itself as the power of life, nakedly revealed and of surpassing efficacy; thus:

$$\text{defilement} \xrightarrow{\text{(blood)}} \text{purgation}$$

state of	pure power	state of
(negative)		(positive)
power		power
	strongly	
	positive	

To be sure, blood itself is a force of ambivalent nature. While it serves as the medium of purgation, in other contexts it may be a defiling agent. That is:

$$\text{defilement} \xrightleftharpoons[\text{blood (negative)}]{\text{blood (positive)}} \text{purgation}$$

The difference lies in the point of view: where blood is manifested in terms of the extension of life, it appears as a positive power, an agent of purgation; but where it appears in terms of the diminution of life, it assumes the character of a defiling agent, a negative force.

This peculiar ambivalence of blood is to be accounted for by the religious desire to affirm *life*. With blood we meet, as it were, the very essence of life, life-power itself. But it is a power that may flow toward or away, in the one case bringing purification with all the blessings of new life, in the other signifying the ebb of life, when it becomes death-power.

Let us pause to inject a few examples which highlight the dynamic relations of defilement, blood, and purgation as we have endeavored to lay them out. We shall call upon four illustrations: one from an anthropologist, one from a dramatist, and two from widely diverse cultuses.

In his careful study of the Ndembu, V. Turner found that they distinguished three basic colors in their world-ordering: white, red, and black.[211] These three colors were associated with the forces of the cosmos and were viewed as three rivers: "the rivers of whiteness, redness, and blackness (or

---

211 Turner, *Forest of Symbols*, 59–92.

darkness)."[212] Turner then attempted to show that the same three colors were significant across a wide range of societies, including both primitive and ancient, and to draw the following conclusion as to that significance:

> The physical experiences associated with the three colors are also experiences of social relationships: white = semen is linked to mating between man and woman; white = milk is linked to the mother-child tie; red = material blood is linked to the mother-child tie and also the processes of group recruitment and social displacement; red = bloodshed is connected with war, feud, conflict, social discontinuities; red = obtaining and preparation of animal food = status of hunter or herder, male productive role in the sexual division of labor, etc.; red = transmission of blood from generation to generation = an index of membership in a corporate group; black = excreta or bodily dissolution = transition from social status to another viewed as mystical death; black = rain clouds or fertile earth = unity of widest recognized groups sharing same life value.[213]

While Turner's work is concerned with the data from an anthropological perspective, we see it as lending support to the basic tenor of our study. That is, the structure

$$\text{defilement} \xrightarrow{\text{(blood)}} \text{purgation}$$

finds its expression in terms of colors as

$$\text{black} \xrightarrow{\text{(red)}} \text{white}$$

We come again to Shakespeare. After Macbeth has been party to the gruesome murder of his rivals, he is filled with remorse:

> What hands are here? Ha! They pluck out mine eyes.
> Will all great Neptune's ocean wash this blood
> Clean from my hand? No, this my hand will rather
> The multitudinous seas incarnadine
> Making the green one red.[214]

---

212 Ibid., 61.
213 Ibid., 89.
214 *Macbeth*, II, 3.

In these famous lines we see, as it were, the state of defilement in cameo. Defilement is physical, but more than physical: it brings with it feelings of the strongest intensity; it calls for the only suitable solution, which is cleansing; and here the defilement is felt to be of such power that even all the oceans of the world could not avail to bring about the desired purgation. Shed blood has defiled Macbeth; no water will suffice to purify him. It is a picture of humanity's "numinous uneasiness" such as has not been rivalled in literature.

Let us take up two illustrations from cultus—first, an ancient chant to the sun from the scriptures of Zoroastrianism, and finally a Christian hymn.

> We sacrifice unto the undying, shining, swift-horsed Sun....
>
> And when the sun rises up, then the earth, made by Ahura, becomes clean; the running waters become clean, the waters of the wells become clean, the waters of the sea become clean, the standing waters become clean; all the holy creatures, the creatures of the Good Spirit, become clean.
>
> Should not the sun rise up, then the Daevas would destroy all the things that are in the seven Karshvares, nor would the heavenly Yazatas find any way of withstanding or repelling them in the material world.
>
> He who offers up a sacrifice unto the undying, shining, swift-horsed Sun—to withstand darkness, to withstand the Daevas born of darkness, to withstand the robbers and bandits, to withstand the Yatus and Pairikas, to withstand death that creeps in unseen—offers it up to Ahura Mazda, offers it up to the Amesha-Spentas, offers it up to his own soul.[215]

Oh now I see the crimson wave,
The fountain deep and wide;
Jesus, my Lord, mighty to save,
Points to His wounded side.
The cleansing stream I see, I see,
I plunge, and O, it cleanseth me!
It cleanseth me, yes, cleanseth me.[216]

In the ancient hymn of the Avesta, the accent falls heavily on the social and cosmic accompaniments of sacrifice. We see here a strong sense of the

---

215 Khorshed Yasht, 1–4.
216 Mrs. Phoebe Palmer.

interdependence of person, society, and cosmos. In the Christian hymn, defilement and purgation as religious counterparts are particularly related to the life of the individual. The physical allusion is to baptism, yet the watery bath has been transmogrified by assimilation to the "crimson wave"—the blood of Christ. With both examples we see strongly in evidence the power of blood to mediate new life.

The above examples, selective though they have had to be, nevertheless serve to point out the deep significance of the terms "defilement," "blood" and "purgation" in the religious life of humanity. Indeed, the modern person, no matter how they pride themselves in their education or emancipation from the past, cannot hope to divest humanity wholly of the ideas we have outlined. They are part of its mental fabric; they are primordial; they continually surface in desacralized contexts. We bring our discussion of the interrelations of defilement, blood, and purgation to a close by summarizing the views of humanity, deity, and cosmos that are implied.

First, the symbology of evil as stain or defilement points to humanity's continuing "numinous uneasiness." Before thought, the stain is *there*: humanity is defiled. Evil is not seen as something external so that humankind can avoid responsibility and say, "The devil made me do it." Nor are is it concerned with locating the historical moment, in its own lifetime or in that of an ancestor, when the stain first appeared. Defilement points to humanity as they now *are*: the stain is *there*.

Because the stain is *there*, it appears and reappears, it is transmuted and transmogrified, but it is abiding in its root significance. To talk of it in terms of its transformations, whether ritual/moral or external/ internal, in no wise can lessen its essential character as a religious category.[217]

Second, what shall we say of this spot—is it a *necessary* part of "human nature"? Not at all, because the spot is a spot on the good. It is not mere absence of the good nor is it part of the good, but it stains the good. It is something to be removed. Thus, humanity is always to be viewed in the light of what they *might be*. Not only *might* be, but *ought* to be.[218] For the religious counterpart of defilement is purgation. If the phenomenology of defilement

---

217 Mattias Vereno, "Ritual and Bewusstseinswandlung als zwei Aspekte von Sühne and Versöhnung," *Kair*, VIII (1966), 125–29, argues that all religions show the twin aspects of "interior" (spiritual death) and "exterior" (the overcoming of forces hostile to life through ritual acts). Where the latter predominates, evil is seen as "material"; where the former is in the ascendancy, rites may be denied altogether. The phenomena of defilement-blood-purification clearly point to *both* aspects with the emphasis falling on the latter.

218 A possibility other than the quest for purgation is to *affirm* defilement. This is a course which has occasionally been followed. Douglas mentions the death rituals of the Nyakyusa in such a context, *Purity and Danger*, 207–10.

is in the minor key, that of purgation is clearly in the major: purgation signifies *hope*.

Consequently, there arises the curious oscillation associated with defilement and purgation:

defilement ⇌ purgation

Purgation is attainable but cannot long be held: there is a continual falling-back, a re-defiling which calls for a new purging. Humanity's religious efforts are never quite able to match its religious aspirations. So, while purgation, which sounds the optimistic note, is the balance of pessimistic defilement, it is on the *is*, that is, defilement that the accent falls, and which must inevitably form the starting point of the religious structure. So, we hear the note of pathos which cannot be blocked out when we consider what the defilement-purgation structure implies for the human situation.[219]

Fourth, the natures of defilement and purgation are such that the means of passing from one to the other shall be something external to the person. They will be involved—they must do their part—but it is only as the agent of transition comes into play that the *rite de passage* is possible. Indubitably, it is blood which is manifested as the supreme agent for this transition.

Fifth, the patterns of defilement, blood, and purgation lead to an emphasis on humanity rather than on deity. This by no means suggests that deity is excluded or assumes the role of an onlooker. To the contrary: humanity's numinous unease, their dread finds its peculiar intensity precisely because humanity as defiled cannot approach deity, being cut off from the cultus. Furthermore, it is deity that prescribes the necessary means of cleansing. That is, humanity's states of defilement or purgation are understandable only when viewed against the background of deity as the norm of "purity."

But if it is humanity in view of deity with which we have to do, it is nonetheless *humanity* where the focus of interest is to be put. Defilement is a human problem, even as purgation is a human state. Defilement and purgation point us to the deep issues of existence—those of life and death—and to the problems of disorder/order of society and cosmos. The language of these states can only be intensely personal: "We are defiled," or "We are purged."

Finally, one of the most interesting points to emerge from the structures we have drawn up is the interrelation of humanity and cosmos. We see humankind as bound up in the cosmos in religious unity. It is a life *among* the

---

[219] Thus, out of the oscillation between defilement and purgation emerge two motifs: nostalgia (the myth of primal time) and hope.

powers; and in this life no one lives to himself as no one dies to himself. One person's defilement, like their purgation, has ramifications which reverberate throughout the cultus, their society, and ultimately the cosmos.[220] That is, it is quite wrong to think of the individual per se in this schema. That there are, of course, subjective feelings associated with defilement and purgation—indeed, intense feelings—we have already noticed frequently during the course of this chapter; but our point is that these subjective feelings are inevitably accompanied by objective effects. So, if we grant that it is *humanity* upon whom the limelight falls in these structures, we must never forget that it is "collective" humanity of which we speak. It is an understanding of humanity and cosmos which is quite at odds with our modern view of the individual par excellence who "does his own thing," yet it is one which we must not put aside if we are to comprehend the dynamic relations of humanity, deity, and cosmos as expressed in the terms "defilement," "blood," and "purgation."

Conclusion

In this chapter we have suggested a methodology appropriate to the cultic language of Hebrews. We have posited that it is the insights of phenomenology of religion which will provide entree into the argument of the cultus. Phenomenology of religion provides the exegete with the attitude necessary to approach the cultus in its own right—that of "epoch." At the same time, it brings a content of religious data from the religious experience of humanity from which "structures" or "patterns" may be discerned by employing the "eidetic vision"—the search for religious essences. Accordingly, after discussion of the methodology of phenomenology of religion in formal terms, we have set out the nature and interrelations of defilement, blood, and purgation as manifested by religious evidence apart from Hebrews.

Now it is time for us to come to the text of Hebrews, bearing in mind the methodological and phenomenological foundation which has been laid in the work of this chapter. To what extent do the "structures" of defilement, blood, and purgation which we have arrived at shed light on these terms in Hebrews? Do the nature and interrelations of these terms in Hebrews conform to the religious data exclusive of Hebrews? At what points does the understanding of Hebrews diverge from the "patterns" and thus display its individual character as a religious text? And finally—and most importantly for our concerns in terms of biblical scholarship—what help if any is offered

---

220 220 Cf. M. Hermanns, "Schuld un Reinigungsriten unter den Primitiven Indiens," *Kair*, VIII (1966), 107–13: the individual's sin and purgation have cosmic repercussions.

by the methodology in coming to grips with the perennial problems raised by the cultus which we already have noticed in the first two chapters of the study? That is, what illumination of the cultic argumentation employed by the *auctor ad Hebraeos* will be available to the exegete?

It is these questions and others which will come into focus as we embark upon the task of Chapter 4. That task involves us in the exegesis of Hebrews 9–10, with special reference to the use of the terms "defilement," "blood," and "purgation."

CHAPTER 4

Defilement, Blood, and Purgation in the Book of Hebrews: An Exegesis of Hebrews 9–10

The ninth and tenth chapters of Hebrews provide the logical focus for our study as we turn from the consideration of general religious "structures" and concentrate our energies upon Hebrews. For a start, it is manifest that here we find the summit of the author's cultic reasoning. That 7.1–10.18 is a tightly woven unity seems incontestable—an argumentative unity which skillfully rises to a peak in Hebrews 9–10 and establishes the base for the powerful parenetic appeal which commences with the ἔχοντες οὖν ἀδελφοί ("Therefore, brothers, since we have ... ") of 10.19. Second—and as a corollary of the above fact—it is here that we find most clearly expressed the writer's understanding of the nature and interrelations of blood, defilement, and purgation. Thus, a careful study of these two chapters will inevitably illumine the enigma of the cultus as the anthropology implied by the cultus is held up to the light.

Let us pause to notice the vocabulary and occurrence of the terms "defilement," "blood," and "purgation" in Hebrews. It is clearly the second of these—blood (αἷμα)—which is predominant with regard to the frequency of usage. Αἷμα occurs a total of twenty-one times in the letter, of which no less than fourteen are found in the ninth and tenth chapters.[1] Of the remainder, one has reference to the humanity of Jesus (2.14—he was a sharer in our "blood and flesh"), one to martyrdom (12.4—not yet resisted "to the extent of blood"), one to the passover (11.28), one to the Old Testament cultus (13.11), and three to the blood of Christ (12.24; 13.12, 20). Defilement on the other hand comes to expression through several words. At 9.13 we find κοινοῦν[2] with reference to

---

1 The compound word αἱματεκχυσία which is used in 9.22 has been included in these totals. The other references to αἷμα in Hebrews 9–10 are 9.7, 12–14, 20–22; 10.4, 19, 29.

2 Κοινοῦν = "make common or impure, defile in the ceremonial sense," or "consider or declare (ceremonially) unclean." See William F. Arndt and F. Wilbur Gingrich, *A Greek-English*

the old cultus, while 10.29 speaks of the condemnation of those who regard the blood of the new covenant as κοινός ("common" or defiled). Hebrews 12.15 uses μιαίνειν[3] with regard to the "root of bitterness" which causes many to be "defiled," while 13.4 has ἀμίαντος for the marriage-bed ("uncontaminated"). Purgation, however, comes to expression chiefly in terms of καθαρίζειν[4] and its cognates. We have already had occasion to refer to the καθαρισμός of 1.3b; it suffices to observe that the other five occurrences of καθαρίζειν and its cognates are in chapters 9–10.[5] Two related words should be mentioned. λούειν,[6] used at 10.22, and βαπτισμός,[7] used at 6.2 and 9.10.

The bare data from vocabulary are useful at this point to demonstrate that our concentration upon Hebrews 9–10 is soundly based. But we would underline that a lexical study alone, or an approach along the lines of Kittel's *Theological Dictionary of the New Testament*, is inadequate for the understanding of defilement, blood, and purgation.[8] These terms do not represent discrete concepts; rather, they are windows into the same "structure." It is only as the entire "structure" comes into view that we can arrive at understanding. We shall find in our exegesis in this chapter that this "structure" will involve a wider vocabulary than that which we have noticed above. In particular, we shall be forced to give consideration to the ideas behind ἁγιάζειν ("consecration" or "sanctification"),[9] τελειοῦν ("perfection," "consummation"),[10] and συνείδησις ("conscience," "consciousness").[11]

Let us make clear at the outset what we conceive our task in this chapter to be: it is to attempt to recover the author's original intent in employ-

---

Lexicon of the New Testament and Other Early Christian Literature (4th rev. and augmented ed.; University of Chicago Press, 1969), 439.

3 Μιαίνειν = "stain, defile," of either "ceremonial impurity" or "moral defilement by sins and vices"; ibid., 522. This setting out of the meaning of μιαίνειν by Arndt and Gingrich points to a perpetuation of the moral/ritual dichotomy which we have already had occasion to call into question.

4 Καθαρίζειν = "make clean, cleanse, purify." Arndt and Gingrich again divide as to literal or figurative. ibid., 388.

5 9.14, 22–23; 10.2, 22.

6 Λούειν = "wash, as a rule of the whole body, bathe." It may be employed in religious or non-religious settings. See Arndt and Gingrich, *Greek-English Lexicon*, 481–82.

7 Βαπτισμός = "dipping," "washing," "ritual washings." ibid., 132.

8 A devastating critique of such approaches has been given by James Barr in a series of works, especially, *The Semantics of Biblical Language* (Oxford University Press, 1961), and *Biblical Words for Time* (2nd rev. ed.; Naperville, Ill.: Alec R. Allenson, Inc. 1969).

9 Ἁγιάζειν = "make holy, consecrate, sanctify," of things or persons. By extension it comes to = "treat as holy, reverence" or "purify." See Arndt and Gingrich, *Greek-English Lexicon*, 8–9.

10 Τελειοῦν = "complete, bring to an end, finish, accomplish"; "bring to an end, bring to its goal or accomplishment." With the mystery religions, τελειοῦν = "consecrate, initiate." ibid., 817–18.

11 Συνείδησις = "consciousness"; "moral consciousness, conscience"; or "conscientiousness." ibid., 794.

ing the cultic argumentation in Hebrews 9–10. We desire to understand *with him* as he proceeds to discuss humanity's "problem" and its "solution." We are not concerned with the significance of the discussion for the modern person, that is, our understanding of exegesis follows the traditional view as set out by Stendahl[12] rather than that of Bultmann.[13] Furthermore, while we have taken note of the scholarly treatments of the passage, our purpose is to provide an individual interpretation based on the methodology we have proposed. That is to say, our exegesis will be much less a debate with previous positions than an attempt toward a positive construction.[14]

Our study of the passage will take us through a series of stages. We may dispense with a formal discussion of text-critical questions, since the text is singularly free of significant variants.[15] Nor do we need to set out at the beginning a new translation which, by showing marked departures from previous ones, forms the basis for a particular exegesis. What we must concern ourselves with, however, are the following matters: the context of the passage; the leitmotif(s) of the passage; the nature and interrelations of defilement, blood, and purgation in the passage; and the explication of the cultic argumentation of the passage. Finally, we shall take account of the occurrences of defilement, blood, and purgation outside of the chapters which we have exegeted. Let us now take up these matters in order.

Contextual Considerations

Here we consider the aspects of external context (the passage in relation to the letter as a whole), internal context (the general plan or structure of the passage itself), and the limits of the passage.

---

12 See Krister Stendahl, "Biblical Theology, Contemporary," *IDB*, I, 418–32. Stendahl makes the distinction between exegesis as "what it meant" and hermeneutics as "what it means."

13 Bultmann's understanding of exegesis is governed by the weight he gives to the *Vorverständnis* and the *Selbst-verständnis*. A good summary in provided by W. Schmithals, *Die Theologie Rudolf Bultmanns* (J. C. B. Mohr, 1967), 226–53.

14 Our exegesis is thus characterized by two features: (1) we will especially attempt to elucidate the anthropology of Hebrews 9–10; and (2) we will emphasize our own individual interpretation, showing how our approach has illumined not only the total argument but also portions of the text which long have presented serious problems of exegesis. According to the first feature, we do not find it necessary to dwell upon christological or cosmological aspects of the text which do not bear upon the anthropology. According to the second, we will take account of the major arguments against our interpretation but at the same time will not divert from the ongoing discussion to set out lists of interpreters who agree or disagree with us for each detail. It will be obvious, therefore, that we have no intention of producing another exegesis of Hebrews 9–10 along the lines of the commentaries. Our hope is to clarify the *argument* of the passage, especially as it comes to expression in the anthropology.

15 The one major exception is in 9.11, which is considered in our discussion; *infra*, p. 133.

Hebrews 9–10 forms the climax of the cultic argumentation which commenced at 7.1. The seventh chapter was concerned with Christ as high priest after the order of Melchizedek—an order which is superior to the Levitical because it brings with it "perfection" (τελειοῦν). But not only is the order superior, Christ himself surpasses the Levites by virtue of his moral character, his endless life, the oath of his office, and his priestly act. This, then, is the thrust of the seventh chapter: *a better priest*. In chapter 8, the *auctor ad Hebraeos* states that he has now arrived at the "chief point" (κεφάλαιον) of his argument: Christ is priest over a better sanctuary, even the heavenly. At the same time, he is the mediator of a better covenant—a covenant prophesied by Jeremiah. The eighth chapter, therefore, establishes the following: *a better sanctuary and a better covenant*. Now we are ready to enter upon a discussion of Christ's work. Already 7.27 had thrown out the hint: Christ offered himself once for all. Chapters 9–10 will pick up this thought and explicate it. In so doing there will be a subtle but significant shift in emphasis—for Christ's work can only come to meaningful focus in terms of the human dilemma. Thus, in discussing Christ's work, we see laid bare the "problem" of humanity to which Christ offers the "solution." So we are prepared for the shift from the emphasis on what Christ has accomplished in relation to humanity's problem to its logical correlate: how humanity should respond in view of Christ's accomplishment—a move that occurs only at 10.19 but which has been most skillfully prepared.

Yet it would be a grave mistake to see Hebrews 9–10 as forming merely the climax of the cultic argumentation of 7.1–10.18. There are numerous earlier anticipations of the passage, even as there are reflections upon it in the subsequent chapters. The "when he had made purgation of sins" of 1.3b is a direct announcement of the argument to be presented in detail only in the ninth and tenth chapters; likewise do 2.5–18 (the priesthood of Jesus rooted in his humanity), 4.14–5.10 (Jesus a priest by virtue of his sufferings and the divine call), and 6.19–20 (Jesus the high priest as forerunner) look toward the exposition of 7.1–10.18. With 10.18 we have reached the peak: the remainder of the book is to be comprehended under the οὖν of 10.19. The immediate parenetic consequence comes as a dire warning; then follow the exhortations to emulate the faithfulness of the old "heroes" and to "draw near" in the fulness of access to the divine presence which the blood of Christ has provided.[16] It is striking in these chapters after the peak of 10.18 to see the valence attached to the "blood" of Christ. In fact, αἷμα does not occur in a cultic sense before

---

16 The warning (10.26–31); the emulation of heroes of old (11.1ff); the invitation to draw near (12.18–29).

chapter 9; after 10.18, however, it occurs seven times with reference to the cultus—five times signifying Christ's "blood."[17] In all of these seven occurrences there is an obvious looking back to the discussion of chapters 9–10.

It seems apparent, therefore, that the ninth and tenth chapters of Hebrews place us, as it were, at the Everest of the letter. This is true whether we consider the cultic argumentation alone or whether we seek to trace the overall discussion of the author.[18]

Turning to the internal context of Hebrews 9–10, we discern the following clearly distinguishable parts:

9.1–10: Brief description of the earthly sanctuary and its ministry. Emphasis: lack of access to God, lack of perfection of συνείδησις.
9.11–28: Christ a minister of the heavenly sanctuary. Emphasis: Christ achieves access to God by a once-for-all offering.
10.1–18: Christ's blood deals decisively with sins.
10.19–39: The believer's response to Christ's work.

It is tempting to see chapter 9 as primarily referring to *access* and chapter 10 as emphasizing the *finality* with which Christ's blood deals with sins. In this way the contrast with the old cultus would very neatly be made. Such an analysis, however, is too simple, since in both chapters the concern is with access and a purged συνείδησις.

Yet it seems obvious that there is a break in the argument between the chapters. The final verses of Hebrews 9 move away from the consideration of the heavenly cultus to sound the eschatological note, but 10.1 returns abruptly to talk of the old cultus. How then are we to see the general outline of the argument? Specifically, does chapter 10 repeat the basic point of chapter 9?

An observation made earlier points to the solution to the problem: there is a shift in the argument from a christological to an anthropological emphasis. That is, chapter 9 is concerned with "objective" benefits of Christ's offering,

---

17 Signifying Christ's blood. 10.19, 29; 12.24; 13.12, 20; with reference to the old cultus. 11.28; 13.11.

18 The agreements and disagreements with Vanhoye's analysis of Hebrews will be apparent. He sees 8.1–9.28 as the central section of the letter. We hold that his attempt to set forth the structure of Hebrews upon "external" criteria—chiasm and hook-words—is not only prima facie unlikely but fails in terms of the argument of Hebrews. In particular, the division into 8.1–9.28 and 10.1–18 is clearly in error in that it obscures the continuing argument of Heb 9–10 which reaches its indubitable climax in the parenesis of 10.19ff. A convenient outline of Vanhoye's analysis is available in Albert Vanhoye, *A Structured Translation of the Epistle to the Hebrews*, trans. James Swetnam (Pontifical Biblical Institute, 1964), 20–27.

while chapter 10 deals with its "subjective" effects in the life of the Christian.[19] What we have, therefore, in the course of the argument of Hebrews 9–10 is, first, a summary statement of the old cultus to highlight its limitations (9.1–10); a summary statement of the blessings of the new cultus—blessings both "objective" and "subjective" (9.11–14); and an explication of these benefits—"objective" in 9.15–28, and "subjective" in 10.1–18. Thus, 9.11–14 stands as the essence of the author's argument, at once contrasting with the old cultus and outlining the subsequent discussion.

We would suggest, therefore, that the internal structure of Hebrews 9–10 is as follows:

I. Denigration of the old cultus (9.1–10)
    Brief description of the earthly sanctuary (9.1–5)
    The ministry of the old sanctuary
    Emphasis: lack of access, no "perfection" attained (9.6–10)

II. The benefits of the new cultus (9.11–10.18)
    A. A summary of its benefits, both "objective" and "subjective" (9.11–14)
    B. "Objective" benefits (9.15–28)
    The new covenant (9.15–21)
    The blood rule (9.22)
    The cleansing of heavenly things (9.23)
    A ministry in heaven itself (9.24–26)
    The eschatological consummation (9.27–28)
    C. "Subjective" benefits
    Man's problem: the συνείδησις (10.1–4)
    The offering of Christ brings "perfection" (10.5–14)
    The "subjective" blessings of the new covenant (10.15–18)

III. "Therefore"—the believers' response (10.19–39)
    A. Exhortation to "draw near" in full confidence (10.19–25)
    B. Warning against despising Christ's blood (10.26–31)
    C. Looking toward the consummation (10.32–39)[20]

---

19 Throughout this chapter, we use "objective" to signify the work of Christ apart from personal reflection and feelings, in contrast to "subjective" which points to personal "experience" or knowledge.

20 Again we may compare and contrast with Vanhoye's analysis. He arranges 8.1–9.28, the "central section," according to a chiasm: c (8.1–6), b (8.7–13), a (9.1–10), A (9.11–14), B (9.15–23), C (9.24–28). The principal objection to this structure is that it fails to give 9.11–14 the correct weighting for the argument of Heb 10 as well as for the rest of Heb 9. The reference to the purgation of συνείδησις at 9.14 is manifestly taken up only in 10.1–18. The chiasm in fact breaks down if we examine the argument of Heb 9–10 carefully; e.g., it is an error to lump together all

This outline, we are convinced, does serve to show the manner in which the author has developed his argument. We do *not* see these two chapters as having a watertight structure based on "external" criteria such as chiasms and hook-words; rather, the structure is "internal" and logical.

The contextual considerations above lead naturally to a discussion of the limits of the passage we have to exegete. No doubt it could well be argued that the strict boundaries of the cultic argumentation are 9.6 and 10.18. We have chosen to include the full chapters for several reasons, however. So far as the beginning of the passage is concerned, it is certain that 9.6 is more closely tied to 9.1 than is 9.1 to 8.13. The author moves from discussion of the covenants at 8.13 to consideration of the sanctuary services in 9.1, a shift that is also signaled by the οὖν of 9.1. Furthermore, the μὲν of 9.1 is answered by the δὲ of 9.6; thus, it could be strongly contended that a beginning at 9.6 rather than at 9.1 would be artificial. With regard to the final limit of the passage, again it seems manifest that 11.1, with its obvious turning to a discussion of πίστις, marks a more distinct break with the foregoing than does 10.19.[21] We have already noticed how the accent has fallen more and more upon the human side as the argument has moved into the tenth chapter, so the transition to parenesis at 10.19 is not at all a sharp one. Furthermore, in the section 10.19–39 we encounter a number of arresting statements. Some of these *prima facie* appear to bring to a head the discussion of the interrelation of blood, defilement, and purgation, while others have proved to be perennial matters of dispute among the exegetes. We refer especially to the τουτ' ἔστιν τῆς σαρκὸς αὐτοῦ (literally: "through the curtain, that is, his flesh") of 10.20 and the severe warning against sins committed ἑκουσίως ("deliberately") in 10.26–31. By concluding our exegesis at 10.39 instead of 10.19, therefore, we shall not only demonstrate how imperceptibly thesis and parenesis are blended by the author, but we shall also be able to show how the methodology we have proposed may illumine traditional *cruces interpretum*.

The Leitmotif(s) of the Passage 9.1–10.39

As we study carefully the writer's language in this passage, the overwhelming impression is of the use of cultic terminology. The argument proceeds step by step via talk of priests and high priests, sacrifices and offerings, days of atonement and a once-for-all "happening," earthly holy places and heavenly holy

---

the section 9.15–23 under the rubric "the new covenant," since in 9.21–23 the argument moves away from covenant per se to cultus. *Structure Translation*, 22–23.

21   Here we find ourselves in agreement with Vanhoye. He divides the letter into five principal parts, of which 5.11–10.39 is the third. Ibid., 15–27.

places, things on earth and things in heaven defiled and cleansed, an earthly access to God and a heavenly access to God. Out of the currents and cross currents of this cultic maelstrom, is it possible for us to discern one which is clearly constitutive of the whole?

We think it is: that of blood. Over the whole stands the rubric "better blood": just as the preceding argument of the writer established a better name, a better priesthood, a better priest, a better sanctuary, and a better covenant, so here in the climax of the development we see the better *means* by which the new age has come about—the blood of Christ.

A series of reasons support this view of blood, and Christ's blood in particular, as the leitmotif of Hebrews 9–10. First, of course, is the frequency with which αἷμα occurs in the passage—fourteen times in all. It would be folly to think of biblical scholarship as primarily a matter of the concordance and word counts, yet we cannot ignore this evidence so immediately given.

More significant than this statistic, however, is the *manner* in which αἷμα constitutes the framework of the argument. This comes into view most dramatically in connection with the cultic presuppositions which undergird the train of thought. These might be set out as follows:

Overriding axiom: "the blood rule" of 9:22 = no ἄφεσις without blood

Correlates: (1) Animal blood is efficacious to the extent of purgation τῆς σαρκός (9.13), but
(2) Animal blood cannot take away sins (10.4); however,
(3) Christ's blood extends even to the purgation of the συνείδησις (9.14).

Accordingly, we notice the way in which the author consistently emphasizes the "not without blood" theme in 9.6–22. At 9.7, it is blood which provides entree for the earthly high priest on atonement day: he dares not enter χωρὶς αἵματος; at 9.18, the first covenant could not be inaugurated χωρὶς αἵματος: blood provides dedication or inauguration: and thus, the ground is laid for the "blood rule" of 9.22—χωρὶς αἱματεκχυσία no ἄφεσις. Again, we should observe the valence which the four places in the passage where αἷμα is specifically linked to Christ have in the total argument. In 9.12, it is Christ's *blood* which enables him to gain access to the "real" sanctuary; in 9.14, it is Christ's *blood* which brings in purgation of the συνείδησις and enables true worship; in 10.19, it is Christ's *blood* which enables the Christian to approach the heavenly cultus with confidence; and in 10.29, it is Christ's *blood* which is the medium of consecration under the new covenant and which the one who sins deliberately holds in contempt.

We may summarize this syntactical evidence concerning the author's use of αἷμα in Hebrews 9–10 thusly: in all fourteen occurrences, αἷμα is a key term which directs the force of the argument.

Finally, we would draw attention to a point made early in this study:[22] the argument, which appears to be moving away from αἷμα, in fact returns to this term for its climactic affirmations. To recapitulate: superficially, the course of the argument moves from αἷμα to θυσία (sacrifice) to σῶμα (body) to θέλημα (will), but there is a dramatic "return" to αἷμα. From 10.19ff., as the author is concerned with the οὖν, ἀδελφοί ("Therefore, brothers ... "), he discards any talk of sacrifice, body, or the divine will and employs the blood of Christ for his strongest appeal and warning.

The evidence is to us decisive. We suggest that it brings with it two important conclusions for the interpretation of the passage. First, the "blood rule" of 9.22 becomes extremely significant: it controls the logic. This by both exclusion and inclusion: on the one hand, all means of purgation other than blood are ruled out of court as being ultimately ineffective; on the other, animal sacrifices here find their common ground with the self-offering of Christ. Thus, it becomes imperative to understand the "blood rule" precisely: the highly unusual form αἱματεκχυσία and peculiar usage of ἄφεσις call for careful investigation.

Second, we are able to make good sense of the passage as a whole. In particular, the view that Hebrews 10 stands in tension with Hebrews 9 is to be discarded: Michel has introduced into the text a difficulty which was never in fact present.[23] It seems likely to us that, because many students of Hebrews have been afraid of a grossly materialistic explanation (perhaps springing from the impassioned concern of certain Christians with the "blood" of Christ), they have endeavored to see a shift in the argument from αἷμα (grossly material) to πνεῦμα (spirit) or θέλημα (divine will) at 10.5–10. But no such "shift" is to be seen. Both before and after these verses, the argument of chapter 10 proceeds by way of "sacrifices" and "blood."[24]

A final comment concerning our view that "better blood" is the leitmotif of the passage is in order. It is undeniable that the argument of the third chapter of this study has provided the preparation for this insight. Not, we hope, in that we have been given a bias to "see" blood everywhere as significant—but rather by providing the necessary *attitude* to the cultic terminolo-

---

22 *Supra*, p. 5.
23 *An die Hebräer*, 334.
24 Thus, αἷμα occurs at 10.3, 19, 29; θυσία at 10.1, 5, 26; προσφορά at 10.14, 18.

gy of Hebrews 9–10. That is, we have been enabled to "hear" this language for what it is in essence—*religious* language. We have been alerted to its power to evoke primordial values and have been able to discard such burdens to understanding as the view that αἷμα represents a grossly materialistic, primitive (used derogatively) concept of the work of Christ.

But, granted that "better blood" is the leitmotif of the passage, how in fact does the *auctor ad Hebraeos* understand its nature and function? Does he conceive of "actual" blood of Jesus being offered in heaven? And how does this blood relate to the problem of defilement and its religious counterpart, purgation? To these problems we are now ready to turn.

The Nature and Interrelations of Blood, Defilement, and Purgation

The first thing to be said about the author's understanding of this αἷμα is this: it is the medium of approach to deity. At first sight, the reader of Hebrews is puzzled by the strange way in which the writer lumps together daily sacrifices, the red heifer, the covenantal sacrifices, and the Day of Atonement ceremonies in our passage.[25] Likewise, he finds it surprising that so careful a writer apparently makes mistakes concerning the types of animals used in these sacrifices.[26] But the changes from "goats and calves" to "goats and bulls" or to "calves and goats" or to "bulls and goats"[27] are of no significance in themselves; the *auctor ad Hebraeos* is as little concerned with such matters as he is with the details of the earthly sanctuary. What all these sacrifices have in common is the single point of blood: blood provides the medium of drawing near to God. Thus, it is a mistake to try to press the author's argument too rigidly into a framework of the Day of Atonement: while the ceremonies of this day do provide him with a point of comparison helpful to his purpose, they themselves are comprehended under the general rubric of blood.[28]

---

25 Daily sacrifices are referred to in 10.5–6, 8.11 (also 7.27); the Day of Atonement sacrifices in 9.6–7, 12, 21, 23, 25; 10.1–3; covenant sacrifices in 9.15–20; and the red heifer ceremony in 9.13 (possibly 10.22 also). The blending of these sacrifices is highlighted in 9.13, where Day of Atonement sacrifices are coupled with the red heifer ritual, and in 9.19, 21, where the author merges the sprinkling of the book and the people at the time of the covenant-making with the annual purging of the sanctuary on the Day of Atonement.

26 He refers to "calves and goats" at the covenant ceremony (9.19). But the MT has "oxen" (פָּרִים) and the LXX μοσχάρια ("young calves"). Likewise, the account (Exod 24.3–8) mentions only that the blood was thrown on the altar and the people—no mention is made of the "book" (βιβλίον). Nor does it make any reference to marjoram or scarlet thread.

27 9.12–13, 19; 10.4 respectively.

28 We have already noticed how the covenant-ceremony is merged with the Day of Atonement in 9.15–21. Again, in 10.1–11 the argument at first emphasizes the annual recalling

Thus, blood is set forth as a medium of *power*. Not on holy day per se, not on sacred ritual, not on consecrated persons, not on water, fire, or hyssop does the accent fall—but on blood. And that accent signifies potency. Specifically:

Blood provides access to God (9.7, 12, 25; 10.19)
Blood sanctifies, or consecrates (9.13)
Blood cleanses (9.14, 22)
Blood inaugurates covenant (9.20; 10.29)
Blood "perfects" (9.9, 14; 10.14)
Blood brings ἄφεσις (9.22)

The nature of blood as power comes to expression most clearly in terms of comparisons and contrasts as the blood of animals is juxtaposed to that of Christ. Blood is the medium of power: this is the general basis of the comparison; Christ's blood is the more powerful medium: this is the conclusion which the author wants to make. The comparison and contrast come into sharpest focus at 9.13–14—*if* the blood of goats and bulls avail to the extent of a purgation concerning the σάρξ, *how much more* will Christ's blood bring purgation of conscience for true worship. Yet they are seen throughout the course of the argumentation: animal blood provides access only for the high priest to the earthly inner sanctum—and that only once each year, but Christ's blood opens the way for all Christians to draw near to deity in heaven itself at any moment;[29] animal blood is offered repeatedly, but Christ's blood was offered once for all;[30] animal blood could never give a purged συνείδησις, but Christ's blood avails to "perfect" the συνείδησις.[31]

It is blood as *medium* of power rather than as agent to which the author's usage points. His employment of ἐν with αἷμα is suggestive:[32] everything (it might almost be said) is purged *in* blood according to the law;[33] the high priest enters the Most Holy *in* the blood of another;[34] believers may approach the inner sanctum in the blood of Jesus;[35] and Christ was consecrated (sancti-

---

of sins (the Day of Atonement) but then hammers home the idea of repetition by referring to daily sacrifice. Contrast Montefiore, *Epistle to the Hebrews*, 37: "The author of Hebrews, however, does not merely use sacrificial imagery: he gives an elaborate explanation of Jesus's death and ascension in terms of the most important of all sacrifices described in the Old Testament, that of the Day of Atonement."

29 9.6–7, 25; 10.18–22.
30 9.12, 24; 10.1–2, 10–14.
31 9.9, 14; 10.2–4, 15–18, 22.
32 The author prefers to use ἐν with αἷμα; however, διά is used at 9.12.
33 9.22.
34 9.25.
35 10.19.

fied) *in* the blood of the covenant.³⁶ The original locative sense of ἐν has not been wholly taken over by the instrumental sense; ἐν signifies "means" here, as Oepke has observed.³⁷ As in so many other aspects, Westcott showed more perception of blood as a medium to bring about religious passage than many subsequent commentators.³⁸

Finally, we should note that blood is associated with *life*. Here Heb 10.19ff comes to the fore: the "new way" into the presence of God opened in the blood of Jesus is a "living" one. Again, it is from "*dead* works" which defile the conscience that the blood of Christ provides purgation.³⁹ Further, the deity to which that blood offers access is emphasized as being the "living" God,⁴⁰ while it is the indissoluble life of the high priest Jesus, who offers his own blood, which is heavily stressed.⁴¹

Indeed, any attempt to understand the author in these chapters must take account of the way in which this motif of life dominates the discussion. While it is true that there is a brief reference to the death of Jesus,⁴² this is altogether a minor theme in the argument. Since it is death that makes blood available, the exegete is inclined to be impressed by the tragic element, with the result that blood is equated with death. Such a view, however, quite misses the author's perspective: his concern is not so much with the *means* of obtaining blood (death) as with the *life*-giving power that the symbol indicates.

The functions of blood correspond to its nature as a powerful, living medium. We have already listed these functions: to provide access, to purge, to inaugurate, to bring access, to consecrate (ἁγιάζειν), and to perfect (τελειοῦν). We shall return to these functions, especially the last two, later when the rela-

---

36 10.29.

37 Albrecht Oepke, "'Ἐν,"*TDNT*, II, 536–43. Oepke lists ἐν αἵματι under the classifcation of ἐν used as "means." He cites Rom 3.25 as an example where the phrase is "purely spacial" in significance, and Rev 7.14 as an example of its crossing over to the instrumental sense. This ambivalence of the sense of ἐν perhaps reflects a more general problem of the use of this preposition with liquids. For instance, A. T. Robertson, *A Grammar of the Greek New Testament in the Light of Historical Research* (Hodder & Stoughton, 1914), 584–90, emphasizes the locative use of the preposition and holds that texts such as Matt 3.11 (baptism ἐν water and fire) are probably not examples of the instrumental usage.

38 Cf. his *Epistle to the Hebrews*, 268: "Blood was the characteristic means for cleansing, though fire and water were also used. It is the power of a pure life which purifies. Under this aspect the Blood becomes, as it were, the enveloping medium in which (ἐν), and not simply the means or instrument through or by which, the complete purification is effected."

39 9.14.

40 9.14—"to serve the living God." In 12.22, "the city of the living God." Cf. 10.31; 3.12—the peril of falling away from the "living God."

41 7.3—Melchizedek, like the Son of God, continues forever; 7.9—"he lives" (i.e., forever); 7.16—Christ is priest "by the power of an indestructible life"; 7.23–25—Christ "continues forever ... always lives."

42 9.15–17; see the exegesis of this text, *infra*, p. 140.

Defilement, Blood, and Purgation in the Book of Hebrews: An Exegesis of Hebrews 9–10

tion of blood to defilement and purgation must be brought sharply into focus; for the moment it is sufficient to remark that all these functions mentioned above signify religious transition equals change of status.

It is manifest that the nature and function of blood as we have seen it set out in Hebrews 9–10 bear a very strong resemblance to the phenomenology of blood which we met in the previous chapter. We note especially the following aspects: those of power, life, and the effecting of transition.

At the same time, we notice the individuality of the representation given by the *auctor ad Hebraeos*. The most striking point, of course, is in the value assigned to a particular "blood," namely, the blood of Christ: while, as we have seen, the "blood rule" stands over the lintel of the discussion, it is one specific case of blood applied which stands out as having pre-eminent efficacy. A second point of divergence concerns the univalent role assigned to blood. We saw in the general "structure" that, while blood is an agent of surpassing power, that power may be either positive or negative: blood is the agent par excellence of *either* defilement or purgation. In Hebrews, αἷμα is repeatedly set out as the means of purgation; its ambivalent character is not at all in evidence.[43]

Thus, the "structures" of blood as revealed by phenomenology of religion at once illumine the ideas of "blood" in Hebrews 9–10 by showing their essential conformity and also their particularity. We would suggest, furthermore, that they are of significant help to us in our attempt to grapple with the argument of the passage. In particular, we refer to the emphasis on life in the passage, to the manner in which deity comes into view, and to the longstanding problem of the "materiality" to be assigned to the author's view of blood. Each of these matters calls for careful examination in turn.

Concerning the motifs of life and death in the passage, commentators have felt two problems. On one hand, there is the question as to why blood should be set forth only in terms of purgation: did not blood defile as well as cleanse in the Old Testament?[44] and should not Christ's blood, since it involves his death, also be a means of defilement?[45] On the other hand, the continual references to θυσία (sacrifice) and προσφέρειν (to offer) in the argument have led to an emphasis on the death of the sacrificial victim. But this em-

---

43 The one possible exception is in terms of those who despise the blood of Christ; see *infra* on 10.26–31, pp. 161ff.

44 E.g., Num 35.33—"Blood defiles the land"; Ps 106.38—"The land was polluted with blood"; Isa 59.3—"hands defiled with blood"; Lam. 4.13—"polluted themselves with blood" (cf. Ezek. 9.9; 16.6, 9, 22).

45 Purdy, *Epistle to the Hebrews*, 692, has felt this difficulty: "Is he suggesting that the blood of Christ not only caused no defilement, but that his blood purified even the conscience?"

phasis has been clearly out of harmony with the accent on life in the passage. How then are the motifs of life and death to be balanced?

The insights from phenomenology of religion point to the solution of these difficulties. As we saw in Chapter 3, blood *may* be seen as an ambivalent power; it is not *necessarily* so. Further, in any one situation blood is not at once positive *and* negative: it can only be positive *or* negative. The difference arises according to the view of its function: whether it is seen as increasing or diminishing life.[46] With regard to the argument of Hebrews, the point of view is manifestly directed toward the life-affirming side, so to introduce the negative aspect in the present form of the argument would not only be unnecessary but unexpected. There is only one point in the passage where the negative aspect might come into view. This is in the strong warning of 10.26–31 against regarding Christ's blood as κοινός ("common," "non-sacred"). Here that blood, which everywhere else has functioned as the medium of cleansing, consecration, and perfection, may turn against its despiser in fiercely destructive potency.

It is difficult for the Western exegete to assign to blood, sacrifice, and offering the positive sense which the passage clearly calls for. An accumulated weight of negative attitudes from the past has first to be laid aside—the ready equation of "blood" with "death" taken over from Pauline studies,[47] dogmatic theories of atonement which have heavily stressed the death of Christ as a "necessary" vicarious punishment so that sacrifice and offering signify a *victim*,[48] and the general response of his culture to "blood." That response seems invariably to point to the tragic element in human existence: blood signifies the sudden and violent loss of life. We are creatures of our time: perhaps the enormities of two world wars, together with numerous other conflicts around the world, and the assignation of important world leaders have made a negative evocation by blood inevitable. Certainly, the tables have been turned on centuries past: where once it was sex that was the unmentionable topic and death was discussed by pen and pulpit, today death is taboo, and sex is dominant. Only rarely does blood appear in its positive role for us. At the superficial level, blood in terms of blood donors and transfusions lays bare its function as the medium of life. At the specifically religious level, there have

---

46 *Supra*, Ch. 3, "The Multivalent Character of Blood."

47 Arguing from Rom 3.25; 5.9 (cf. 5.8); in the light of our study, however, it may be questioned whether such an equation holds true even for the Pauline corpus.

48 Schmoller's concordance affords a mute testimony to this type of thinking. He groups references to αἷμα which deal with animal sacrifices under "*sanguis victimarum.*" See Alfred Schmoller, *Handkonkordanz zum griechischen Neuen Testament*, 7. Aufl. (Privilegierte Württembergische Bibelanstalt, n.d.), 16–17.

been stirrings of recognition of the positive results which have ensued from the violent death of a Mahatma Gandhi: that such a person may have accomplished more in his dying than in his living. But generally the concern of our generation with the apparent senselessness of death—humans no longer die at childbirth; the old pass away out of sight and out of mind; it is the young, the beautiful, and the brave whose full cup is in a moment dashed from their hands—has blocked the insight into the positive valuation of "blood."[49]

Thus, if, as Moffatt suggested, the priest in ancient times was really a "holy butcher,"[50] that office signified hope to his people, however much it may offend our modern sensibilities. It is by assuming such a stance that we may grasp the force of the argument of the writer of Hebrews as he speaks of sacrifices and offerings, and dwells so often upon blood itself. For him, these expressions signified a way to overcome the religious problems of humanity, so that "blood" is a medium of life-giving power. In such a context it is utterly out of place to emphasize the note of tragedy.

We turn now to the matter of the role of deity in the argument of Hebrews 9–10. This is a subject which has received no serious consideration; yet *prima facie* the evidence poses a strong difficulty, namely, that deity seems to occupy a secondary place in the discussion. In view of the motifs of sacrifice, presentation of offerings, blood, and access, we would expect deity to be at the fore. In fact, θεός is used only eight times and in almost all of these places in a sense subsidiary to the main train of thought. In four cases, it is on Christ as the one who comes to do God's will, who sits down at the right hand of God, who is the great high priest over God's household, or who as the Son of God is not to be despised[51] that the interest rests; in another, it is on Christians who must patiently perform God's will in order to receive the promised reward.[52] Only at 9.14 does θεός appear with significant import, but even here the limelight is firmly on the blood of Christ: it is the blood of the one who through eternal spirit has offered himself faultless to God and which avails to purge the συνείδησις so that we may serve the living God. The most surprising omissions are to be found with regard to the offering of sacrifices: not once does the indirect object (τῷ θεῷ) occur with reference to the old cultus, while only once is it related to the offering of Christ.[53] Indeed, the

---

49   Amos Wilder's penetrating essay, "The Cross: Social Trauma or Redemption," *Symbolism in Religion and Literature*, 99–117 well expresses the difference between the early Christians' understanding of blood (positive) and the view of many moderns (negative: obsession with pain, or blood-lust).
50   *Epistle to the Hebrews*, xlvi.
51   10.7, 12, 21, 29.
52   10.36.
53   9.14. At 9.28, the passive προσενεχθείς is used with reference to Christ's sacrifice.

person of deity does not come to the fore at all in the strictly cultic argumentation of our passage. We see a marked change, however, as we enter upon the exhortations: it is God who stands ready to avenge the deliberate sinner and who guarantees the Parousia.[54] This evidence is all the more noteworthy when we bear in mind that the institutions of the Aaronic priesthood and Christ's Melchizedekian office were earlier underlined as being of specifically divine appointment.[55]

The immediate consequence of this data must be understood: it is utterly in error to think of an *offering demanded by deity* in Hebrews 9–10. The emphasis upon blood in the passage must not be construed to mean that God "requires" blood: this is never stated or implied. With such ideas are to be discarded all theories of substitution or "satisfaction" made to God or devil. Just as it is easy for the exegete to move from "blood" to the idea of victim, so he is likely to assign deity a place in the argument concerning blood which the text will not support. The one error is as obfuscating as the other: both detract from the force of "blood" as the key motif in the logic.

But how are we to account for this de-emphasis of deity in the cult? Certainly, it would be an unsatisfactory solution to posit that because the spotlight is on Christ and his blood (which is true), deity is at the fore. While it is clear that Christ's blood has a special character, apparently more than would derive from its character as human rather than animal blood, and while the letter does manifest a "high" christology,[56] just as surely does the author make a clear distinction between Christ the high priest and θεός at whose right hand he sits in the heavens.[57] No; it is not a matter of Christ's blood being powerful because it is "divine"; rather, the argument is that *all* blood is powerful but that Christ's is *most* powerful.[58]

At this point the general religious understanding of blood which we had earlier gained provides helpful insights. It reminds us that blood is a religious term evocative of such direct, immediate potency that it tends inexorably to autonomy, actually attaining independence of deity in some cultures.[59] Thus,

---

54 Especially 10.31—"It is a fearful thing to fall into the hands of the living God!" and 10.38—"My righteous one will live by faithfulness."

55 Necessity of divine call (5.4–6); the oath (6.15–20); the divine oath appoints a new order (7.11–12, 20–21, 28).

56 Especially in 1.1–4. Christ is Son, heir of all, agent of creation, reflects the divine glory, bears the stamp of the divine nature, upholds the universe, and is above the angels.

57 At 1.3, Christ, after purging sins, sits down at the right hand of "the Majesty on high"; at 10.12, he sits down after his sacrifice at the right hand of θεός.

58 The question of what it is that gives to Christ's blood its superlative power is discussed *infra*, pp. 138ff.

59 *Supra*, p. 71.

it is not surprising that, in an argument which has as its leitmotif "better blood," deity should not be assigned a prominent place.

We might well bring to a head this discourse concerning the relation of blood to deity in Hebrews 9–10 by pointing out the two extremes in presenting the argument of the author which must be sedulously avoided. First, for the *auctor ad Hebraeos* it is the blood of Christ that is the medium of approach to God, since it is the means of purgation. There is no thought here of Christ leaving for us a noble example in suffering, nor of giving us a demonstration of God's love which melts our hearts; just as there is no hint that blood is something which God *requires* or demands; certainly there is a denial of "salvation" as a gift without any reference to Christ. The first distortion of the writer's argument, then, is any schema which fails to assign pre-eminent place to the blood of Christ *in itself* as the "saving"[60] means. The other extreme consists in raising Christ's blood to the level of an autonomous medium. Christ is high priest by divine appointment; the offering of his blood was by the divine will; he sits at the right hand of the Majesty in heaven; the ancient scriptures had foretold his accomplishment; it is access to the living God which Christ's blood has provided.[61] By so many affirmations does the writer insist that the element of the "divine" is not to be excluded in considering the operation of Christ's blood.

Thus, there is a tension of ideas here: the term "blood" tends to religious autonomy in the face of the overarching divine will. Clearly, in Hebrews 9–10 the scale is weighted toward "blood" rather than toward God. But both this tension and weighting of the argument are readily comprehensible in view of the character of blood as revealed by the phenomenology of religion.[62]

With the above remarks concerning the nature and function of "blood" in Hebrews as basis, we are now ready to enter the fray concerning the "materiality" of Christ's blood in the author's understanding. It will be recalled that two diametrically opposed views have been advocated. Windisch holds to a

---

60 We use "salvation" here in a non-specific sense for Christ's work on behalf of humanity and the universe. For the *auctor ad Hebraeos*, it is apparent that he views σωτηρία as the final good only to be attained at the Parousia (9.28; 1.14; 2.3, 10; 5.9; 6.9). See *infra* on the exegesis of 9.28.

61 High-priest by divine appointment: 5.4–6; 6.15–20; 7.11–12, 20–21, 28; the divine will: 10.10; the heavenly session: 1.3; 10.12; the prediction: 10.5–10, 16–17; access to the living God: 9.14; 10.19–22 (also 4.14–16; 6.19–20; 12.18–24).

62 I find Spicq's contention that the theology of the letter is not christocentric but theocentric extraordinary (*L'Épître aux Hébreux*, I, 325–29). It is significant that he makes few references to Hebrews 9–10 in presenting his case. In this matter we see well the advantages of the approach followed in this study over previous efforts: in particular, the motif of blood is able to emerge in its full valence in the argument.

strict literalism while others, particularly Catholic scholars, have argued for a "spiritualized" conception such as the glorified blood of the Mass.[63]

In moving toward a resolution of this problem, the first point to observe is that while Christ's blood is indeed set forth as of surpassing excellence, it nevertheless finds its place in the argumentation under the general category of blood. That is to say, the "blood rule" of 9.22 stands over the whole discussion. It therefore appears to us to be a serious misunderstanding of the author's reasoning to introduce a dichotomy between "material" blood (that is, of animals) and "spiritualized" blood (that is, of Christ). In fact, there is absolutely no grounds for seeing some sort of "spiritualized" blood with regard to Christ. The only possible point of contest, 9.14, cannot provide support, since the διὰ πνεύματος αἰωνίου ("through eternal spirit") has reference only to the self-offering of Christ—it clearly does not define the nature of Christ's blood.[64]

Why then has there been this continued concern to see a "spiritualized" blood of Christ? For at least two reasons: material (literal) blood is a symbol which tends to offend modern sensibilities, as we have already suggested, and because of speculative theology. Catholic scholars in particular have endeavored to probe the question as to *how* Jesus could die on earth and yet offer himself to God in heaven above.[65] A "spiritualized" body of Jesus—with "spiritualized" blood—was sufficiently nebulous to overcome the difficulties of time and space.

We have already given our view of the modern Western revulsion to blood; let us now comment on the speculative attempts at a solution. It seems to us that they must be judged to have failed because they have endeavored to provide answers to questions which the author of Hebrews did not have in mind. The question of *what sort of* blood Christ offers in heaven is our question, not his, and we err if we try to put answers into his lips. That the writer did conceive of a heavenly cultus seems indisputable; that such a heavenly cultus was the "real"—the *real* sanctuary the *real* high priest, and the *real* offering—is likewise given; but that Christ's "blood" in the argument is therefore some sort of "spiritualized" substance does not necessarily follow.

---

63 *Supra*, Ch. 2, "The Question of the Spiritualizing of the Cultus."

64 It is incontestable that the διὰ πνεύματος αἰωνίου in 9.14 has reference to Christ, not to his blood. Only indirectly can the phrase have significance for αἷμα and that only under the rubric of the πόσῳ μᾶλλον.

65 Davidson, *Epistle to the Hebrews*, 146–54, shows how this question and the related problem as to when Jesus became high priest were significant in the Socinian controversies. For continuing Roman Catholic concern with these questions, cf. the bibliography of recent articles by Catholic scholars (n. 4, p. 27), and works such as Cody, *Heavenly Sanctuary and Liturgy*, 199–202, and Bonsirven, *Épître aux Hébreux*, 40ff.

The mistake in such speculative attempts is in shifting the focus of the argument. In Hebrews 9–10 that focus is *on earth*: it is concerned with the here and now, with humanity's "problem" which cries out for solution, and for the way in which Christ offers hope and help. "Heaven" must be in view, of course, since the work of Christ must avail to bring humanity into the presence of God, yet it is definitely not the point of emphasis.[66] The argument starts with humanity *as* they are and *where* there are, and *how* they are to come to God. This is why speculations concerning a "heavenly" type of blood have quite missed the mark, and, though understandable in view of our questions, must be adjudged improper and fruitless.

These remarks appear to drive us back to the literal, "material" view of blood. It is because many Protestant students have sensed this difficulty that they have endeavored to draw a line between the argument of Hebrews 9–10, positing a tension between the two or putting the accent on divine will or obedience or a "moral" sacrifice of Christ as opposed to a "grossly material" bloody sacrifice.[67] But our study of the two chapters has clearly demonstrated their unity—a unity comprehended under the leitmotif of blood. Are we not then obliged to take our place with Windisch's literalizing explanation?

We think not. Windisch's "materialistic" emphasis is as misplaced as the "spiritualizing" view—it is based on the same sort of speculation about happenings in heaven. The solution, we suggest, is rather to be found by taking into account our earlier studies concerning blood as a religious phenomenon. There we noticed that "blood" comes to expression as *force*—life-force manifested with direct, immediate potency. The "material" character of blood in such manifestation is not at all in view. The Ndembu with his "river of redness," Macbeth whose guilty hand will "incarnadine" the oceans, the evangelical Christian who sings "washed in the blood of the Lamb"—in all these cases it is a blood as an agent or medium of power that is being experienced.

Thus, we hold that it is mistaken procedure to attempt to "decode," as it were, the term "blood of Christ" in Hebrews 9–10. The author does not intend some spiritual or mystical connotation: the language is *religious* rather than theological. That is, it is essentially mythopoetic. As such, it bears its own peculiar intensity as it evokes ideas of a medium par excellence of access to

---

66 Thus, the *auctor ad Hebraeos* attempts no description of the heavenly sanctuary beyond stating that it is the real (8.1–2—ἀληθινῆς), nor does he embark upon an elaboration of cosmology beyond the basic idea of a two-story cosmology. So far as "heaven" is concerned, the author merely states (and states repeatedly) that Christ's self-offering is presented in the "real" sanctuary, i.e., before God. That is, "heaven" enters the argument only as the guarantee of Christ's work, not as a matter of interest in itself.

67 E.g., Michel, A. B. Bruce, F. F. Bruce (*supra*, Ch. 2).

God—a medium of life-potency. In such religious understanding, talk of metaphor is as wide of the mark as is that of "gross materialism."

Defilement and Purgation

In terms of vocabulary and word counts, we have seen that defilement does not come to prominence in Hebrews 9–10 or indeed elsewhere in the letter. But the manner of the author's argumentation as we consider the ideas of humanity's "problem" and its "solution" clearly brings defilement to the fore as *the* issue of existential concern.

Thus, the proem states that Christ has made *purgation* (καθαρισμός) for sins.[68] Here sin is set forth as a quasi-material "substance" which must be dealt with. The ninth and tenth chapters of Hebrews, which expatiate this statement, continually make the same point. Defilement may be a matter of flesh (σάρξ) or mind (συνείδησις), but in either case it calls for purgation (καθαρίζειν); thus, those who have been fully purged have no more consciousness of sins: they are washed (λούειν) in body and sprinkled clean (ῥαντίζειν) in mind.[69] The other verbs used in connection with the sin problem—ἀναφέρειν (to bear away),[70] ἀφαιρεῖν (to take away)[71] and περιαιρεῖν (to remove, take away)[72]—likewise point to ἁμαρτία as that which must be *removed*.

We note: humanity's problem here is *not* that it lacks righteousness, so that it cries out for "right-wising";[73] nor is it a debt that it owes, so that it seeks forgiveness;[74] still less is it a will in bondage, with freedom seen as the *summum bonum*.[75] No; these ideas are not to be imported into Hebrews 9–10; here humanity faces the difficulty of the stain, the blot, the corruption of its person—that is, defilement. And when we have said this, we see that the anthropology of Hebrews 9–10 finds its genre[76] in the language of defilement which we have already considered at some length in Chapter 3 of this study.

---

68 1.3b.

69 The old cultus could not bring "perfection" of "conscience" (9.9–10); the sprinkling of animal blood availed to purify "the flesh," but the blood of Christ purges the "conscience" (9.13–14). Heb 10.1–4 repeats the inadequacy of the OT offerings to cleanse "the conscience." In 10.22, Christians draw near to God "with hearts sprinkled clean from an evil conscience and our bodies washed with pure water."

70 Ἀναφέρειν= "to bring or take up ... to take away," Arndt and Gingrich, *Greek-English Lexicon*, 62.

71 Ἀφαιρεῖν= "to take away"; ibid., 123–24.

72 Περιαιρεῖν "to take away, remove"; ibid., 65.

73 As in the Pauline corpus, e.g., Rom 1.17, 3.20, 23–26; 4.5, 25; 5.9.

74 As in Luke 7.36–50 (the two debtors); 15.11–32 (the prodigal son).

75 As in John 8.30–36; Rom 7.14–25, 8.14–16, 22; Gal 4. 1–11.

76 We have used "genre" here in a non-technical sense (i.e., not according to its particular usage in form criticism) to indicate a religious type.

Indeed, we cannot escape the strong conformity of humanity's problem of defilement in Hebrews to the general "structures." We have noticed above the *quasi-material* character: defilement may extend to the very "consciousness," as well as to the body. Its *contagious* nature is also brought out by the *auctor ad Hebraeos:* not in these chapters, but at 12.15 where the "root of bitterness" may lead to the defilement of "many." The fatal aspect is also in evidence: defilement bears the stench of death,[77] it is inimical to the approach to the "living" God.[78]

The effects of sin as defilement likewise reflect the general patterns in a most striking way. Here there comes into view a feature of the argumentation of Hebrews which has not escaped the notice of various students, namely the "collective" view of humanity which is set forth.[79] It is fair to say that the individual person as such is nowhere under consideration in this passage: the high priest of the old order offers the sacrifices of the Day of Atonement for the sins of the *people*;[80] the covenantal sacrifices are likewise for the *whole* congregation;[81] while Christ's self-offering is for *all* people.[82] Thus, there is no mention of the offering of the individual's sacrifice which was provided for under the priestly regulations,[83] nor does the author turn to the individualistic emphasis at points in his discussion which would conveniently call for it. For instance, the mention of the red heifer obviously could suggest the cleansing of the defiled individual, but the point is lost in the argumentation concerning αἷμα;[84] again, in referring to the danger of treating lightly Christ's blood, we find the collective ἡμῶν where a τίνος, which would serve to underline that such an attitude is exceptional, might be expected.[85]

While this "collective" understanding of humanity has been discerned, its significance in terms of humanity's "problem" of defilement has escaped previous studies. The conceptual patterns are clearly congruent with those

---

77 9.14—Christ's blood purges the "conscience" from "dead works."

78 9.14—those who are purged "serve the living God"; 10.19-22—the purified in body and mind "draw near" in full assurance to God.

79 Spicq, for instance, has caught this sense of "collectivity" in his discussions of the conceptions of pilgrimage and cultic people: *L'Épître aux Hébreux*, I, 269-83. Grässer likewise has noticed that the "corporate" view of humanity deriving from the cultus entails that faith cannot have an individualistic meaning (*Der Glaube im Hebräerbrief,* 216-18).

80 9.7—The high priest takes blood "for himself and for the errors of the people."

81 9.19—Moses sprinkled with blood "all the people."

82 The plural is used consistently: Christ's blood purges your (our) conscience (9.14); he entered heaven "on our behalf" (9.24); he appeared "to put away sin" (9.26); he bore the sins of "many" (9.28); the heavenly sanctuary has been opened to "us" by his blood (10.19ff.).

83 As in Lev 1-7.

84 That the ritual of the red heifer was clearly intended for individual cases of defilement is manifest from the account of Num 19.

85 10.26.

which we encountered in Chapter 3: there is a strong sense of the *interrelatedness* of humanity, society, and cultus. And we would go further: even as we saw in the general "structures" a strong sense of the *interdependence* of humanity, society, cultus, and cosmos, so here. The enumeration of the effects of defilement in Hebrews 9–10 will provide the sharpest data.

We see in these chapters both "subjective" and "objective" effects of defilement. "Subjectively"—that is, in terms of the experience of the people—the passage brings out a marked contrast in feeling tone. On the one hand, there is the stress on the uneasy συνείδησις, on the continual remembering of sins, and on the terror which may be anticipated for the despiser of Christ's blood—"it is a fearful thing to fall into the hands of the living God!"[86] On the other, there is the stress—just as pronounced—on the confidence, even boldness, with which the believers may draw near to the living God because of the new way opened through the blood of Christ.[87] That is, the "subjective" effects of defilement—dread, aloneness, ostracism from society and cult—are precisely those which were noticed in the previous chapter. "Objectively"—that is, in terms of relations of defiled persons—the effects also conform to the general "structures." The defiled person may lead to the defilement of others;[88] the tent and all the vessels of ministration had to be sprinkled with blood in the old order;[89] likewise, it is necessary that the heavenly things themselves be purged.[90] The conceptual framework here cannot be denied: sin as defilement is a foul contagion whose effects extend not only to other members of the society but to the very inanimate vessels of the cultus and even to the cosmos itself. That is, while the "heavenly things" of which the *auctor ad Hebraeos* speaks are the "real" (the "*really* real"), they are not to be thought of as existing in utter separation from, and independence of, the less real things of earth.

We are now in a position to consider the issue of the morality of the category of defilement in Hebrews 9–10. It will be recalled that various attempts have been made to find a contrast between ritual (equals external) and morality (equals internal) in this passage.[91] Our study so far in this chapter will

---

86 Quoting Heb 10.31. In 10.1–3, the emphasis falls on the *continually* offered sacrifices of the old cultus: in them "there is a reminder of sin year after year." This is because they cannot purge the conscience (9.9, 14).

87 9.14—They now may "serve" God; in 10.19–22, they "draw near" to the "heavenly sanctuary" in "full assurance." In 4.16 and 10.35, the author speaks of "confidence" in approaching God.

88 12.15—The "root of bitterness" may spring up and by it "many may become defiled."

89 9.21—"He sprinkled with the blood both the tent and all the vessels used in worship."

90 9.23—"Thus it was necessary for ... the heavenly things themselves to be purified with better sacrifices than these."

91 *Supra*, Ch. 2, "The Question of the Spiritualizing of the Cultus."

have made it abundantly clear that such a dichotomy is not to be found here: the *total* argument is in terms of ritual, with the categories of defilement and purgation shown as common to both the old and the new orders, so that the high point of the discussion finds the Christians with *bodies* washed and *hearts* clean.[92] Further, we have noticed that the individual nowhere comes to view: the "collective" community is always to the fore.

Indeed, the manner of reasoning of the author might appear to indicate a "mechanical" sort of soteriology. Thus, the efforts by the commentators to sound the note of morality are readily understandable. They fail because they do not comprehend that defilement is pre-eminently a *religious* category and so cuts beneath distinctions of external/internal and ritual/moral. Defilement is quasimoral, even as it is quasi-material—but its essence concerns neither morality nor materiality but humanity's sense of "numinous uneasiness."

As with the general "structures" of Chapter 3, purgation in Hebrews 9–10 is the religious counterpart of defilement. As there are degrees of defilements, so there are degrees of purgation, namely of only the body or embracing the συνείδησις.[93] As the defilement has as its prime representation stain, blot, or mark, so purgation comes to expression as the state where that stain, blot, or mark has been sprinkled, washed, cleansed, or taken away.[94] As defilement is a state of negative power, so purgation is a state of positive power.[95] As defilement produces unease of mind and numinous dread, so purgation results in confidence before God and peace of mind.[96] As defilement leads to exclusion from the cult of earth and of heaven, so purgation qualifies for full participation in the cultic community on earth and the worship of heaven.[97] As defilement reaches beyond the immediate person to contaminate society, earthly cultus, and cosmos, so purgation is ultimately all-embracing in its scope, reaching even to the heavenly things themselves.[98]

The particular vocabulary of the writer with regard to purgation, however, calls for careful examination. We have to consider not only καθαρίζειν (to cleanse,

---

92 10.22.

93 We have noticed this point already in 9.9–10 and 10.1–3, 22. The sharpest contrast occurs at 9.13–14: whereas animal blood "sanctifies for the purgation of the flesh," Christ's blood avails to "purify your conscience from dead works to serve the living God."

94 Cf. the verbs used in the passage: καθαρίζειν, λούειν, βαπτίζειν, ἀναφέρειν, ἀφαιρεῖν, περιαιρεῖν.

95 Shown by its privileges: access to the living God by means of incorporation in the heavenly cultus; 10.19–22; 12.18–24.

96 As we already observed in 9.13–14; 10.1–3, 19–22.

97 12.22–24: "You have come to Mount Zion and to the city of the living God, the heavenly Jerusalem, and to innumerable angels in festal gathering...."

98 9.23—The necessity for purifying τὰ ἐπουράνια.

purify), but also ἁγιάζειν (to consecrate) and τελειοῦν (to perfect). How do these three terms relate to each other and to the general category of purgation?

In Hebrews 9–10, τελειοῦν seems clearly to be used as the *summum bonum* realized for the believer by Christ. In 7.11 the author had argued that "perfection" was not attainable via the Levitical priesthood and at 7.19 that the law perfected nothing; now he summarily states the conclusion that by one offering Jesus Christ has perfected the sanctified ones forever.[99] The manner in which he has used τελειοῦν as well as the general drift of his argumentation serve to indicate that this "perfection" consists of a twofold benefit: access to God and purification of the συνείδησις. Thus, in 7.19, after stating the inefficacy of the old order to perfect, he announces that the new hope in Christ enables us to "draw near" (ἐγγίζειν) to God. Again, 10.1 argues that the animal sacrifices can never "perfect" the offenders and is immediately connected with the "consciousness" (συνείδησις) or "remembering" (ἀνάμνησις) of sins. The elaboration of 10.14 (Christ has perfected the sanctified ones) in 10.15–18 likewise highlights the removal of the remembering of sins. In 10.19ff., both of these aspects flow together under the οὖν, ἀδελφοί: "let us draw near with a true heart in full assurance of faith"—although τελειοῦν as such is not used.

This, then, is the understanding of τελειοῦν in Hebrews 9–10: believers with all unease due to sin removed participating in the heavenly cultus. It seems to us that instead of the *loaded* word "perfection" a better term would be "incorporation." Incorporation signifies a state rather than an act of becoming, of entering into, such as "consecration" or "initiation" would point to. It is this view of τελειοῦν as a state which is indicated by the data of Hebrews 9–10; thus, we feel that those who have argued for τελειοῦν meaning consecration on the basis of the LXX have made too easy an equation.[100] Indeed, the

---

99 10.14.

100 For instance, O. Moe, "Der Gedanke des allgemeinen Priestertum im Hebräerbrief," *TZ*, V (1949), 161–69; and Spicq, *L'Épître aux Hébreux*, II, 221. While τελειοῦν is used with reference to the ordination of the Levitical priests in the LXX, the parallel with Hebrews is not complete: the LXX adds τὰς χεῖρας in every case (Exod 29.9, 29, 33, 35; Lev 4.5; 8.33; 16.32; Num 3.3) except one (Lev 21.10). The idea of τελειοῦν in Hebrews has long been a matter of debate among scholars. Their interest has been along christological lines, since the letter speaks of τελειοῦν with reference to Christ as well as to Christians. This raises the issue of whether τελειοῦν is used in an ethical sense for Jesus; cf. O. Michel, "Die Lehre von der christlichen Vollkommenheit nach der Anschauung des Hebräerbriefes," *ThSK*, CVI (1934–35), 333–35; Frederik Torm,"Om τελειοῦν i Hebraeerbrevet," *SEA*, V (1940), 116–25; P. J. du Plessis, *ΤΕΛΕΙΟΣ: The Idea of Perfection in the New Testament* (Uitgave J. H. Kok, 1959), pp. 206–33; and Allen Wikgren, "Patterns of Perfection in the Epistle to the Hebrews," *NTS*, VI (1959–60), 159–67. Our concern in this study is with the implications of τελειοῦν for anthropology rather than for christology—although, since Christ shared our flesh and blood (2.14), these motifs can be distinguished but not separated. We pay attention to the author's employment of τελειοῦν outside of Heb 9–10 later in this chapter (*infra*, p. 168).

fact that, as we shall notice below, the author distinguishes between τελειοῦν and ἁγιάζειν would make τελειοῦν mean "to consecrate" highly unlikely. N. A. Dahl proposes "initiation" for τελειοῦν in order to set it apart from "consecration" (ἁγιάζειν);[101] our suggestion of "incorporation" seems to be less confusing, however.

Hebrews 10.14 distinguishes ἁγιάζειν from τελειοῦν making the former the logical preparation for the latter: Jesus Christ has perfected (incorporated) forever those who are sanctified. That the present passive ἁγιαζόμενος here has the sense of a state attained is made apparent from 10.10 with the periphrastic ἡγιασμένοι ἐσμέν "we have been sanctified" (that is, in 10.14, it would be inadmissible to read as: "he incorporated those who are being sanctified," making τελειοῦν logically prior to ἁγιάζειν).

The two other occurrences of ἁγιάζειν in our passage serve to make manifest its meaning. At Heb 9.13, the author argues that in the old order blood "sanctifies" for purity of the flesh, while at 10.29 he speaks of the blood of the covenant in which Christ was "sanctified." That is:

Old order: ἁγιάζειν, no τελειοῦν (explicitly excluded)
Christ: ἁγιάζειν, τελειοῦν
New order: ἁγιάζειν, τελειοῦν[102]

In this light, it appears that the *auctor ad Hebraeos* understands ἁγιάζειν as consecration, sanctification as separation for divine service. That is, ἁγιάζειν marks the point of transition, of separation from the profane, in the approach to the Sacred. Under the old order, such a separation was made, but full access was not attainable: there was ἁγιάζειν but no τελειοῦν. Under the new order, there is a corresponding separation from the profane (the letter as a whole is written in an atmosphere of total disregard for the "world"),[103] brought about by the blood of Jesus—but that blood further avails to blot out all unease due to sin and to provide full access to deity. That is,

ἁγιάζειν  τελειοῦν
Separation   Incorporation

---

101 "A New and Living Way—the Approach to God according to Hebrews 10.19–25," *Int*, V (1951), 401–12. We feel, however, that in common parlance the two terms are so close in meaning that his purpose is not well served. "Consecration" and "incorporation" seem more easily distinguishable—the first denoting an act of separation into the realm of the Sacred, and the second the state of full participation in the life of the cultus.

102 Old order: 9.13, 9; 10.1; 7.11, 19; Christ: 10.29; 2.10, 5.9; 7.28; 12.2; new order: 10.10, 14.

103 Apart from vague references to persecution, the author seems oblivious to the larger world outside his own cultic circle. Thus, there are no references to the state or to social ethics.

The author's usage of καθαρίζειν (to cleanse, to purify) indicates an interesting difference from that of ἁγιάζειν and τελειοῦν. καθαρίζειν is used both of people and things,[104] the others only of people. The data in fact point to a broad spectrum of meanings for καθαρίζειν: it is the *general* word used to indicate purgation. For example, in the parallel construction of 9.13–14, καθαρίζειν is used as the equivalent of ἁγιάζειν; but comparison with 9.9 makes it apparent that "purgation of συνείδησις from dead works" is equivalent to τελειοῦν of συνείδησις—that is, καθαρίζειν embraces both ἁγιάζειν and τελειοῦν. Again, at 10.2 the κεκαθαρισμένους is qualified by the ἅπαξ, to distinguish a purgation with finality ("once for all") from a purgation which will have to be repeated: clearly καθαρίζειν in itself does not carry this idea of finality. No; καθαρίζειν itself merely points to the religious phenomena of purgation: the context must determine differentiations as to persons or things, old order or new order, repeated or once-for-all. Thus, in 10.22 we read of the Christians approaching deity having their bodies washed in ὕδατι καθαρῷ (pure water) and we discern very clearly the *religious* category that is operating in the term καθαρίζειν. In such an understanding, it is quite out of place to introduce questions of morality in an attempt to draw a sharp line between external (ritual) and internal (moral) purgation.

As to the agent(s) of purgation in Hebrews 9–10, our previous remarks make it manifest that the means par excellence is αἷμα. While water is referred to in a passing manner,[105] the total argument is built around the power of blood. Here two distinct levels of potency are brought to view: animal blood avails to consecrate but cannot provide full access to God and must be applied over and over, but Christ's blood has brought incorporation (τελειοῦν) by a once-for-all operation.

We see at this point in sharp outline the congruency and also the contrast of the data of purgation in Hebrews 9–10 vis-à-vis the general "patterns" from phenomenology of religion. In the nature of purgation, in its effects, in the means used to bring it about—all aspects show precise parallels. The divergence is likewise sharp: it is not blood in general but a particular blood, even Christ's blood, which is the supreme purging medium; and further, this medium is of such potency that the state of purgation may not only be attained but held. Thus, whereas the general patterns continually looked to purgation as that which once was or which might be, since the melancholy force of the

---

104 People: 9.14; 10.2, 22 (all refer to the συνείδησις); things: 9.22—"almost everything under the law"; 9.23—τὰ ἐπουράνια.

105 9.10—"various ablutions" (of the OT); 9.19—the covenant ceremony at Sinai involved blood, wool, hyssop, and water; 10.22—Christians approach God with "bodies washed with pure water."

is with its note of recurring defilement could not be pushed aside from center-stage, there is a dramatic shift in Hebrews 9–10. The accent continues to fall on the "now" time—but with a reversal of religious "tone." Whereas in the general "structure" the present is the time of continued and repeated defilements and is therefore somber, in Hebrews 9–10 the note is of a lasting purgation *now* achieved. The somber note is wholly in terms of the past, as the repeated attempts of the old cultus to attain a decisive purgation are described. That is, the author is fully aware of the oscillatory pattern

$$\text{Defilement} \rightleftarrows \text{Purgation}$$

but his argument is that this pattern has been broken through by the "once-for-all" blood of Christ. Now we have

$$\text{Defilement} \longrightarrow \text{Purgation}$$

Defilement, Blood, and Purgation in Dynamic Relation

We may now bring together the results of this discussion of defilement, blood, and purgation. It is clear that the three terms are bound up in the closest interplay in the argument of Hebrews 9–10. We may conveniently set out the relationships by a series of diagrams, for which the basis is indubitably:

$$\text{Defilement} \xrightarrow{\text{blood}} \text{Purgation}$$

If we place alongside this the general "structure" from Chapter 3, we see at once the individuality of the argument of Hebrews 9–10:

$$\text{Defilement} \; \overset{\text{Blood (cleansing)}}{\underset{\text{Blood (defiling)}}{\rightleftarrows}} \; \text{Purgation}$$

That *is*, the *auctor ad Hebraeos* conceives of blood only as a purging medium.[106]

But that this individual representation is intelligible only within the general patterns is likewise manifest. Just as the general patterns come to expression in terms of power, death, and order, so in Hebrews.

First, in terms of power, we find again the network of forces:

---

106 The possible exception is at 10.29.

Defilement	Blood	Purgation
Negative power	Strongly Positive	Positive power

Defilement is the state of danger: the polluted one is also a polluter.[107] It is the state of separation, of cutting off from society and cultus.[108] Purgation implies the reverse of defilement: it is a state of positive power wherein one has participation in the heavenly cultus.[109] Blood—particularly Christ's blood—is manifested as the medium of unrivalled potency to effect the transition, the *rite de passage*.

Again, we see expressed the dynamic relationships in terms of life and death:

Defilement	Blood	Purgation
`Death	Life-Power	Life

The smell of death hangs over κοινοῦν: its bundle of νεκρῶν ἔργων droops like an albatross from the συνείδησις.[110] Purgation, on the other hand, is the state of worship of the living God.[111] It is αἷμα that effects the change of status: the αἷμα of one who is ἄμωμος and ἀμίαντος and who has the power of an indestructible life.[112]

Finally, the relationship in terms of order/disorder is in evidence:

Defilement	Blood	Purgation
Disorder	Blood	Order

In Hebrews 9–10 we see, on the one hand, the *necessity* to apply blood to even the items of service of the earthly sanctuary and ultimately to the "real"—the heavenly things themselves; and, on the other, the restoration of order among the holy things of earth and of heaven when this has been done.[113]

Likewise, when we lay out the data of Hebrews in terms of the nature and concomitants of defilement and purgation, the resemblances to the "structures" in Chapter 3 are most striking:[114]

---

107 12.15—the "root of bitterness" leads to the "defilement" of "many."
108 10.26–31—the one who counts as κοινός the covenant blood awaits punishment without mercy.
109 10.19–22—"let us draw near ... in full assurance of faith."
110 9.14—Christ's blood purges the "conscience from dead works to serve the living God."
111 9.14; 10.19–22; also 12.18–24—participants with angels in the heavenly cultus.
112 7.26—Christ is an "unstained" priest; 7.16—he became priest "by the power of an indestructible life"; 9.14—he offered himself "without blemish to God."
113 9.21–23: the purging of earthly copies and τὰ ἐπουράνια themselves was necessary.
114 *Supra*, p. 123.

		Defilement → Blood → Purgation	
Nature	{	Basic idea: spot, stains Quasi-material Quasi-moral Contagious	Basic idea: stain removed Quasi-material Quasi-moral –
"Subjective" Effects	{	Dread Uneasy συνείδησις No access to God	Confidence Συνείδησις at peace Worship God
"Objective" Effects	{	Society endangered Earthly cultus defiled Heavenly cultus defiled	Society strengthened Earthly cultus cleansed Heavenly cultus cleansed

In Hebrews 9–10 we also see agreement with, and departure from, the oscillatory pattern:

Defilement ⇌ Purgation

derived in Chapter 3. Indeed, the emphatic argumentation centering in the terms ἅπαξ and ἐφάπαξ[115] has its focus in such a context. On the one hand, the *auctor ad Hebraeos* is concerned to emphasize that the old order functioned according to the pattern:

Defilement ⇌ Purgation

He argues that the very repetition of its most significant ceremonies—those of Atonement Day—point to the fact that purgation was never achieved in finality.[116] The blood of Christ, however, breaks the pattern completely; now we have:

Defilement → Purgation

This concern with the purgation effected by the once-for-all offering of Christ's blood leads the author to introduce a particular vocabulary into the general concept of purgation. Blood purges defilement: this is his working principle,

---

115 The author does not seem to distinguish between these terms.
116 9.6–7, 25; 10.1–3.

so he cannot deny all purgative power to the sacrifices of the old cultus. Yet he wishes to differentiate strongly the purgation effected under the old order from that available under the new. Hence, we find introduced the categories of ἁγιάζειν, ἐφάπαξ, and τελειοῦν. Whereas ἁγιάζειν stands for that separation from the profane which marked the old cultus, only under the new order is incorporation into the heavenly cultus (τελειοῦν) possible. We may conveniently diagram the relationships which result as follows:

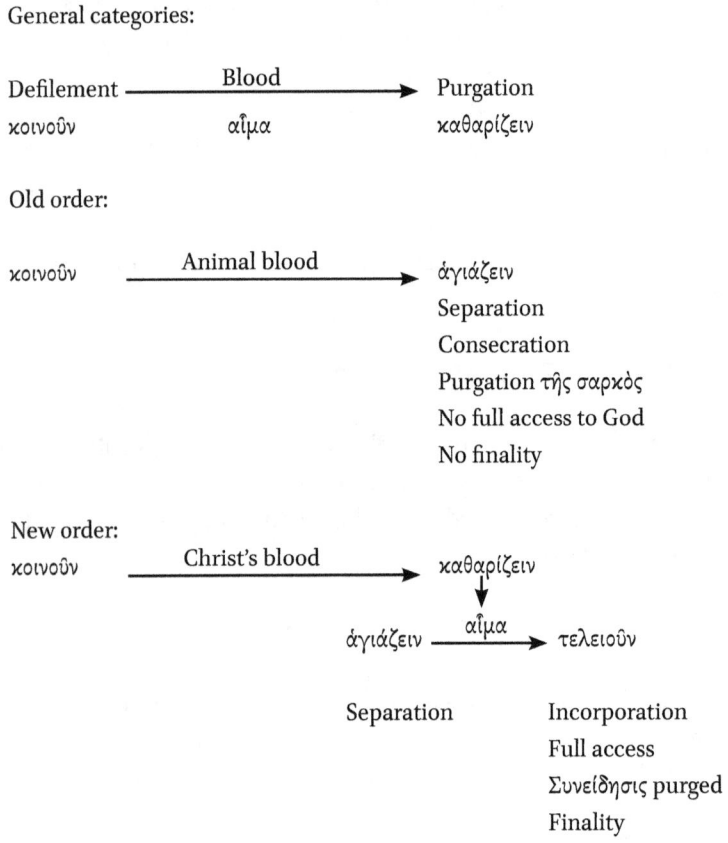

It seems incontestable that the methodology we have adopted has illuminated the argumentation of Hebrews 9–10, particularly as it concerns the notions of blood, defilement, and purgation. But our presentation so far has not taken account of certain points in the text which might appear to lead in a different direction: for instance, the reference to λύτρωσις (redemption),[117]

---

[117] 9.12—"having secured an eternal redemption" (in 9.15, ἀπολύτρωσις is used).

and the mention of divine will.[118] Besides, we must consider what light may now be shed upon the *cruces interpretum* from the discussion we have already concluded. It is time, therefore, for us to take up the text and trace its developing argument step by step.

The Progress of the Argument in Hebrews 9–10

Rather than considering the passage in a verse-byverse fashion, it seems more helpful to deal with it in its logical parts as we have previously isolated them. In this way, traditional "hard nuts" will be taken up with due regard to their context in the argument.

9.1–5. One should not endeavor to attach too much significance to these verses; nor, on the other hand, should they be put aside. The author here sets out a quick description of the earthly sanctuary, basing his remarks on the portable tent of the wanderings rather than on the Jerusalem temple. But we are not to attach meaning to the various items of the sanctuary which he lists: he has no interest in them is underlined by his περὶ ὧν οὐκ ἔστιν νῦν λέγειν κατὰ μέρος that ("We cannot speak in detail about these things here"). The point is important: it shows us that the argument is not to be conducted via an allegorizing or "spiritualizing" of each item in the earthly sanctuary. The *auctor ad Hebraeos* is no more concerned with drawing correspondences between the earthly items of furniture and their counterparts in the heavenly sanctuary than with a homiletical "application" of each item to the work of Jesus Christ.

Indeed, the items mentioned in these verses are not alluded to again. Why then does he trouble to list them? Manifestly, in terms of defining the *two divisions* of the earthly sanctuary: the Ἅγια (Holy Place) and the Ἅγια Ἁγίων (Holiest of all). Introducing his discussion in this way accomplishes two apparent purposes: (1) on a broad level, the point is being made that humanity's approach to God is not an easy matter: the old sanctuary was a system of *barriers* between humanity and God; and (2) more specifically, the two compartments are to be used as an illustration for the contrast between earthly and heavenly that he is shortly to make.

These observations shed light on two omissions from the list of sanctuary appurtenances which might appear surprising. In view of the argumentation concerning purgation and the offering of blood, which is to follow, we might have expected to see included the laver and the altar of burnt offering. But

---

118 10.10—"by that will we have been sanctified through the offering of the body of Jesus Christ once for all."

when we see what the *auctor ad Hebraeos* is about, the omissions are altogether in order: first, these two items were placed outside the first compartment of the sanctuary and hence could not come into view in an argument concerned with access to God in terms of the two compartments; and second, the author clearly shows no interest in drawing parallels from items of the sanctuary to the work of Christ. The altar of burnt offering, in fact, would turn the argument in a direction contrary to his purpose: it was the place of killing and burning, whereas he is dealing with blood as a medium of access and purgation.[119]

The passage contains one error of fact: the author places the altar of incense in the second apartment instead of in the first. It seems impossible to find any justification for the statement, whether from the particular edition of the LXX which he used or from the manner in which he develops the argument of Hebrews 9–10. We must underline this latter point: the golden altar is not at all the focus of interest to the author in 9.1–5 nor can it in any way be conceived of as entering into the subsequent argument. That is, this puzzling misplacement of an item of the earthly sanctuary's furniture is no more than a curiosity to the exegete.[120]

This is not the only place where the author's description of the cultus is at variance with the LXX: at 7.27, he seems to have the high priest offering daily sacrifices, while there is a curious blending of cultic animals and ceremonies in 9.6–22. These errors in detail appear to present the exegete with three options: the author had a "defective" edition of the LXX, or he misunderstood the LXX (not having personal acquaintance with the cultus), or he simply was not concerned with the details of the cultus. The first position lacks manuscript support; the second must always remain purely conjectural; the third, however, does allow of investigation. Admittedly, such investigation involves the "feel," as it were, of the author's manner of argumentation. It seems to me that with the *auctor ad Hebraeos* we are dealing with a master whose convolutions of thought are developed very carefully but whose mind grasps religion in terms of a series of striking motifs rather than in a mass of minutiae.[121]

---

119 At the close of his work, he makes a homiletical application from the idea of the altar of burnt offering in 13.11–13. The offhand mention of the altar there is in marked contrast to the closely woven argumentation of Heb 9–10.

120 It is because certain views as to the nature of Scripture seem to be threatened by this error of fact that commentators have frequently given considerable space to this problem. A recent discussion from a conservative viewpoint is provided by F. F. Bruce, *Epistle to the Hebrews*, 184–87. That Bruce finds the author's "mistake" a problem is obvious; his eventual attempt to diminish its force—"there was, however, a special connection between the incense-altar and the holy of holies, no matter on which side of the veil the altar stood" (p. 186)—is itself quite unsatisfactory in meeting the point, however.

121 Elsewhere in the letter we may discern evidence of the author's impatience with minutiae, e.g., in the list of the ABC's of Christ (6.1–3), in the abrupt termination of the list of

In Hebrews 9–10, these motifs are blood, access, defilement, purgation, and "conscience" (συνείδησις). Details are only in view as they are lumped together in the service of the motif which is in focus. From one point of view, then, the author is careless in his examples and makes mistakes of fact; from another, however, he is seen at work as a master painter whose broad canvas reduces such talk of mistakes to mere quibbling.

9.6–10. The δέ of verse 6 picks up the μέν of verse 1, showing that a forward movement in the argument is about to be made. What this movement is becomes quite clear: it is an explicit proof of the imperfection of the old order. This is shown in two respects: lack of access to God and no purgation of συνείδησις—ideas which we have already seen to be internally related.

Indeed, the preparation of the argument in the description of the earthly sanctuary in verses 1–5 and its full development here show the old cultus as a system of *barriers*. No access to the outer compartment of the earthly sanctuary was possible for the layman, while the Holiest of All was even more restricted: only the high priest, and that but once a year, could approach the second compartment. Yet even the high priest, as he entered the Most Holy on Atonement Day, could not be said to have realized the fulness of access to deity, for the earthly sanctuary was no more than a symbol pointing to the present age.[122] In this age, a way to the "real" sanctuary,[123] which is heaven itself, has been manifested: here only is true access to God.

Before we look into the anthropology which comes into view here, we should pause to note that the passage exposes the limits of our thesis. We are concerned in this study with the defilement-purgation syndrome as a way of explicating the anthropology of Hebrews. But in verses 8–9 we seem to confront another symbolism: the outer tent equals this age and consists of barriers. That is, the defilement "structure" is crossed by a cosmological (gnostic?) one. Since we are investigating anthropological rather than cosmological aspects of Hebrews, we can do no more than to take notice of this second sym-

---

the heroes of faithfulness (11.32–38), and in the description of the privileges of the heavenly cultus (12.22–24).

122 Παραβολὴ εἰς τὸν καιρὸν τὸν ἐνεστηκότα. We have followed Arndt and Gingrich, *Greek-English Lexicon,* 617, at this point.

123 The author's usage of τὰ ἅγια in Heb 9–10 has evoked considerable comment. We agree with the assertion by A. P. Salom, "TA HAGIA in the Epistle to the Hebrews," *AUSS,* IV (1966), 59–70, that the term denotes the sanctuary in general, rather than with Swetnam, "Hebrews 9.2 and the Uses of Consistency," 205–21, that it signifies the Holy of Holies. Swetnam is right to the extent that the stress in the author's usage of the term in 9.12, 24–25; 10.19 is clearly on full access to God. It seems to us that no distinction of two "compartments" in the heavenly sanctuary is to be made on the basis of the author's argument. His point in dealing with the Holy and Most Holy in 9.1–5 manifestly is to show the lack of access under the old cultus and to provide the base for the symbolism of outer equals earthly, inner equals heavenly.

bology. By this means, however, we may guard against overextending our thesis: clearly, the defilement syndrome is not to be forced so as to attempt to cover all issues (its primary thrust is anthropological). It is obvious that investigation of the cosmology of Hebrews, along lines analogous to the anthropological concerns of this study, is called for.

Turning from cosmology, we observe that the *auctor ad Hebraeos* uses τελειοῦν instead of καθαρίζειν with reference to the "consciousness" (συνείδησις) of sin here. We have seen that τελειοῦν for him signals finality—here, such a removal of sin from the consciousness that it does not again come into remembrance. What he wishes to deny, apparently, is not a temporary purgation of the consciousness under the old order, but rather the ability of that cultus to effect a permanent purgation (τελειοῦν). The qualification of the κεκαθαρισμένους by ἅπαξ at 10.2 confirms this interpretation.

It is time for us to consider the author's understanding of the term συνείδησις. In doing so we cannot escape giving attention to his usage of σάρξ, since the two terms appear to be juxtaposed: while the old cultus could not "perfect" the συνείδησις of the worshipper, it consisted only in δικαιώματα σαρκός ("fleshly regulations");[124] again, animal blood brought purgation τῆς σαρκός, but Christ's blood purged the συνείδησις.[125] On this basis, commentators have argued for a συνείδησις-σάρξ dichotomy, which has been equated with an "internal"/"external" equals moral/ritual cleft.[126] Thus, the issues raised from a consideration of the author's intent in using συνείδησις are ultimately of crucial significance in the exegesis of Hebrews 9–10.

Our earlier study of defilement and purgation in Hebrews 9–10 has pointed to the manner in which συνείδησις is to be understood. The word has obviously negative connotations—connotations of sin, remembering, and repetition. With the συνείδησις there comes into view the "subjective" aspects of humanity as defiled: that is, the personal sense of "sin." Συνείδησις is the internal witness, as it were, that all is not well; it is the uneasy consciousness. Though the old cultus with its ritual of the Day of Atonement might effect temporary relief, the purgation of mind was short lived: the very need for the rituals to be repeated was the damning evidence that "sin" had again come into remembrance.

We must beware of reading into the text modern ideas of "conscience" as the moral arbiter, the influence of the superego on the ego.[127] Conscience in

---

124 9.10, translating literally.
125 9.13–14.
126 *Supra*, Ch. 2.
127 Cf. Gove, *Webster's Third New International Dictionary*: "the sense of right or wrong within the individual ... inmost thought or sense ... conscientious observance ... sensitive regard for fairness or justice."

this sense denotes the intuition of "right" as well as "wrong"; it is involved in decision; and, above all, it is eminently individualistic. We would underline that in all of these three points there is a yawning gulf between "conscience" in common parlance and συνείδησις in Hebrews 9–10. For the *auctor ad Hebraeos*, συνείδησις concerns only the sense of "wrong"; it is not involved in decision-making but in "remembering" or "consciousness"; and it is collective: the community, not the individual, is in view.[128] It seems to us, therefore, that it would be wise for students of these chapters to eliminate all talk of "conscience" as they discuss the argumentation.

Obviously, while "consciousness" and "remembering" serve to give a general idea of what the author is about when he refers to the συνείδησις, they are awkward in translation; furthermore, they themselves introduce misleading connotations. We would suggest that Bouquet's expression, "numinous uneasiness," provides an attractive alternative. The author of Hebrews clearly intends to convey the sense of unease by συνείδησις: it is the collective unease of the congregation which leads over and over to Atonement Day. At the same time, this unease receives its peculiar sharpness because the sense of defilement is above all with reference to deity: it is a *numinous* unease.

Συνείδησις is thus a word of deep significance to the author. Above all, we must recognize it for what it is: deeply evocative of *homo religiosus*. With συνείδησις we see, as it were, humanity's efforts at self-sufficiency peeled away and his feelings of inadequacy before the divine—that is, coming to expression as defilement—laid bare in his innermost consciousness; and with that we see his repeated efforts to seek the "solution" held out by the cultus—purgation from defilement—only to fall, fall back again into defilement. It is a picture which, of course, accords exactly with the anthropology of defilement indicated by phenomenology of religion.

---

128 Our conclusions concerning the use of συνείδησις in Hebrews find precise support in C. A. Pierce's penetrating study: *Conscience in the New Testament*, SBT (Alec R. Allenson, Inc., 1955), 99–102. Pierce shows that συνείδησις, although used sparingly, is employed with great skill by the author of Hebrews; he also points the need of understanding the author's use of the term without interpreting it by other NT occurrences. In Heb 9.9, he finds that "conscience is the real obstacle to worship." The badness of the "conscience" is implicit in the description: the old ritual could not "perfect" the συνείδησις. In 9.14, the badness is explicit: "dead works." In 10.2, the author describes a συνείδησις decisively purged: it is essentially "empty" (cf. p. 26). In 10.22, the badness of the "conscience" is again explicit: it requires purgation. Pierce's account agrees with ours in showing the negative connotation which συνείδησις has: it stands in the way of worship and calls for cleansing. When it has been purged, it is marked by an *absence* of "numinous uneasiness" rather than having a positive content. Pierce, however, has not brought out the "collective" aspect as he might have done. He seems to take for granted that the argument of Hebrews has in view a *cultus*—that is, a *group* of worshippers.

What then of the author's understanding of the σάρξ (flesh)? Apart from these two occurrences of σάρξ in conjunction with συνείδησις, there are four references to σάρξ in the letter.[129] One of these, that at 10.20, involves the *crux interpretum* of the apparent equation of flesh with "curtain" and must be left for full treatment later. The other three, however, seem to share a common idea of σάρξ—that of a mere designation for human nature. The reference at 5.7 is especially clear: the earthly experiences of Jesus are comprehended under ἐν ταῖς ἡμέραις τῆς σαρκὸς αὐτοῦ ("in the days of his flesh"). Again, 2.14 speaks of Christ's children, and thence Christ, sharing blood and σάρξ; while 12.9 contrasts our fathers τῆς σαρκὸς with God as father.

In all these three cases, it is quite clear that σάρξ is not a term of derogation. There is no suggestion of "fallen" human nature in view, for instance, even as there is absolutely no hint of a σάρξ-πνεῦμα dichotomy of a metaphysical (Greek philosophy) or ethical (Pauline) type. No; σάρξ is used without special theological weight: it does no more than designate the *sphere of humanity*. The only contrast here is the general one that pertains throughout the Bible: the inferiority of the human to the divine.[130]

We are now ready to consider the significance of σάρξ in 9.10. Is it possible that here we find the term used with special—that is derogative—significance to indicate a dichotomy with συνείδησις? The evidence is overwhelmingly against such a view, even if we set aside the use of σάρξ elsewhere in Hebrews. For a start, we noticed already the curious preference of τελειοῦν for καθαρίζειν at 9.9, which would indicate, not that the old cultus could not bring purgation of συνείδησις, but that it could not effect a lasting purgation. If this is correct, then there could obviously be no dichotomy of σάρξ-συνείδησις in view. The conclusion of 10.19ff is decisive to settle the issue beyond all doubt: there the Christian comes to God purged in *both* body and συνείδησις. In fact, the *auctor ad Hebraeos* had already clearly revealed that he had no objections to ritual on the grounds that it was "external" instead of "internal": he included lustrations (βαπτισμοί) among the ABC's of catechetics.[131]

In 9.10, therefore, we should translate δικαιώματα σαρκὸς "human regulations."[132] The contrast is yet to be made: it will be between the earthly sanctuary

---

129   In addition, the adjective σάρκινος is used at 7.16.
130   Cf. E. Schweizer,"Σάρξ," *TDNT*, VII, 142, writing concerning σάρξ in Hebrews: "In all these passages σάρξ denotes the earthly sphere which is separated from the world of God. But the thought of sin is never linked to it."
131   6.2.
132   Cf. RSV—"regulations for the body" and NEB—"outward ordinances." Both of these transactions reveal the outworking of the bias against ritual which we have noted frequently before. Schweizer, "Σάρξ," *TDNT*, VII, 142, however, agrees with us: "One may ask, then, whether the phrase in 9.10 does not mean 'statutes of the earthly sphere.'"

with which these human regulations are concerned and the new order which finds its focus in the heavenly sanctuary.

The author's view of the old cultus comes clearly into view in this paragraph. On the one hand, there is obvious denigration: it is a system of barriers; it brings no finality in dealing with the numinous uneasiness of humanity, because it belongs merely to the human order. Yet it is not to be wholly deprecated: it was significant in its time, serving as a symbol of the new order to come. Thus, there is a delicate balancing of discontinuity and continuity. This continuity is, above all, pointed to by the οὐ χωρὶς αἵματος ("not without blood"): it is blood that provides access and purgation in both orders. Thus, as we move into the next paragraph, it is blood that forms the axis of the argument.[133]

9.11–14. One of the very few textual variants of significance immediately presents itself. The question is whether Christ is high priest of the "good things" γενομένων (which have come) or μελλόντων (which are to come, that is, about to come). The manuscripts and interpreters of Hebrews are divided on the issue.[134] Furthermore, both readings are entirely understandable in view of the tension which the author maintains between the "now" and the "not yet" throughout the letter. On the one hand, he stresses the ἐφάπαξ (once-for-all) work of Christ, which has brought in the new order;[135] but on the other, the hope of the Parousia is clearly in evidence.[136] In fact, while the two chapters we are considering revolve around the *now* time, the future aspect even here is never completely out of sight. We cannot involve ourselves in an elaboration of the author's eschatology; it suffices to notice that an intentional change of either word to the other would be quite understandable,

---

133 We may pause at this point to summarize the manner in which our treatment of Heb 9.6–10 has varied from that of the commentators. We take, by way of contrast, Michel's work—as a whole probably the best commentary on Hebrews. Michel's strong *religionsgeschichtliche* interest is of no significant help to him in this passage. Apparently he can see no value in religious ritual, so that the defilement-purgation anthropology not only is not sighted but is obfuscated by a strong contrast of "flesh" versus "conscience": "Opfer und Gaben einerseits, Gebote und Verbote andererseits, die Speisen, Getränke und Waschungen angehen, sind letzlich immer nur auf das Fleisch bezogene und durch das Fleisch begrenzte Handlungen und Satzungen. 'Fleisch' ist aber der Mensch in seiner natürlichen Beschaffenheit, die sich Gott im letzen entziehen kann; Gegensatz zum Fleisch ist das 'Gewissen', dem dem Wort und Gebot Gottes ausgesetz ist" (pp. 308–9). The value of our approach via phenomenology of religion in showing the *holistic* character of defilement-purgation and "conscience" as "numinous uneasiness" as a means to understanding the text will be obvious.

134 Among the interpreters, F. F. Bruce, RSV, NEB, Westcott favor γενομένων; Michel, Montefiore, Moffatt, and Spicq favor μελλόντων.

135 9.28; 10.37–38; 12.26–28.

136 9.28—Christ to "appear the second time"; 10.37–38—"Yet a little while and the coming one shall come and shall not tarry"; 12.26–28—"Yet once more I will shake not only the earth but also the heaven."

depending on whether the scribe was more in sympathy with the present or future viewpoint of soteriology.[137]

The immediate context, however, seems decisive for settling the issue. We noticed how 9.6–10 is concerned to show the imperfection of the old order. The final statement is both a summing up and a preparation for the argument of verses 11–14: the old cultus consisted only of human regulations (equals regulations of the human order) incumbent *until* (μέχρι) the time of the new order. The full transition comes in verse 11, the δέ having an adversative sense: "but (or now) since Christ has become a high priest of the good things." In this setting, the "good things" obviously have come, otherwise the contrast evaporates.

That such a contrast is precisely the point which the author wishes to make is further shown by the way in which verses 11–12 balance verses 6–10. We may set out the evidence as follows:

Old Order (verses 6–10)	**New Order (verses 11–12)**
Earthly high priests	Christ
Earthly sanctuary	Greater tent (σκηνή)
Made with hands equals human order	Not made with hands equals not of human order
Animal blood	Christ's own blood
Repetition	Once for all
Limited access; barriers	Access to the "*real*"
Until the time of the new order	Good things *realized*

What then are the "good things" of verse 9.11? Manifestly, those very things which the old order could never provide—full access to God with a purgation of numinous uneasiness. In a sense, then, verses 1–10 hang together under the rubric of "the good things not yet realized but pointed to" while all the subsequent discussion falls under "the good things that have come." This is the setting in which the leitmotif of "better blood" comes to focus. Christ's blood answers the question of *how* the good things have been brought about.

Before turning to verses 13–14, we should briefly note two matters which, while not of significant weight in the development of the argument, nevertheless call for comment. The first concerns the author's understanding of the greater and more perfect σκηνή (tent) in verse 11. The genesis of the problem of

---

137 It is also possible that the text has assimilated to either the παραγενόμενος of 9.11 or the τῶν μελλόντων of 10.1.

understanding is grammatical: in verses 11–12 we have in a continuous statement three uses of διά with reference to the work of Christ. Since the last two are indubitably instrumental in function, students of the passage have long argued that the first must also have the instrumental sense, that is, "Christ entered the holy places by means of the greater and more perfect σκηνή."[138] This interpretation, however, seems *prima facie* impossible: how can a heavenly tent be the instrument of Christ's access? Thus, a number of exegetes have endeavored to "spiritualize" the meaning of σκηνή, making it signify Christ's body in some way.[139]

I consider all such attempts to be unsuccessful. They display a failure to discern the immediate argument, the context of the argument, and the parallel passages found elsewhere in Hebrews. Let us quickly amplify these points. First, with regard to the immediate argument: according to the "spiritualizing" view, the argument runs—"by means of his body ... not by means of animal blood, but by means of his own blood, he entered." That is, the last διά is essentially repetitive in function: the argument in effect stops at σκηνή. More than this, however, is the description of the σκηνή: it is greater, more perfect, not made with hands, not of this creation. Surely the author is making a point by all this, but what is it? If it is a description of the body of Christ, we must frankly state that it is extremely obscure. The facts are these: there has been no hint for the reader that such a "spiritualizing" interpretation is coming; instead, the thrust of the argument from 8.1 to this point would lead one immediately to link this description with the "true (that is, *real*) tent" of 8.2.[140] Sec-

---

138 Cf. Westcott, *Epistle to the Hebrews*, 256: "It seems best to take the preposition in each case in the same general sense and to join both διὰ τῆς μ. καὶ τ. σκ. and διὰ τοῦ ἰδ. αἵ. with εἰσῆλθε. Christ employed in the fulfilment of His office 'the greater Tabernacle' and 'His own Blood' (compare the corresponding though not parallel use of διά in I John 5.6)." More recently, Montefiore, *Epistle to the Hebrews*, 152: "It would be bad style and unparalleled NT usage to use the same preposition twice in the same sentence with the same case but with different meanings."

139 E.g., James Swetman interprets the σκηνή as Christ's body as Eucharistic sacrifice: "The Greater and More Perfect Tent," 91–106; "On the Imagery and Significance of Hebrews 9, 9–10," 155–73; "Sacrifice and Revelation in the Epistle to the Hebrews," 227–34. Albert Vanhoye, however, argues for the glorified body of the risen Christ: "Par la tente plus grand et plus parfaite ... ," 1–28. Westcott himself is forced to adopt a "spiritualizing" view: he traces the interpretation as "flesh" or "humanity" back to the Fathers, both Greek and Latin (*Epistle to the Hebrews*, 257).

140 In 8.2, Christ is "minister of the real (ἀληθινῆς) tent, which the Lord—not man—pitched"; in 9.10, the tent is "greater and more perfect, not made by human beings—that is not of this creation." Likewise, the stress on the earthly tent's being made according to the pattern (8.5–6) leads in the same direction. Finally, in view of the earlier underlining of the humanity of Jesus (2.5–18; 5.7–8) and the subsequent reference to the body of Christ in terms of his sacrifice (10.5–10), it seems incredible that the author could here (9.11) intend σκηνή to refer to Christ's flesh, body, humanity, or "spiritual" body.

ond, with regard to the context of the argument: we have already noticed that verses 6–10 are clearly meant to prepare for, and to balance, verses 11–12. Now, in verses 6–10 the concern is first with place, then with instrumentality. To suggest that the first διά in verse 11 has no reference to locale destroys this correspondence. Finally, with regard to parallel passages: two other statements of the author seem to have provided the base for the statement that Christ has entered διά the heavenly tent. In 4.14, Christ is a great high priest who has *passed through* the heavens, while in 7.26 he is exalted *above* the heavens. That both of these references have a local significance is beyond dispute.

All these considerations demand that the first διά be local in function. What then of the syntactical problem? In fact, it has recently been demonstrated that a local διά followed by an instrumental διά is admissible;[141] this is surely what we must see here.[142] With this interpretation we are able to illuminate the argument in its immediate development, its context, and its anticipations in the letter.

Granted, then, that the greater σκηνή of 9.11 has local reference, questions as to its precise significance to the author might still be raised. With them, however, we would be forced to embark upon a discussion of the author's cosmology—altogether a full topic in itself.[143]

The second matter calling for comment is the curious phrase αἰωνίαν λύτρωσιν εὑράμενος ("having found eternal redemption") which is used in 9.12. The motif of redemption stands strangely apart from the argument, which has dealt with access to God, numinous uneasiness, priest, and blood. Nor is it picked up in the subsequent discussion:[144] it is *blood* which is the pivot for the argument—blood as purging, not as redeeming.

Michel has pointed to the probable solution of the inconsistency: αἰωνίαν λύτρωσιν εὑράμενος has a liturgical ring.[145] That the *auctor ad Hebraeos* understood humanity's "problem" in terms of defilement and its "solution" as purgation we have already demonstrated, yet, after all, he could not fail to be exposed to other interpretations of Christ's work. Just as there was a brief allusion to the *Christus victor* idea early in the letter,[146] so here, as the au-

---

141 So Otfried Hofius, "Inkarnation und Opfertod Jesu nach Hebr 10, 19f.," *Der Ruf Jesu und die Antwort der Gemeinde*, ed. Eduard Lohse, Christoph Burchard, and Berndt Schaller (Vandenhoeck & Ruprecht, 1970), 132–41; also J. Jeremias, "Hebräer 10.20: τοῦτ' ἔστιν τῆς σαρκὸς αὐτοῦ," *ZNW*, LXII (1971), 131.

142 So Hofius in Lohse, *Ruf Jesu*, 136–37.

143 As noted at the outset of the chapter, cosmological questions have been avoided except where directly significant for the task of elucidating the anthropology.

144 Only in 9.15, where ἀπολύτρωσιν occurs, is there any echo of this motif.

145 Michel, *An die Hebräer*, 312.

146 2.14–15.

thor gave in brief his view of the "good things" realized in Christ, the hymnic phrase came to mind. Even so do we find in modern times that Christian writers quite uncritically blend motifs of redemption (buying back), forgiveness (debt), and purgation (washing) when they express themselves concerning soteriology.[147]

We have already given attention to verses 13–14 in our discussion of blood, defilement, and purgation earlier in this chapter. Here we find in capsule form the author's understanding of blood: it is the medium of purgation. Here the leitmotif of "better blood" is set out in an argument of vivid force by means of the πόσῳ μᾶλλον. Here we see the balancing of the old cultus against the new: both rest on blood, but the new has *better* blood.

The author's statement in these verses provides a splendid example of the advantages of the methodology we have adopted in this study. We see, first of all, the barrenness of *Religionsgeschichte* as an approach to the argument. The argument proceeds from a base of the blood of bulls and goats and the ashes of the red heifer: all that *religionsgeschichtliche* methodology can do is to lead us back to the Old Testament cultus. But for getting "inside" that cultus, as it were, we are left without any help.[148] The statement, however,

---

147 We noticed in the history of the investigation of our topic (Ch. 2) that very often commentators moved, apparently unconsciously, from the vocabulary of the text of Hebrews in terms of purgation to talk of atonement, forgiveness, or redemption. We find the same sort of merging in Christian hymnody; cf. Charlotte Elliott's

> "Just as I am, thou wilt receive,
> Wilt welcome, pardon, cleanse, relieve;
> Because thy promise I believe,
> O Lamb of God, I come, I come."

148 The reference to the δάμαλις ("heifer") in 9.13 points up the weaknesses of traditional exegetical methodology when confronted with the cultus. The author's reference is manifestly to the ceremony of the red cow (Hebrew: פָּרָה), which is found only in Num 19. This chapter, however, has long presented a puzzle to OT scholarship. In fact it was a continuing source of debate among the rabbis: the Mishnah has a whole tract (Parah) dealing with it. The peculiar difficulty of the passage was in the religious ambivalence it manifested—the ritual of the red cow was instituted for the purpose of providing purification but it acted itself as a source of pollution. Blau, "The Red Heifer," 70–80, suggests that it was this character of an unsolved puzzle which prompted the long line of rabbinic speculation. The methodology of literary criticism does not provide the solution to the difficulties of the passage: it reveals a series of inconsistencies, repetitions, roughnesses, and general lack of clarity which point to two or three discrete literary units, all of which are priestly material (Cf. G. C. Gray, ICC, *Commentary on Numbers* [Charles Scribner's Sons, 1903], 242–43.). Nor does form criticism take us further: whether we have two, three, or more pieces of disparate material brought together by a priestly editor, the *Sitz im Leben* of each is clearly the cult. *Religionsgeschichtliche* methodology likewise leads to an impasse. Apparently no Canaanite parallel to the ceremony of the red cow has so far come to light. Commentators have searched far afield, even mentioning the sacrifice of red puppies and red-haired men in Roman religion, or suggesting that the use of the cow in this rite points to Iranian (i.e., Zoroastrian) roots. All this, however, is quite imprecise. Tradition history

immediately glows with significance when we turn the searchlights of phenomenology of religion on it. Now we begin to see the text in its religious context as a witness to humanity's existential strivings. Specifically, the passage is setting forth the play and counter-play of religious forces (powers). We see a network of six interlocking powers, four of which are active forces (powers of transition or agency). We may briefly recapitulate our earlier findings by means of the following schema:

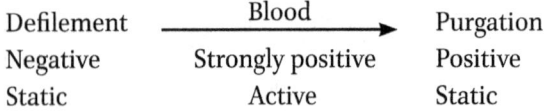

Defilement	Blood	Purgation
Negative	Strongly positive	Positive
Static	Active	Static

Within this general schema there is a hierarchy of forces, in descending order as follows:

Level one: Christ's blood equals supreme power, direct and positive.
Level two: Defilement (negative) or purgation (positive) of the συνείδησις.
Level three: Animal blood equals weakly positive, direct power.
Level four: Defilement (negative) or purgation (positive) τῆς σαρκὸς

It is natural for us to raise the question as to *how* the blood of Christ is able to accomplish what animal blood never could. Is it because it is human blood?[149] spotless blood?[150] because offered διὰ πνεύματος αἰωνίου (through eternal spirit)?[151] because it is the blood of the Son?[152] The *auctor ad Hebraeos*

---

seems to open up the text to some extent: it suggests that Num 19 attempts an amalgamation of two discrete types of instruction relative to defilement through contact with a corpse—one procedure being a self-purgation, the other calling for the use of the "water for impurity." Some writers have attempted to press the ideas of Num 19 to indigenous Palestinian religion; thus, de Vaux, *Ancient Israel: Its Life and Institutions*, trans. J. McHugh (McGraw Hill, 1961), 461; or H. P. Smith, "Notes on the Red Heifer," *JBL*, XXVII (1908), 153–56, who sees its basis in an ancient sacrifice of the dead. In short, it is obvious that the ideas which come to light in Num 19 are extremely baffling to the modern mind, and that the exegetes have been at their wits' end to grapple with them. It is surely significant that they have felt compelled to go beyond the strict boundaries of the methodology of *Religionsgeschichte* in an attempt to deal with this "primitive," "magical" material. Their tentative steps toward phenomenology of religion provide a suggestive background for the full espousal of this sister discipline by the exegete which we have put forward in this study.

149   In 12.24, however, Christ's blood is contrasted with the blood of Abel.
150   9.14: ἄμωμον.
151   Ibid.
152   10.29.

nowhere clearly states his reasoning: the πόσῳ μᾶλλον shows that to him the point is obvious.

The evidence of Hebrews seems to divide into two clear parts. On the one hand, there is the accent on the humanness of Christ. The reference to ἄμωμον here is in agreement with a continual strain of the writing;[153] the argument of 10.1–10 contrasts animal sacrifices with the body of Christ, that is, with his humanness; and there is a pronounced accent on Christ's obedience in the letter.[154] All these indicators lead in the direction that Christ's blood is efficacious because it is human blood—though of a special quality, since Christ is spotless, having been obedient. On the other hand, there is the accent on the more-than-humanness of Jesus. Here, unlike some writers who have argued that the *auctor ad Hebraeos* is emphasizing the "blood of the Messiah" in 9.14 (a very dubious point, in our view), we do not assign particular weight to the use of χριστός.[155] Nor do we consider that διὰ πνεύματος αἰωνίου specifies the blood of Christ per se; rather, it points to the heavenly sphere of its offering, in contrast to the earthly sphere (τῆς σαρκός) of the animal blood.[156] But the strong emphasis on the indissoluble life of Jesus which we have already noticed[157] and the close connections between despising the Son of God and disregarding the blood of his covenant[158] indicate that, although Christ is fully human, he is more than human. Yet it must be noted that the connection between "divinity" and blood is no more than implicit: nowhere is the blood of the *Son* referred to, while the argument concerning his indestructible life is in terms of the priesthood, not offering.[159]

Perhaps in the clash of possibilities which we find here (human blood versus "eternal" blood), we see in stark outline the unresolved tension of the human and the "divine" which characterizes Hebrews. Jesus is the Son, yet he is portrayed as human in strongly realistic colors. In this light, the question of the special power of the blood of Christ is insoluble: the argument is evenly balanced. We would think it most likely that the author, holding both sides in

---

153 He was tempted, but without sin: cf. 2.18; 4.15; 7.26.

154 2.9–10; 5.8.

155 A study of the author's references to Ἰησοῦς (2.9; 3.1; 4.14; 5.20; 7.22; 10.19 ; 12.2, 24; 13.12) and Χριστός (3.6, 14; 5.5; 6.1; 9.11, 14, 24, 28; 10.10; 11.26; 13.8, 21) seems to preclude any distinction in meaning. In terms of the particular context here, it is to be noted that both Χριστός and Ἰησοῦς are used with reference to his high priesthood; thus, the argument from "the blood of the Messiah" at 9.14 seems to us to be extremely tenuous. Spicq, however, speaks of the "dignity of the Messiah" at this point (*L'Épître aux Hébreux*, II, 258.)

156 See note 132 above.

157 7.3, 8, 16.

158 10.26–31.

159 Contrast Spicq, *L'Épître aux Hébreux*, II, 258, on the reason for the superiority of Christ's blood: "dans un cas, des bêtes; dans l'autre, le Fils de Dieu!"

tension, had not thought through to the answer we seek. In any case he certainly does not reason like Anselm.

As we conclude our discussion of this important paragraph, we may make passing mention of the phrase νεκρῶν ἔργων ("dead works"). In view of the earlier discussion in this chapter, it is manifest that to introduce ideas of legalism from this phrase is totally misguided. The phrase is to be understood in the light of the phenomenology of defilement, where it is seen to be peculiarly effective as evocative of the troubled consciousness—the "numinous uneasiness" felt by humanity as defiled.

Reviewing 9.11–14, then, we discern the import of two phrases: τῶν γενομένων ἀγαθῶν and πόσῳ μᾶλλον—"the good things that have come," and "how much more!" Whereas the first points to benefits realized, the second points to the means of that realizing—that is, to the blood of Christ.[160] The remainder of the discussion of Hebrews 9–10 will be concerned to elaborate both the "what" and the "how" in an intricately woven argument.

9.15–21. Probably no other portion of the two chapters we are considering presents such difficulty to the exegete as does this paragraph. The immediate issue is the author's usage of διαθήκη ("covenant"? "testament"? or both?), but the problem extends far beyond this: at stake is the tracing of the argumentative thread. Since we are intensely concerned with the latter, we cannot downplay the problems of the text; if we are finally unable to resolve all difficulties of detail, we hope at least to have shown how the passage is integrated into the ongoing argument.

It is well, therefore, first to discern the general thrust of the passage. Unambiguous affirmations by the *auctor ad Hebraeos* at its beginning, center, and end show what that thrust is. The passage begins with the διὰ τοῦτο ("be-

---

160 We may again notice the differences between our treatment of 9.11–14 and previous studies. *Religionsgeschichtliche* studies are not fruitful; e.g., the author is clearly at odds with Philo, who held that "the rites of the Law cleansed a man both in body and soul" (*De spec. leg.* I, 257f.), while attempts to trace historical links for the red heifer, for instance, are unproductive, as we have seen. The "structures" of defilement, blood, and purgation which we have brought to bear upon the passage have been most helpful, however. While some writers had caught the ideas of relative defilement and cleansing agents of relative efficacy (e.g., Windisch, *Der Hebräerbrief*, 79–80), and even of the basic "structure" being expressed as power (e.g., Westcott, *Epistle to the Hebrews*, 259), these features of the passage were only dimly perceived. We hope to have been able to bring them to much greater clarity. At the same time, we have been able to avoid three errors commonly made by earlier scholars: (1) a placing of the emphasis on λύτρωσις; e.g., D. B. Weiss, *Epistle to the Hebrews*, 187 (concerning 9.12): "the blood which He offered was accepted as a ransom, on account of which He declared men free of guilt and punishment"; (2) drawing a false contrast between "flesh" and "conscience," or between "flesh" and "spirit"; e.g., Ketter, *Hebräerbrief*, 68 (on 9.14) sees Christ's blood as giving the "soul" new life; or (3) a dismissal or denigration of the cultic terminology as being "primitive" or "magical," e.g., Robinson, *Epistle to the Hebrews*, 126; A. B. Bruce, *Epistle to the Hebrews*, 322–43.

cause of this"), showing that we have before us a result of the power of the blood of Christ under consideration. That result is stated at the outset: he is mediator of the new covenant. Hebrews 9.18 embodies one of the "not without blood" statements: the first covenant was not inaugurated without blood. The passage closes with reference to the sprinkling of "the blood of the covenant which God commanded you." It seems beyond contention that the author is dealing with the interrelation of covenant and blood, showing that, just as the first covenant came about by blood, so the new.

We should further notice that the passage does not signal a major shift in the line of thought, so that the motif of διαθήκη is to dominate the subsequent discussion. Not at all: as in Heb 9.11–14 the leitmotif of "better blood" is introduced, so after 9.21 it is αἷμα which links the discussion; διαθήκη is dropped.[161] That is, while in 9.15–21 the idea of διαθήκη is indeed to the fore, it is only properly understandable in view of the general theme of blood-better blood.

Let us now look at the argument in some detail. Indubitably, it is Heb 9.15–18 which poses the major problem to following the argument concerning διαθήκη and αἷμα. It presents three principal difficulties, two of which have been felt by previous exegetes and one which is peculiar to the particular interpretation we have been suggesting in this study. The two traditional difficulties are the usage of διαθήκη and the logical unity of Heb 9.15–18. The peculiar problem concerns the introduction of the death motif: we have throughout suggested that the accent in Hebrews 9–10 is strongly on life.

The problems of the meaning of διαθήκη and logical unity are clearly intertwined. If, as with many commentators, we decide that διαθήκη signifies "covenant" in verse 15, "testament" in verses 15–17, and again "covenant" in verse 18,[162] the logical unity of the passage seems seriously endangered. We must then resort to the defense that the author uses διαθήκη for a play on words. This, of course, is entirely possible; but the interpretation so obtained is not convincing. Apart from certain syntactical objections which we shall mention below, the argument appears to be extremely devious: death suggests covenant, covenant suggests inheritance, inheritance suggests will, will suggests death; while the way in which the argument reverts to διαθήκη as "covenant" cannot be made

---

161 Only at 10.16ff does the writer return to the idea of διαθήκη, but with no direct connection with 9.15–18 since there his focus is not on covenant per se but on the benefits realized under the new covenant.

162 The RSV switches from "covenant" to "will" in vv. 16–17, adding by means of a footnote: "The Greek word here used means both covenant and will." The NEB seeks to reduce the difficulty by translating vs. 15 as: "And therefore he is the mediator of a new covenant, or testament...." Moffatt's version resorts to the expediency of translating vs. 18 as "Hence even the first covenant of God's will was not inaugurated ...." We regard these interpretations by the translators of the NEB and Moffatt as taking undue liberties with the text.

understandable.¹⁶³ On the other hand, if διαθήκη is understood throughout as "covenant," the problem of logical unity does not arise.¹⁶⁴ But an extremely difficult conceptual problem is introduced, namely, as to how the διαθέμενος ("covenanter") can be said to "die" before the covenant has legal standing.

It seems to us that the evidence of the passage itself as well as its context demands that διαθήκη be understood throughout as "covenant."¹⁶⁵ In the first place, it would be altogether unexpected if διαθήκη were to signify "testament" in verses 16–17. The eighth chapter of Hebrews has prepared the ground for the discussion of 9.15–21 by its emphasis on the "better covenant" in Christ. This theme is picked up at 9.15, where διαθήκη unquestionably refers to "covenant." Likewise, in 9.18, and again in 10.16: no other interpretation can be considered. Therefore, that διαθήκη at 9.16–17 refers to "testament" is extremely unlikely *prima facie*: we are not to blur the difference in significance between "covenant" and "testament"¹⁶⁶ Second, the association of διαθήκη with θάνατος (death) in verse 15 and again at verses 16–17 strongly suggests that διαθήκη is used univalently throughout: as we mentioned above, the argument becomes extremely devious if we posit dual meanings for διαθήκη. Syntactical grounds, however, provide for us the clincher. Any interpretation cannot fail to give full weight to the ὅπου γὰρ ... ὅθεν construction, which requires that verse 18 be seen as the logical conclusion of verse 16; since διαθήκη in verse 18 is clearly means "covenant," it must have the same meaning in verse 16. Indeed, it is precisely at this point of transition from verses 16–17 to verse 18 that all interpretations positing a dual significance for διαθήκη appear to us to come to grief: they are unable to account for the internal logic of the argument. Finally, if we take διαθήκη as "testament" in verses 16–17, we are utterly at a loss to explain the plural νεκροῖς of verse 17: the singular of διαθήκη and of διαθέμενος in both verses would demand νεκρῷ.¹⁶⁷

---

163 See the following paragraph.

164 Another possibility, of course, is to translate throughout as "will"; so E. Riggenbach, "Der Begriff der ΔΙΑΘΗΚΗ im Hebräerbrief," in *Theologische Studien Theodor Zahn zum 10. Oktober 1908 dargebracht* (Leipzig, 1908), 289ff., cited by F. F. Bruce, *Epistle to the Hebrews*, 211, n. 119. Adolf Deissmann, *Paul: A Study in Social and Religious History*, trans. William E. Wilson (2nd ed.; George H. Doran Co., 1926), uses "testament" for διαθήκη in Paul's writings (pp. 175, 216). He does not, however, refer to the book of Hebrews. It seems to us impossible to sustain διαθήκη means testament with reference to Hebrews.

165 This is a minority position among the exegetes; nevertheless it has had some supporters, notably Westcott and Nairne.

166 This seems to have been the inevitable tendency when scholars have tried to make a case for a play on the word διαθήκη. The NEB and Moffatt versions display such an error; nor is F. F. Bruce's attempt to comprehend both "covenant" and "testament" under the general idea of "settlement" (*Epistle to the Hebrews*, 210–13) convincing. Bruce argues for a unique idea of διαθήκη in which the mediator is also the testator—an unsatisfactory "solution."

167 Westcott, *Epistle to the Hebrews*, 298–302, argues for διαθήκη meaning "covenant" on the basis of the meaning of διαθήκη in the LXX and elsewhere in the NT, the connection of ὅπου

Understanding διαθήκη as "covenant" throughout, then, we may proceed to trace the development of the argumentation. The reference to the purgation of συνείδησις in 9.14 provides the point of entrée for the idea of διαθήκη since it is this very benefit which the eighth chapter has already set out as being the epitome of the new covenant. That is, the author is saying in effect: "See how powerful the blood of Christ is! See what benefits it brings to us! It therefore fulfills the Jeremianic prediction of the new covenant." Thus, the introduction of the διαθήκη motif is altogether understandable. But while the motif is introduced in terms of its force in chapter 8—that is, with emphasis on the benefits realized by the believer—there is a new development of meaning in 9.15–18. First, the "subjective" benefits are extended to the people of old—those who could not be "perfected" (incorporated) "apart from us."[168] But more importantly, the emphasis shifts from the benefits conferred by the blood of Christ to Christ who gives his blood. At first sight, the ὅπως θανάτου γενομένου ("since a death occurred") of 9.15b is redundant: the διὰ τοῦτο at the beginning of the statement has already provided grounds in the πόσῳ μᾶλλον of the blood of Christ. But only at first sight: the *auctor ad Hebraeos* is now concerned to argue the fact of Christ's death as the means of providing the blood of the new covenant. In verses 16–17, he argues from the general idea of covenant: covenant requires death of the covenanter and therefore is only ratified upon the death of the animals[169] offered in covenant sacrifice. Even so, the first covenant had to be inaugurated with the blood of animals.

The author's general statements concerning διαθήκη in verses 16–17 are significant. The singular διαθέμενος clearly implies a view of covenant as unilateral rather than as contractual. Thus, he is able to provide the basis for arguing concerning the first covenant, which was commanded by God,[170] or with regard to the new, wherein Christ is offered according to the divine will.[171] His reasoning concerning διαθήκη in relation to blood and death is likewise suggestive: covenant is inaugurated by blood, but blood is obtained only by means of death. It is alien to his argument to acknowledge, for instance, that blood could be obtained without death.[172]

γάρ ... with ὅθεν οὐδέ ... and the strangeness of ἐπὶ νεκροῖς and φέρεσθαι for the death of a testator. Nairne, *Epistle of Priesthood*, 30, finds it strange that the mediater of a will should be the testator.

168   Cf. 11.40: "Apart from us they should not be made perfect."

169   That is, in vs. 17 ἐπὶ νεκροῖς means "over the dead bodies" (of the covenant animals), not "over dead people."

170   Cf. 9.20: "the covenant which God commanded you."

171   There is no suggestion in Hebrews that διαθήκη is contractual; rather, it is God who provides covenant (old or new) for man.

172   An obvious (to us) possibility, but his argument at this point arises out of a theological concern with why Christ died; on which, see the following two paragraphs.

The presentation of the argument thus confronts the modern reader with ideas which are especially difficult to accept: the covenanter's death is necessary, and this death may be signified by sacrificial animals. It is to avoid their apparent force that the attempt is made to move to διαθήκη meaning testament in verses 16–17—an unfortunate expediency, as we have shown. Are we able in view of the approach of this study to ease at all the difficulties involved?

We have two suggestions which, while they do not fully dispose of the problems, may nevertheless reduce their force.[173] First, it seems to us that the "structures" from phenomenology of religion already noticed may be helpful. We do not hold that, if the data of religion can somewhere be made to turn up an exotic example which accords with the author's reasoning, the difficulties will be resolved. No; instead of looking for a precise parallel, we would turn to the general picture of humanity vis-à-vis blood that we have come to recognize. That picture is fundamentally one of an interdependent cosmos in which blood provides the medium of religious transition. In such a worldview, the one who offers sacrifice offers himself; the blood which is released is mediately his own blood. To talk of "substitution" in this setting is to distort the interrelatedness of humanity and cult which is operative.[174] Second, it is intriguing to reflect upon the way in which the argument of 9.15–17 plays upon the theme of θάνατος (death). It is clear that this motif is subsidiary to the leitmotif of blood which rules the preceding and subsequent discussion: we note, for instance, how in verse 18 it is "not without blood" instead of "not without death" which is the conclusion of verses 15–17. That is, verses 15b–17 could be seen to be a diversion from the developing argument. Why then this concern with θάνατος? It seems likely to us that we here catch a glimpse of theological debate within the early church: the problem of not only *whether* Christ died but *why* he should have died. While the latter question is not the determining concern of the letter, it is clearly a matter of some interest to the author. Thus, as he earlier argued—again, in a quite offhand way— that Christ's death was for the purpose of destroying the devil,[175] so now he roots that death in the ἀνάγκη (necessity) of covenant provisions. In fine, we would suggest that the author's concern to give a reason for the fact of the

---

173 So far as we are aware, the two suggestions presented here have not been put forward before. Westcott spoke of "representative death" in commenting on 9.16 (*Epistle to the Hebrews*, 265) and approached the point of view of the first suggestion. But neither he nor Nairne advanced the second suggestion—that a theological concern with the reason for Christ's death may have shaped the argument in 9.15–18.

174 Van der Leeuw has brought out this point very clearly; *Religion in Essence and Manifestation*, 350–59.

175 2.14.

death of Christ has shaped the form of the argument of verses 15b-17, even to the extent of his formulating a general principle of covenant which in fact can only be derived from reference to considerations of Christ and the new covenant.[176]

With these considerations we have indicated the answer to the problem of how 9.15-18, with its concern with death, is to be accommodated to the general context of Hebrews 9-10 with its emphasis on blood and life. It is clear that it would be altogether out of place to try to argue for a bland equation of blood equals death on the basis of 9.15-18. If that were so, blood would have a negative (defiling) character, whereas the author consistently views it as a medium of purgation. Nor would it be correct to say that in 9.15-18 the author's principle stress is that blood *implies* a death (that is, no obtaining of blood without a death), although that idea is implicit in the argument. Rather, the brief discussion concerning death is to be understood as an excursus in accord with the author's interest in the question as to why Christ died and the collective import of blood for the community.

This concern of 9.15b-18 serves, as we already noticed, to shift the focus away from the believer and the benefits received from Christ. This shift to an "objective" focus, as we termed it earlier, predominates throughout the remainder of the ninth chapter. Thus, in verses 19-21 we see the power of blood to purge manifested in a far-reaching way, as the book, the congregation, the tent, and all its vessels of ministration are sprinkled.[177]

9.22. This verse is crucial in the argument of Hebrews 9-10. It functions as a general statement: it is an exposé of the previous argument and a bridge to verse 23 and the following discussion concerning the heavenly sanctuary. Here we meet the third and climactic "not without blood" proposition—as there was no access to God without blood, no inauguration of covenant without blood, so there can be no ἄφεσις without blood.

---

176 Apart from these two reasons for Christ's death—the destruction of the devil and the necessity of covenant—it seems likely that the author has in mind a third: the providing of an offering for the heavenly cultus. At 8.3 we find another of the "necessity" statements: "it is necessary for Christ to have something to offer." Nowhere, however, does he explicitly connect the death with the making available of such an offering, although 9.15 would surely have provided a fitting opportunity. Instead, the idea of διαθήκη, introduced in the long quotation in Hebrews 8, provides the point of departure for his remarks as to why Christ died.

177 We have already noted that the author, in specifying that the "book" was sprinkled with blood (v. 19) has taken liberties with the text. In 9.21, he goes further: the sprinkling of the tent is a reference either to its dedication, which was later, or more likely to the annual cleansing of the Day of Atonement. But no actual sprinkling of the tent with blood (instead, oil) is recorded at its dedication (Exod. 40.9), while the actual vessels of the sanctuary are not listed as having been purged in the Day of Atonement ceremonies (Lev 16.14-19).

The issues in interpretation are clearly threefold: the force of κατὰ τὸν νόμον, the translation of αἱματεκχυσία and the meaning of ἄφεσις. We shall take up each in turn.

What is the force of κατὰ τὸν νόμον? If we say that it is meant to embrace all verse 22, that is, that verse 22 is summarizing the previous verses and merely laying down the axiom of the old cultus, we destroy the link with verse 23— for it is manifest that the old law has nothing to do with the new cultus.[178] The κατὰ τὸν νόμον then must be only of limited application, that is, to the first part of the verse: "Almost everything is purged in blood according to the law." Thus, the placing of κατὰ τὸν νόμον is decisive: it *limits* the point.

The second καί is therefore adversative: according to the law, almost everything is purged in blood, *but* there can be no ἄφεσις without blood; that is: whereas according to the law some things were purged without blood, for ἄφεσις blood is essential.[179] Thus, verse 22b is a general principle, one that embraces both old and new cultuses.

We come now to the peculiar term αἱματεκχυσία. Here is a word that is unknown before this occurrence, which is found nowhere else in the New Testament, but which serves exclusively Christian purposes in later writings.[180] Obviously, the word could well be a technical term whose import was confined to the narrow circle of the *auctor ad Hebraeos* and his readers. On the other hand, it is possible that he himself has coined the term for the purposes of his argument in this letter. While the question of origin cannot finally be decided, the data (its absence from the New Testament writings, but later Christian usage) strongly suggest that we have here a composition of the author.[181]

---

178 Cf. 7.22: "When there is a change in the priesthood, there is necessarily a change in the law as well"; 7.18;—the former commandment is set aside because of its weakness and uselessness."

179 This construction (καί ... καί) is, of course, well recognized as a means of introducing contrasts. Cf. Arndt and Gingrich, *Greek-English Lexicon,* 394, and F. Blass and A. Debrunner, *A Greek Grammar of the New Testament and Other Early Christian Literature,* trans. and rev. by Robert W. Funk (University of Chicago Press, 1961), 230.

180 Cf. Arndt and Gingrich, *Greek-English Lexicon,* 22. James Hope Moulton and George Milligan, *The Vocabulary of the Greek Testament Illustrated from the Papyri and Other Non-Literary Sources* (Hodder and Stoughton, 1930), make no reference to αἱματεκχυσία. The word apparently is found only by the latter half of the second century CE. G. W. H. Lampe, ed., *A Patristic Greek Lexicon* (Clarendon Press, 1961), 50, gives as its meaning "shedding of blood," of gladiatorial contests (*Tat. Orat.* 23; *Epiph. Haer.* 399), or metaphorically (*Ant. Mon. hom.* 39).

181 If αἱματεκχυσία had already become a technical term familiar to at least some Christians at the time of its use by the author, it seems likely that it would have been employed in the latest NT writings or in the extracanonical works before Tatian. Furthermore, the use in Hebrews is heavily cultic, but not so with Tatian. No watertight conclusion may be drawn from the data, but the evidence clearly favors the idea that αἱματεκχυσία was a word coined by the

If this is so, we may expect that his meaning will be made abundantly clear from the course of his argumentation.

Before turning to review the context, we should note that the word is a compound of αἷμα with ἐκχύννειν. The latter has a general sense of "to pour out."[182] When associated with αἷμα, it may be used to signify the flow of blood or derivatively to indicate bloodshed, that is, the taking of life.[183] It is in the second sense that almost all translators have taken αἱματεκχυσία in Hebrews 9.22, that is, "without bloodshed, no ἄφεσις."[184] The accent then clearly falls on the *death* of the sacrificial victim.

Such a meaning seems to us to be quite out of keeping with the context in which the author introduces αἱματεκχυσία. Throughout, he has stressed the idea of blood as a religious force of surpassing potency: blood provides access, blood perfects the συνείδησις, blood inaugurates, blood cleanses ritual objects as well as the people, blood purges almost everything under the old law. He does not say: the high priest, after taking the life of the sacrificial animal, was able to enter the Most Holy; nor: Christ by his death perfected the συνείδησις; nor: the death of the covenant animals inaugurated the first covenant; nor: purgation under the old law required the killing of animals. That is the way we are prone to put the argument! If we are willing to let him present the argument in his own way, then by αἱματεκχυσία he must signify the *application* of blood.[185] The contrast between the two parts of verse 22 is not ἐν αἵματι opposed to αἱματεκχυσία, but rather σχέδον (almost) against οὐ (no, none).

The author has shown a predilection for the term ῥαντίζειν (to sprinkle) in speaking of the application of blood.[186] But this verb does not fit all the functions of blood: the earthly high priest, for instance, "offered" or "brought forward" (προσφέρειν) blood as he entered the Most Holy.[187] Thus, in making the general statement of 9.22b, a comprehensive term for the application of blood was called for. In this light it is highly likely that αἱματεκχυσία was his

---

author of Hebrews which eventually passed into Christian usage, but with modified meaning. We recognize, of course, that inferences *e silentio* are always fraught with hazard.

182 Arndt and Gingrich, *Greek-English Lexicon*, 246.

183 I Kings 18.28 (LXX): ἕως ἐκχύσεως αἵματος ἐπ᾽ αὐτούς "until the blood flowed out upon them"; Acts 22.20: καὶ ὅτε ἐξεχύννετο τὸ αἷμα Στεφάνου τοῦ μάρτυρός σου "and when the blood of Stephen your martyr was shed" (cf. Rom 3.15; Rev 16.6; Matt 23.35).

184 So RSV and NEB. Johannes Behm, *TDNT*, I, 176, gives the meaning thus: "the shedding of blood in slaying, and esp. in the offering of sacrifices under the OT cultus.

185 It seems to us that Behm has failed to follow the argument of the passage when he can write: "The main point is that the giving of life is the necessary presupposition of the remission of sins (ἄφεσις)." Ibid., 177. His treatment of αἱματεκχυσία is brief and unsatisfactory.

186 9.13, 19, 21; also 10.22, 12.24.

187 9.7; also 9.14, 25, 28; 10.1, 2, 8, 11–12.

own coinage. It signifies ἐν αἵματι: blood applied, blood as the medium of transition.[188]

Our findings concerning the meaning of αἱματεκχυσία in Hebrews 9.22 have been based primarily on the drift of the author's argument in the passage. They are supported, however, by Thornton,[189] who has carefully considered the rabbinical writings of the period. He notices this saying—"Once the blood has reached the altar, the owners are forgiven"[190] as indicative of the *application* of blood as the highest point of Jewish sacrificial ritual and concludes:

> If, on the other hand, αἱματεκχυσία is regarded as referring primarily to the killing of sacrificial victims, then Heb. 9.22 is given an emphasis which, as far as the available evidence goes, is unparalleled in Jewish sacrificial thought around this period, and which gives the component roots αἷμα and ἐκχέειν unusual overtones for a Jewish sacrificial context.[191]

The final issue in the text concerns the meaning of ἄφεσις. The translation and interpretation as "forgiveness of sins," perpetuated by the RSV and NEB, is unfounded and insupportable: not only is the usual τῶν ἁμαριῶν[192] absent, but the context of the verse in the passage, as well as the total view of the work of Christ in Hebrews, has no view of sin as debt or broken relationship. What then is to be understood by ἄφεσις here? We must look for explanation especially to the argument of the passage, and, in view of its references to the old cultus, to the LXX rendering of Leviticus.[193]

---

188   We should notice also that in the LXX αἷμα and ἐκχύννειν are used in conjunction eight times to indicate the *pouring out* of blood upon the altar: Exod 29.12; Lev 4.7, 18, 25, 30, 34; 8.15; 9.9.

189   T. C. G. Thornton, "The Meaning of αἱματεκχυσία in Heb 10.22," *JTS*, XV (1964), 63–65. We had reached the conclusion that αἱματεκχυσία = *application* of blood in Heb 9.22 before noticing Thornton's article.

190   *Zebaḥim* 26b.

191   Thornton, "Meaning of αἱματεκχυσία," 65.

192   Ἄφεσις is used with ἁμαρτιῶν in Matt 26.28; Mark 1.4; Luke 1.77; 3.3; 24.47; Acts 2.28; 5.31; 10.43; 13.38; 26.18; Col 1.14; and with παραπτωμάτων at Eph 1.7. Ἄφεσις is used without any qualifying genitive in Luke 4.18 to indicate "release" (of prisoners), and also in Mark 3.29. In the latter, however, the context supplies ἁμαρτημάτων so the example is not in fact parallel to Hebrews, where no reference to ἁμαρτία or equivalent is to be found in the immediate context.

193   The interpretation of Heb 9.22 affords an interesting case study of the way in which commentators have tended to read other writings into the text. One frequently finds reference to Matt 26.28—τοῦτο γάρ ἐστιν τὸ αἷμά μου τῆς διαθήκης τὸ περὶ πολλῶν ἐκχυννόμενον εἰς ἄφεσιν ἁμαρτιῶν. But this is manifestly false procedure: the Matthean form of the "cup-word" is patently late; we have no assurance that Hebrews was written after Matthew; and, above all, it is only by gross distortion of the argument that any allusion to the Last Supper is to be discerned in Heb 9–10. Among commentators making reference to Matt 26.28 might be mentioned Spicq, Schierse, Héring, and Nairne; Delitzsch links Heb 9.22 with the Lukan parallel (Luke 22.20).

We noticed that there seems to be an ascending scale of argument through verses 7, 18, and 22, so that ἄφεσις is the summit of the previous benefits available by means of blood (access, inauguration, purgation). This accords well with what we have discerned the function of verse 22b to be in the total argument and with the comprehensive nature of αἱματεκχυσία. Therefore, it seems likely that ἄφεσις here indicates, on the one hand, inauguration and access, and, on the other, a purgation with *finality*. Whereas τελειοῦν ("perfection," incorporation) has the "subjective" benefits of Christ's blood in view (access to God with the συνείδησις purged once for all), ἄφεσις is a broader term, encompassing also the "objective" benefits of that blood. Thus, the following verse proceeds with οὖν—"therefore"—to talk about the purgation of the heavenly things.

Almost half of the occurrences of ἄφεσις in the LXX occur in Leviticus.[194] One of these has to do with the goat released "to Azazel": it is τὸν διεσταλμένον εἰς ἄφεσιν ("commanded for letting go, release").[195] The others refer to the "year of jubilee": it is the ἔτος τῆς ἀφέσεως the "year of release."[196] Thus, the usage of ἄφεσις in Leviticus conforms to the root idea of "letting go," "sending away," "release."[197] In fact, ἄφεσις is not used in a cultic setting in the LXX apart from Leviticus 16.26. Two curious occurrences outside Leviticus connect ἄφεσις with streams (rivers) or water,[198] a translation that derives, as Deissmann[199] has shown, from the Egyptian practice of release of water from the canals.

It is difficult to find a single English word to convey the comprehensive sense which ἄφεσις clearly has in Hebrews 9.22. Obviously, "release" is inadequate, conveying as it does the idea of an emancipation from bondage. On the other hand, the juxtaposing of καθαρίζειν with ἄφεσις in verse 22 and the immediate return to καθαρίζειν in verse 23 show how closely connected are the meanings of these two words.[200] It seems then that we may best bring out the particular sense of the author in verse 22 if we translate ἄφεσις as "definitive putting away" or "decisive purgation." This at once shows the comparison and contrast in terms of καθαρίζειν. Further, this is manifestly the sense in which ἄφεσις is used in its only other occurrence in Hebrews.[201]

---

194 Twenty-one out of a total of forty-nine times.

195 Lev 16.26. Bultmann, however, understands the sense here to be "forgiveness"—a position which seems to me to be unwarranted in view of the context. See *TDNT*, I, 510.

196 Throughout Lev 25; 27.

197 Cf. Arndt and Gingrich, *Greek-English Lexicon*, 125 (ἀφίημι).

198 Joel 1.20, Lam. 3.47 (LXX. ἀφέσεις ὑδάτων).

199 G. Adolf Deissmann, *Bible Studies*, trans. Alexander Grieve (T&T Clark, 1923), 98–101.

200 Thus, Moffatt, *Epistle to the Hebrews*, 130, translates 9.22b—"i.e. even the limited pardon, in the shape of 'cleansing,' which was possible under the old order." His terminology is curious: "pardon" expressed as "cleansing"! But he is obviously aware of the way in which ideas of purgation cannot be excluded from ἄφεσις here.

201 10.18; see *infra* on this verse, p. 159.

We may now paraphrase verse 22 to bring out more distinctly the argument: "Whereas, according to the law, almost everything was purged in blood [but not everything; there were exceptions],²⁰² for definitive putting away of defilement there must be blood applied."²⁰³

9.23–28. In this paragraph, the "objective" benefits of Christ's blood are concluded. These benefits have so far been shown to include inauguration of covenant; now they will be specified in terms of the heavenly sanctuary and cultus, and the divine plan for the ages. In this exposition we may with justification see the passage as the elaboration of verses 11–12, just as the "subjective" benefits of chapter 10 can rightly be viewed as the exposition of verses 13–14.

Yet verses 23–28 are more than a flat elaboration of verses 11–12. The ongoing argument has reached the climactic "blood rule" in verse 22b, and the αἱματεκχυσία—the application of blood—is to the fore, even as it is throughout the following chapter. Thus, in verse 23 we immediately encounter the οὖν (therefore), which demonstrates that the "blood rule" embraces the cleansing of all—both old and new—cultic places; and the ἀνάγκη (it is necessary), pointing to the axiomatic character of verse 22b. Now the significance of θυσία (sacrifice) is made plain: it is in terms of blood-purgation-inauguration, not in terms of an offering to a demanding God.

But the use of καθαρίζειν here engenders grave difficulties in comprehension. The argument of 9.15ff might have pointed to the use of ἐγκαινίζειν (to inaugurate)—an idea that would have been more amenable to many commentators.²⁰⁴ The use of καθαρίζειν, however, shows that the accent throughout has been on the removal of impurity, that is, on the purging rather than the inaugurating side. In the argument, blood provides access by removal of defilement.

---

202 E.g., Lev 5.11–13, the offering of flour by a poor person; Num 31.22–23, purification by fire.

203 We may observe how our treatment of 9.22 complements precious investigation. *Religionsgeschichtliche* studies (e.g., in the commentaries of Windisch, Moffatt, and Spicq) had long established the similarity of the axiom of this verse to rabbinical statements, e.g., *Yoma* 5a: "Does not atonement come through blood?"; *Zebaḥim* 6a: "Surely atonement can be made only with the blood." The difficulty is that, having made such a connection, the meaning of the axiom is still obscure. That is, we are really just as far from understanding the logic of 9.22 as when we first encounter Lev 17.11 ("It is the blood that makes atonement, by reason of the life")—a verse that is regularly quoted as confirmation of the rabbinical aphorisms! We have endeavored to "get inside" the cultic axiom itself, to expose its internal logic. Our interpretation of 9.22 in terms of blood *applied* and putting away of defilement (instead of *bloodshed* and *forgiveness* of sins) graphically illustrates the exegetical results which have accrued from our method.

204 So, e.g., Bonsirven, *Épître aux Hébreux*, 410–11.

This very point chokes many scholars, for the author's reasoning indubitably indicates an impurity of the heavenly sanctuary. Here Spicq[205] cannot bring himself to face the possibility ("non-sens") and others are at their wits' end to avoid the force of the language.[206] Our findings from phenomenology of religion appear to be most helpful, however. They have shown us that, if an individual is defiled, there is a disordering not only of his society but of the cosmos. Even as the individual finds his place only as part of the community in social relationship and cultic acts, so the cult on earth is inseparably linked to whatever view of "heaven" is held. That is, there is a strong sense of solidarity, both in worship and in pollution.

Such a view of humanity in relation to cult and cosmos sounds foreign to our ears. Humanity today has increasingly been concerned with the individual per se; and the individual has been seen as strangely aloof from its world. The world is thought of as that which is to be brought to serve the individual's ends, while the limitless horizons of space have appeared as cold, dark, mechanistic. Yet it must be averred that the view of the author of Hebrews seems strongly to resemble the "solidarity" patterns which phenomenology of religion displayed to us. His teaching of a heavenly cult composed of angels and the spirits of the past heroes who have "now" (that is, since the work of Christ) attained to "perfection" and to which Christians *on earth* may presently belong[207] is a strong evidence for such an understanding. Likewise, the continual

---

205 *L'Épître aux Hébreux*, II, 267.

206 Cf. the expedient of F. F. Bruce, *Epistle to the Hebrews*, 218—"What required to be cleansed was the defiled conscience of men and women; this is a cleansing which belongs to the spiritual sphere." This equating of τὰ ἐπουράνια with human conscience must be dismissed as an unjustified effort to avoid the thrust of the text; yet it is not at all untypical. What we see operating here, as with Spicq, is a perpetuation of the Platonic schema of heavenly things, albeit in attenuated form. That is, the "real" always stands over against the earthly and cannot be conceived of as having our "problem" of defilement.

207 12.18–24. This is a passage which presents numerous difficulties to the exegete in terms of details, particularly with regard to phrasing. We are concerned only with the *thrust* of the passage here. The key issue is the eschatological one: is the author setting forth a thoroughly "realized" eschatology? That issue in turn depends upon the sense one gives to προσεληλύθατε in vv. 18, 22. It seems to us that Montefiore has missed the mark when he translates this word by "you have drawn near" in vs. 22 and comments: "His readers have not yet actually arrived at Mount Zion: they have drawn close (cf. v. 18). This translation is in accord with the author's general viewpoint of a futurist and not a realized eschatology" (*Epistle to the Hebrews*, 229). By so translating he has chosen to ignore the obviously cultic sense of προσέρχεσθαι throughout the letter (4.16; 7.25. 10.1, 22. 11.6), a sense well established outside Hebrews (cf. J. Schneider, "Προσέρχομαι," *TDNT*, II, 683–84). It seems unquestionable to us that any consideration of the eschatology of Hebrews must maintain a tension between the apparently "realized" eschatology which comes into view here and especially in Hebrews 9–10 and the "futurist" eschatology manifested at 9.28; 10.37–38; and 12.26–27. Since the author clearly holds that it is only in the *future* that the "real" order, which now exists but is invisible, will replace the present, earthly order, it seems preferable to speak of *proleptic participation* of believers on

stress on the community and never on the individual, coupled with the congruence of the views of defilement and purgation to the general "structures," point in the same direction. Thus, we hold that it is not only possible but even likely that the *auctor ad Hebraeos* could conceive of a need for purgation with finality to embrace the "heavenly things" as well as the earthly cultus.[208]

It seems to us that difficulties of two types have hindered exegetes in their grappling with the concept of defiled "heavenly things." We have referred to the first of these: our modern view of humanity in the universe. The second has to do with a preconceived notion of the heavenly cultus. So long as it is thought of along Platonizing lines, an absolute break with the earthly must be felt. It is not our purpose to enter into the cosmology of Hebrews in this study; we find it necessary to our task of exegeting Hebrews 9–10, however, to enter a disclaimer against such a Platonizing view, at least at this point. We have already noticed a lack of dichotomy along "spatial" lines: the Christian on earth may *now* be part of the cult of heaven. Furthermore, it is incorrect to see the heavenly cult as a *timeless* entity. The passage which we are here considering directly relates the heavenly cult to the past, the present, and the future. In terms of the past: the author underlines the ἐφάπαξ character of Christ's offering by his use of the striking phrase: ἐπεὶ ἔδει αὐτὸν πολλάκις παθεῖν ἀπὸ καταβολῆς κόσμου—"else then he would have had to suffer many times since the foundation of the world." That is, a *single* offering at a point in time in the past precludes all consideration of the need to repeat such an offering. If there were such need, the author reasons, such repetition would have had to begin with the foundation of the world. But that Golgotha was not the first passion of Christ is unthinkable.[209] With regard to the present: the "now" time is the συντελείᾳ τῶν αἰώνων—the consummation of the ages. It is the time which rests on the ἐφάπαξ of Christ's blood. It is the time when the

---

earth in the heavenly cultus. The author's emphasis on the ἐφάπαξ character of the purgation afforded by Christ's blood is designed to remove all doubts as to the *acceptance* of Christians in the heavenly assembly of angels and "spirits of just men made perfect" (12.23). They are *now* accepted, but their full—in the sense of physical presence—participation lies in the future.

208 Among the very few writers who are prepared to accept the text according to its obvious intention stands Héring: "We think that the purification of the lower reaches of heaven is implied in the victory over Satan which is asserted in 2.14"; *Epistle to the Hebrews*, 82. Why was the purification of heaven necessary?—"because the hostile powers had settled there, in order to oppress men and to separate them from God" (ibid.). The weakness of this explanation is that it has to draw upon parallels outside of Hebrews; it gains no support directly from the letter itself. Windisch suggests that it is the sins of men who defile the heavenly sanctuary, according to the parallelisms between the earthly and heavenly sanctuaries (Heb 8.5). His remarks are extremely terse, however (*Hebräerbrief*, 85).

209 Elsewhere the author relates the heavenly cult to the past: 9.8—the way into the heavenly holy places was not revealed while the old cultus had standing; 11.40—the heroes of old could not attain τελείωσις "without us."

heroes of old along with Christians on earth find incorporation in the heavenly cultus. Concerning the future: the "now" is balanced by the "not yet." While the new age has come with Christ, while believers now enjoy access to God with purged συνείδησις, still the best is yet to be. What that future will bring is not spelled out by the author: here he merely labels it "salvation," while elsewhere he speaks of it in terms of inheritance, rest, country, and city.[210] But the point with regard to the heavenly cultus is clear: that cultus is part of an ongoing divine purpose which is realized in time. It was at a precise moment—the ἐφάπαξ—that Christ "entered" the heavenly sanctuary. Even so comes the precise moment for the Parousia. That is not an event which can add to the purgation already fully accomplished, for Christ returns χωρὶς ἁμαρτίας—"not to deal with sin." Yet that it marks some sort of transition in terms of the heavenly cultus is manifest: whereas Christ is now interceding for those who are to be *heirs* of salvation, salvation then will be realized.[211]

"At the climax of the ages, Christ appeared in order to remove (purge) sins by means of the sacrifice of himself"—this then is the principal point made in verses 23–28. That removal (ἀθετεῖν) of sins must in this context have primary reference to the "heavenly things"; the concern with the "subjective" benefits to the believers on earth is not here in view. Thus, the first argument from the "blood rule" concerns heaven itself: the "better blood" of Christ applied brings purgation with finality to the very "heavenly things."

We may conclude our consideration of this paragraph by briefly noting the contrasts drawn by the author between the old cultus and its ministration and the new. While both cultuses stand under the "blood rule," the better blood of the new at every point achieves that which the old order could not. It is sufficient to set out these contrasts in the following summary form:

Old Cultus	New Cultus
Patterns of the heavenly things	The very heavenly things
Holy places made with hands	Heaven itself
Figures of the "real"	God's presence
Many offerings	One offering
Many entries (annual)	One entry
Continual services	Climax of ages
No final purgation	Sins removed
Sacrifice of animals	Sacrifice of himself

---

210 9.15; 3.11, 18; 4.1, 3, 5, 10–11; 11.14–16; 11.10, 16; 12.22; 13.14.
211 7.25; 9.28. As we have already emphasized above, the author refuses to give details concerning the work of Christ in the heavenly cultus.

Our interpretation of the difficult passage 9.23–28 goes beyond the tentative explanations of Héring and Windisch. Yet, suggestive as it may appear to be, it leaves unanswered many questions. In particular, this one: Is heaven part of the cosmos for the author of Hebrews? If so, this view would separate him from many common assumptions concerning heaven. Again, we see the need for a supplementation of our study with an investigation of the cosmology of Hebrews.

10.1–4. There is an obvious shift in the argument at 10.1. Whereas 9.23–28 had its focus on Christ and his work in terms of the heavenly sanctuary and the divine plan for the ages, the author now turns to elaborate the "subjective" effects of Christ's blood. These benefits are encompassed by the idea of τελειοῦν which is met at the outset—τελειοῦν signifying, as we have already seen, "incorporation" (decisive purgation from numinous uneasiness, with access to God).[212] Throughout the first eighteen verses of the chapter, which bring to a close the strictly cultic argumentation, the concern is with τελειοῦν, especially with regard to the purging of the συνείδησις. Thus, in 10.1–4 the author shows the inability of the old cultus to bring τελειοῦν; in 10.5–10, he finds a prediction in the scripture of a change from the old cultus; while in 10.11–18 he shows how that change—the new cultus in Christ—avails to bring τελειοῦν.

In 10.1, there is an obvious looking back to 9.11, where Christ is ἀρχιερεὺς τῶν γενομένων ἀγαθῶν "high priest of the good things that have come." Now (10.1) we read that the law has a σκιὰν τῶν μελλόντων ἀγαθῶν—"a shadow of the good things to come." (This obvious parallelism confirms our adoption of γενομένων in 9.11.) The paragraph underlines the reasons for the inferiority of the old cultus which we have met before: it is only a "shadow," not the *real*; it could not purge the συνείδησις; it consists in the same sort of sacrifices year after year. It is the contrast between the *repetitive* nature of its sacrifices with the once-for-all character of Christ's blood that is yet again the point of heaviest emphasis. It is a question of a καθαρίζειν versus a ἅπαξ καθαρίζειν. As we noticed in our consideration of 9.6–10, the *auctor ad Hebraeos* does not deny that animal sacrifices can bring purgation, even of the συνείδησις; what is at stake is whether they can achieve a decisive cleansing, so that humanity's sense of numinous uneasiness is dealt with. The author argues that it is obvious that they cannot: the annual Day of Atonement ceremonies are proof positive of the collective consciousness of defilement.[213]

---

212 *Supra*, p. 120.

213 This is the sense of the ἀνάμνησις ἁμαρτιῶν—not the idea of a public confession of sins. This view of the author of Hebrews is also at variance with Philo's assertion that the

We are now able to appreciate the intent of his axiomatic statement: "For it is impossible that the blood of bulls and goats should take away sins." To suggest that with this affirmation the author announces his opposition to all ritual, that here he discards the old cultus as having no value in itself, that he now lays the foundation for an "internal," moral religion—all such interpretations of his statement fly in the face of the immediate context and the progress of the argument in chapter 9.[214] The question is not whether the blood of animals has any power but as to its *relative* power. The axiom, in fact, is a restatement of the εἰ γὰρ ... πόσῳ μᾶλλον ("For if ... how much more!") of 9.13–14: whereas the latter emphasized the *adequacy* of Christ's blood, this stresses the *inadequacy* of animal blood. That is, the ἀφαιρεῖν ἁμαρτίας here refers to that decisive removal of numinous uneasiness—something which animal blood could never accomplish.

We notice how the exegesis turns on the correct balancing of continuity and discontinuity of the old and new cultuses. The author's point here is obviously to accent the discontinuity; but that accent must not be allowed to obscure the underlying basis of continuity (namely, the "blood rule") on which he is able to frame his argument.

10.5–10. This balance of continuity and discontinuity must be maintained if we are to grasp correctly the author's discussion centering in the quotation of Psalms 40.6–9. It seems indisputable that the argument is rooted in the concept of offerings (sacrifices). Whereas the axiom of verse 4 had stressed the inadequacy of animal offerings, the conclusion of verse 10 plays on the "offering of the body of Jesus Christ." Likewise, the verses immediately following continue to contrast the *many* offerings of the old cultus with the once-for-all self-offering of Jesus.

That is, in verses 5–10 we have to do with the *relative efficacy* of offering—on the one hand, those of the old covenant, and on the other, the offering of Jesus. The *auctor ad Hebraeos* uses the citation from the LXX to argue forcefully his point: already it had been predicted that a σῶμα (body) would be accorded superior status to the cultic offerings.[215]

---

sacrifices of the wicked put God in remembrance of their sins (cf. F. F. Bruce, *Epistle to the Hebrews*, 229, n. 19).

214 Contrast the findings of our method with F. F. Bruce's comment on 10.4: "Moral defilement cannot be removed by material means. Such spiritual value as the sacrificial ritual might have lay in its being a material foreshadowing or object-lesson of a moral or spiritual reality" (*Epistle to the Hebrews*, 229–30).

215 This quotation shows the author's dependence on the LXX. The MT has "ears you have dug for me" instead of "a body you have prepared for me"—a reading which would altogether be unacceptable to the author's contrast between animal sacrifices and Christ's self-offering.

We may now discern the function of the quotation in the author's plan. As elsewhere, he sees the Old Testament as an arsenal for the Christian pastor: its sayings are pregnant with significance for the followers of Christ.[216] Thus, he allows the Holy Spirit, as it were, to bring to his readers the point he wishes to make, which is *the end* of the old cultus because of the coming of the new. Already he had hinted at this: the old was only a parable, a shadow, an example, incumbent until the time of the new order.[217] But now the point is made sharply: the old is taken away with the establishment of the new. And this very transition, he argues, had already been predicted in Scripture.

What significance is to be attached to σῶμα in the author's argument? It seems necessary to guard against both minimizing and maximizing tendencies. On one hand, commentators such as F. F. Bruce have taken the former view: σῶμα signifies obedience, and the *auctor ad Hebraeos* could as well have used the ὠτία (ears) demanded by the Hebrew.[218] But this view quite misses the point of verse 10, where the author underlines the "offering of the body of Jesus Christ"; it fails to discern that one set of offerings (animal) is being opposed by another (Christ's body). Inversely, we should probably be careful not to read too much meaning into σῶμα here. We earlier noticed the difficulties which the exegete faces when one endeavors to establish the author's reason for the efficacy of Christ's blood.[219] Certainly, the use of σῶμα at this point seems to carry a qualitative distinction: a *human* sacrifice is being opposed to animal sacrifices.[220] Yet the author uses σάρξ rather than σῶμα to indicate the humanity of Jesus,[221] so that his use of σῶμα in this paragraph is assuredly to be explained on the basis that this was the word which the "prediction" in the LXX happened to use. Thus, while σῶμα is to be accorded significance in the argument, as setting off a qualitatively superior sacrifice, that significance is not to be pressed.

The place of θέλημα (will, wish) in the paragraph will have been made apparent from the above considerations: the offering of Christ is the offering according to the divine will. We have noticed in our discussions how deity is

---

216 Cf. Schröger, *Der Verfasser des Hebräerbriefs als Schriftausleger*, 172–77; and Kistemaker, *The Psalm Citations in the Epistle to the Hebrews*, 124–30.

217 8.5; 9.9; 10.1.

218 Cf. F. F. Bruce, *Epistle to the Hebrews*, 232–33: "But if our author had preferred the Hebrew wording, it would have served his purpose almost as well, for in addition to reminding him and his readers of the psalm from which it was taken, it might have reminded them also of the Isaianic Servant's language in the third Servant Song...."

219 *Supra*, p. 138.

220 But at 12.24 Christ's blood is *contrasted* with the blood of Abel, so this point is not to be pushed too far.

221 5.7—"the days of his flesh"; 2.14—he shared "blood and flesh."

not in the forefront in the argument of Hebrews 9–10. Yet it must be said that deity is always there in the background, even if Christ and humanity are on center stage; and occasionally the light reflects from the main actors to fall on that backdrop. That is the case here: the divine will predicts that σῶμα replace animal sacrifices; Christ comes in accord with the divine will; and by that same divine will, when Christ has been offered as a once-for-all sacrifice, Christians are "sanctified" (separated, consecrated). That is, while the *immediate* grounds of purgation is blood, the *ultimate* source is divine will.

Our interpretation of Hebrews 10.5–10 in terms of the *relative efficacy* of offerings is not new. Before the turn of the century Davidson had written concerning the passage:

> The passage in the Epistle is far from saying that the essence or worth of Christ's offering of Himself lies simply in obedience to the will of God. It does not refer to the point wherein lies the intrinsic worth of the Son's offering, or whether it may be resolved into obedience unto God. Its point is quite different. It argues that the Son's offering of Himself is the true and final offering for sin, because it is the sacrifice which, according to prophecy, God desired to be made.[222]

These insights seem to have been lost in the intervening years. There has been a tendency to view the passage in terms of a radical disjunction between priestly ritual and prophetic religion.[223] The positing of such a dichotomy in Hebrews 10.5–10 wreaks havoc with the argument, which up to this point has presupposed continuities based on the cult. Then the exegete is forced to conclude with Michel that the argument of the ninth chapter stands in tension with that of the tenth. At the other extreme we find a hypersensitivity to ritual in Hebrews 10.5–10, so that the exegete sees in the references to σῶμα allusions to the Mass.[224]

Our interpretation, however, is not a mere repetition of Davidson's work. The method we have followed has enabled us to detect the ebb and flow of the argument from cult as it proceeds through the ninth chapter and into the tenth at a deeper level than Davidson's insights. We hope to have been able to show the internal logic of religious statements which he could do no more than to recognize as axioms.

---

222   *Epistle to the Hebrews*, 193–94.
223   Cf. Héring, *Epistle to the Hebrews*, 87: "the author aligns himself with the anti-ritualist tendencies which can be glimpsed in certain prophets and Psalmists."
224   Cf. Ketter, *Hebräerbrief*, 75.

10.11–18. These final verses of the cultic argumentation proper serve as a satisfactory rounding out of the discussion which commenced at 9.1. The author had first set out in brief the old cultus and its limitations; then in two brilliant affirmations[225] he had given in succinct form the "good things" which had come with Christ—objectively, the institution of a heavenly cultus, and subjectively, the incorporation of the follower of Christ in that cultus. The thrust of the ninth chapter was on the first of these benefits, pointing out the inauguration of the heavenly sanctuary and Christ's ministry in it. With the tenth chapter, the focus has moved to the subjective aspect. In this chapter, he points to the repetitive character of the animal sacrifices as testimony to their inability to purge decisively the numinous unease of the people; then he shows that the divine will called for a replacement of these sacrifices by a σῶμα. Thus, in verses 11–18 the argument moves inexorably to its finale: an elaboration of the purgation of συνείδησις. As such, it may rightly be seen as an exposition of 9.13–14.

As previously, the author makes his point by both arguing from contrast and by reference to the Old Testament. His earlier underlining of the repetitive character of the sacrifices of the old cultus provides the basis for the contrast. Again, he scores this idea: the earthly priests *stand* (that is, their work is never completed); they minister καθ' ἡμέραν (daily); they offer the *same* sacrifices; they offer πολλάκις (frequently); these sacrifices can never remove (περιαιρεῖν) sins. But Christ offered only *one* sacrifice for sins, by which he perfected for all time his separated ones. The contrast is made particularly effective by picking up the idea of "sitting" to signify a completed work—an idea introduced in the proem but only here shown in its significance for the argument. The sustained contrast hammers home the point: the repeated animal sacrifices show that incorporation was not attainable under the old cultus, whereas the completed offering of Christ establishes that it has now been made possible.

The argument from Scripture again introduces the Jeremianic description of the new covenant. There is an obvious dislocution in the text, however: the μετὰ γὰρ τὸ εἰρηκέναι ("after he said ... ") of verse 15 calls for something like τότε εἴρηκεν before verse 17. Since the only manuscript support for some such addition is very weak,[226] we must suppose that either a scribal error was made at a very early copying of the autograph, or (more likely) that the autograph itself was defective, due to a mental slip on the part of the *auctor ad Hebraeos* or his amanuensis. But the presentation of the argument as it stands makes

---

225 9.11–14.
226 Later MSS add either ὕστερον λέγει or τότε εἴρηκεν.

quite clear the point which the author intends to bring out: the citation is to show that it is the purgation of the very συνείδησις which the new covenant is to bring.

The author's use of the covenant motif in Hebrews 9–10 is illuminating to show the course of the argument. The idea of the purgation of the συνείδησις provided the link to introduce the motif at 9.15. But that idea (the subjective benefit) is not developed in the ninth chapter. Instead, the author seems to drag in the idea of διαθήκη for apologetic purposes (why Christ died). Nor do the subsequent references to covenant in Hebrews 9 have to do with συνείδησις; instead, they are subordinated to the leitmotif of blood: blood inaugurates covenant. But in the tenth chapter, as the cultic argumentation has unfolded to almost full flowering, the Jeremianic quotation appears to give the final, convincing touches, now in the service of the subjective benefits of Christ's work.

It seems incontestable that 10.18 echoes 9.22b as its corollary: "no definitive putting away of defilement without blood applied," therefore, "where there is definitive putting away of sins there is no longer need of bloody offerings." With 10.18 we have reached the finale of the cultic argumentation: the rest of the chapter rests under the compelling οὖν (therefore) of verse 19. Further, in view of the masterly development of the argument that we have noticed all along, it would be unthinkable that the author's case should peter out with some weak generalization in verse 18. No; we are surely justified in seeing in his use of ἄφεσις here an indication of a comprehensive, powerful term. This itself tends to confirm the weight which we assigned to the other occurrence in 9.22b. The matter in which the idea of "remembering" is brought into this concluding paragraph of the argument may likewise support our understanding of ἄφεσις as "purgation with finality." Whereas he had argued earlier in terms of the collective consciousness of the community of defilement, here the citation refers to *God's* no longer remembering sin. This indeed is purging with finality![227]

Thus, with 9.22b and 10.18 we see in cameo the play and counter play of the author's discussion in Hebrews 9–10. On one hand, there is the axiom, applicable to both cultuses: no decisive purgation without blood applied. But on the other, we see the particular emphasis which the author is so concerned to bring out through various ways in these chapters: definitive purgation *has* come by means of the blood of Christ.

---

227 This paralleling of God's not remembering sin with the putting away of sin of course derives from the Jeremianic quotation (31.31–34). But the parallel is found elsewhere in the OT, e.g., Isa 43.25—"I am He who blots out your transgressions … and I will not remember your sins."

10.19–22. With verse 19, the focus shifts from cultus per se to the believers' response. "Therefore, brothers, since we have ... " sets the tone for the remainder of the chapter. There is first a summation of the benefits subjectively realized by Christians in the "now" time, with the call to appropriate living in view of them.

Thus, in verses 19–22 we see exactly balanced Christ's work and humanity's response. Christ is the one who has opened or inaugurated the way of the heavenly sanctuary. It is a *new* way: the heroes of old had not been able to attain to it before the coming of Christ.[228] And it is a living way, for it is a way that leads through the heavenly curtain itself, that is, into the real Holy of Holies, the very presence of God. So, in verses 19–20, the *auctor ad Hebraeos* gathers together in a single, comprehensive statement his argument concerning the work of Christ which began at 9.1 and with the mention of καταπέτασμα (curtain) brings the discussion full circle to its starting point. Likewise, verses 21–22 give in summary form the benefits to the believer upon which the believer has been so insistent. The Christians may now "draw near" (προσέρχεσθαι) to God: at last all barriers are down. Furthermore, such approach to God is to be in πληροφορία (boldness)—gone are the feelings of dread, removed is the numinous uneasiness which has been the perpetual burden of the community. For, whereas it was once defilement that burdened the συνείδησις and led to exclusion from deity with feelings of dread, now has come decisive purgation: purgation of body and purgation of mind.

With verse 20, we encounter a *crux interpretum*. The τοῦτ'ἔστιν τῆς σαρκὸς αὐτοῦ has long been a fruitful field for speculation. The majority opinion, perpetuated in the RSV,[229] has put this phrase in apposition to καταπετάσματος, opening the door to marvelous explanations as to how the "curtain" is metaphorically Christ's "flesh." Naturally, those who have sought to "spiritualize" the whole argument of sanctuary-sacrifice have seized on this passage.[230] Yet the interpretation flies in the face of all that has gone before in the argument of the passage. Further, in the immediate context, we would expect that

---

228 11.40—"apart from us they should not be made perfect."

229 RSV: "through the curtain, that is, through his flesh." The NEB, however, translates as "the new, living way which he has opened for us through the curtain, the way of his flesh," with a footnote giving as alternative "the curtain of his flesh." Michel, Moffatt, Käsemann, F. F. Bruce, Windisch, and Purdy favor the first (equals RSV) interpretation. Westcott, Spicq, Héring, and Montefiore, however, favor the second.

230 Cf. William Manson, *Epistle to the Hebrews*, 67–68: "Here by a mystical-allegorical touch the writer identifies the Veil with the 'flesh' of Christ. The Gospels speak of the veil of the Temple, the barrier which hung between God and man, as rent at the death of Christ. The writer to the Hebrews, as Dr. Moffatt trenchantly puts it, 'allegorizes the veil as the flesh of Christ; this had to be rent before the blood could be shed, which enabled him to enter and open God's presence for the people.'"

the believer's approach to God would find its parallel (and source) in Christ's approach "through the curtain." Again, the use of καταπέτασμα here seems clearly to be echoing the local use in 9.3. But the decisive point must be given at 6.19–20, where, in a manifestly parallel passage, καταπέτασμα is used non-metaphorically. Surely the exegete cannot have it both ways—a literal veil when it suits his purposes and then a sudden switch to the flesh of Christ.

The thrust of the passage, as of the epistle, calls for an interpretation of "flesh" in the *instrumental* sense. We were pleased to note that this view, which had forced itself upon us already from a pondering of the argument of the passage, has found recent supporters. The long-standing objection to it was based on the inadmissibility of a local sense of διά followed by an instrumental διά. Both Hofius and Jeremias in recent writings[231] have successfully disposed of this objection. Hofius points to the chiastic structure of Hebrews 10.20, so that ἐνεκαίνισεν ἡμῖν (he inaugurated for us) corresponds to the τοῦτ'ἔστιν (διὰ) τῆς σαρκὸς αὐτοῦ (that is, by means of his flesh), and he argues that σάρξ in Hebrews signifies the incarnation of Jesus—a conclusion already reached in our study.[232] In his brief article supporting Hofius's position, Jeremias[233] points to the parallel structure of verses 19–20:

10.19
a. εἰς τὴν εἴσοδον
b. τῶν ἁγίων
c. ἐν τῷ αἵματι Ἰησοῦ

10.20
a. ὁδὸν πρόσφατον καὶ ζῶσαν
b. διὰ τοῦ καταπετάσματος
c. τοῦτ'ἔστιν τῆς σαρκὸς αὐτοῦ

On the grounds of both the internal logic of the argument of Hebrews 9–10 and the syntax of verses 19–20, we therefore feel justified to translate these verses as follows: "Therefore, brothers, since we have boldness to enter the heavenly sanctuary in the blood of Jesus, by a new and living way which he opened for us through the curtain—that is, the way of his flesh, let us...."

10.23–30. The summary statement of accomplishment-response of verses 19–22 now gives away to specific pareneses. The passage is most significant for the light it sheds on the community itself: its present tendencies (neglect, wavering), its past trials (persecution, fellowship), and its future expectation (the coming Parousia). We shall not enter into a discussion of these details, since our concern in this study is with the cultic argumentation and its view of humanity's problem as defilement. We need merely to note that in verses

---

231 See note 141 above.
232 *Ruf Jesu*, 138–41.
233 Jeremias, "Hebr. 10.20," 131.

23–25 and 32–39 the "problem" changes: the danger to be avoided is ὑποστολή (timidity, drawing back) and the supreme need is ὑπομονή (endurance, faithfulness).

This is surely curious: humanity's "problem" and its "solution" seem to be viewed altogether differently when we leave the framework of the cultic argumentation. It is this difficulty which must be our concern in the fifth chapter of this study.

We shall, however, pause to give some consideration to verses 26–31, inasmuch as in this portion of the parenesis the *auctor ad Hebraeos* mingles his warning with argument concerning the blood of the covenant. We do not propose to trace the long course of debate over this and related passages in the history of interpretation;[234] instead, we shall limit ourselves to insights which might be suggested from our study of blood, defilement, and purgation in general and in Hebrews 9–10.

The first point to be made is that these verses logically belong to the discussion of 9.1–10.22, rather than to the strictly parenetical portions in 10.23–25 and 10.32–39. Just as in 10.19–22, the argument moves subtly away from cult to parenesis, so in 10.26–31 the parenesis turns back to the cult: it is cultic sanctions (θυσία, αἷμα) which furnish the writer with the grounds for his most severe warning. That is, we may conveniently look upon verses 26–31 as the corollary of verses 21–22. The latter verses set forth the *appropriate* response, the former the *wrong* response. But in both cases, it is the cultic argumentation which determines or judges the response: *since* Christ has done this, therefore *do*; or, *since* Christ has done this, *beware* of doing.

Whereas in verses 19–22 the accent falls on confidence, now it falls on *dread*: "it is a fearful thing to fall into the hands of the living God." Whereas in the first case the approach to deity is opened, here there is no prospect of mercy but only of the "flaming fire." This is because the πόσῳ μᾶλλον of the blood of Christ is now turned to the πόσῳ χείρονος of judgment: instead of that blood leading to incorporation in the heavenly cultus, there is no longer a θυσία for sins. Although the author does not develop explicitly the point, we now witness the power of blood to act in a negative, destroying direction. The willful sinner has treated the blood of the covenant—the blood which sanctifies—as κοινός (common, defiled) and that blood now turns upon the sinner with death-dealing potency.

It seems undeniable that ἑκουσίως (deliberately, willfully) is the key word in the author's description of the offender. This attitude is elaborated in verse 29 by the use of three verbs: καταπατεῖν (to trample under, treat with dis-

---

234 A good summary is provided by Grässer, *Der Glaube im Hebräerbrief*, 192–98.

dain),[235] ἡγεῖσθαι (to consider, regard),[236] and (to outrage, insult).[237] In this light his employment ἀγνοήμα ("sins of ignorance") to designate the "sins" which were purged under the old cultus[238] seems highly significant. Apparently, the author knows of no purgation of sins committed with a high hand in either cultus. He sees sin as a defilement, a stain which comes *on* man. It is infectious, it is dangerous, as we have already noticed; but it may be purged by blood. But deliberate sin, sin with a high hand, cannot be purged with blood.

Why is this? Manifestly, because sins committed ἑκουσίως are a rejection of the cultus itself. While, as we have seen, sin as defilement extends its miasma to pollute the cultus, yet the cultus makes provision for dealing with it. But for the one who rejects the cultus there can be no hope of removing the defilement. This one has become a permanent "non-person," a being without hope, without social or cultic privileges and benefits. Their case corresponds closely with that of the extreme offender which came to light in the consideration of the general "structures" of defilement and purgation.[239]

Thus, it seems to us that any explanation of this "hard nut" must be grounded firmly in the cultic argumentation of the *auctor ad Hebraeos*. It must give full weight to the "collective" understanding of humanity which we have viewed throughout and appreciate that it is the *cultus* in which the group finds its *raison d'être*. It must see that to be cut off from the cultus is to be put in a position of peculiar religious dread in which one has ceased to be truly a human and which can only call for obliteration. It must give full weight to the religious ideas centering in defilement and purgation, showing that it is the cultus where these ideas find their focus. And above all, it must be alert to the deep religious power which αἷμα endeavors to express—power to cleanse, to sanctify, to inaugurate, to purge decisively even the very consciousness, but also power to turn in destructive force upon its despiser.[240]

---

235 Arndt and Gingrich, *Greek-English Lexicon*, 416.
236 Ibid., 344.
237 Ibid., 269.
238 9.7.
239 *Supra*, p. 61.
240 The parallelism of Heb 10.26–31 to the thought and vocabulary of the Qumran writings, e.g., "For one sin of inadvertence (alone) he shall do penance for two years. But as for him who has sinned deliberately, he shall never return; only the man who has sinned inadvertently shall be tried for two years that his way and counsel may be made perfect according to the judgement of the Congregation" (1QS ix, 1–2)—has not passed unnoticed. But a *direct* connection of Hebrews and Qumran is not necessary. Rather, we should view the communities of Qumran and Hebrews as sharing the same sort of self-image—that of a cultic community. We hold to have illuminated this self-image by the general "structures" of Ch. 3 of this study and also its particular form with regard to the community of Hebrews by our study in this chapter. The community of Hebrews, as we have seen, finds its *rasion d'être* in terms of

Our tracing of the argument of Hebrews 9–10, particularly as it concerns blood, defilement, and purgation, has come to a close. It merely remains for us to take account of the way in which these ideas occur elsewhere in Hebrews.

Blood, Defilement, and Purgation Elsewhere in Hebrews

Αἷμα occurs seven times in Hebrews outside chapters 9–10, five of which appear in a cultic setting. The other two references are clearly not of significance: at 2.14, Christ shares in "blood and flesh," while at 12.4, the believers have not yet resisted "unto blood." The first reference is non-specific and indicates Christ's humanity (incarnation), while the second refers to martyrdom. With both, the idea of blood as life-power is only weakly in view—Christ takes human life; the Christians have not yet gone to the point of losing their lives.

Let us take up the five cultic references in turn. At 11.28, the author pauses in his recital of the deeds of faith from old times to make mention of the blood which delivered the firstborn children of Israel. The reference is wholly casual, yet it conforms exactly with the function of blood as a life-imparting medium that we have observed already. As before, the blood is mentioned as having been applied (πρόσχυσις: pouring, sprinkling, spreading).[241] The specific benefit imparted by blood is an addition to those which were seen in chapters 9–10: it is here *apotropaic*.

In 12.24, the blood of Christ is contrasted with the blood of Abel. The terminology is strange to our ears: the idea is that of "speaking" blood. It is an idea which the author has taken from the story of the murder of Abel, where the voice of Abel's blood is said to be crying out from the ground.[242] The *auctor ad Hebraeos* had picked up the thought in his roll-call of the faithful, when he commented that Abel, though dead, yet continues to speak.[243] Now, in 12.24, he makes the point that Christ's blood speaks better (RSV: "more graciously") than Abel's blood. That the author should find the curious reference in Genesis amenable to his purposes illumines his conception of blood. In this personification of blood itself we see momentarily magnified that view of blood as a positive, highly potent medium which we have noticed so often

---

the defilement-purgation syndrome in which the blood of Christ is the pre-eminent power. A deliberate rejection of that blood seems to us to be indicated in Heb 10.26–31. We find, for instance, quite unsatisfactory Montefiore's interpretation of the passage in terms of neglect of the Eucharist (*Epistle to the Hebrews*, 177–80).

241 Arndt and Gingrich, *Greek-English Lexicon*, 727.

242 Gen 4.10.

243 11.4. Parallels to the author's expression have been observed by the commentators. Windisch in particular has underlined belief in the atoning efficacy of a martyr's blood in the Judaism of the period (*Hebräerbrief*, 82–85; cf. F. F. Bruce, *Epistle to the Hebrews*, 379).

in Hebrews 9–10. Furthermore, the contrast here between Christ's and Abel's blood clearly rests on an overarching view of blood per se, just as we argued for Hebrews 9–10. Again, the point rests on "better blood," except that now the contrast is not Christ's/animal blood but Christ's/human blood. It is obvious that the author assigns special value to Christ's blood above that of any other human, but, as we have seen before, he nowhere specifies what imparts to it the added power. Finally, it is again blood *applied* ("sprinkled") which speaks the better things.

In 13.11–12 there is a direct comparison of the ministration of the old cultus with that of the new. The reasoning is this: just as the carcasses of animals were burned outside the camp if their blood was brought into the earthly sanctuary, so Jesus, whose blood was brought into the heavenly sanctuary, died "outside the gate." This is one of the few instances in Hebrews that seems to lend support to those efforts of earlier scholars to find precise analogies of the old cultus with the new. All along in this chapter we have taken issue with such an approach; nor is an exception to be made here. The context of the verse indicates that the comparison is made in the service of verse 13—"Therefore let us go forth to him outside the camp...." That is, the author is not endeavoring to show the precise correspondence of the old and new but rather is making a homiletical-type comparison.[244] The passage is significant, however, to point out again the high valency which blood has in the author's mind. In terms of the homiletical analogy which we have pointed to, the mention of blood is not really necessary: the author could as well have reached his conclusion in verse 13 by arguing: "Just as the carcasses of the sacrificial animals of the old cultus were burned outside the camp, so Christ suffered outside the gate. Therefore, let us...." But no, he cannot touch on the idea of sacrifice without bringing in blood as the medium of power. As before, we noticed that it is blood *applied* that is spoken of; while here Christ's blood separates (consecrates, sanctifies) the people collectively.

The final reference to αἷμα occurs in the benediction of 13.20. The new ideas which occur here—Christ's resurrection, shepherd, sheep, eternal covenant—strongly suggest that the verse is not an original composition of

---

244 Cf. H. Koester, "'Outside the Camp'. Hebrews 13.1–14," *HTR*, LV (1962), 299–315. Koester sees a homiletical-type comparison here also, but his assertion that the *auctor ad Hebraeos* advocates "the disgrace of worldliness" seems to us quite out of keeping with the cultic "atmosphere" of the letter. Koester's interpretation requires correction in view of the defilementpurgation syndrome which our study has disclosed—a study which renders his explanation of "outside the camp" as "the uncleanness of the world" clearly untenable. It seems to us that the author's point is not to advocate a separation from cult to world, but rather to underscore the *reproach* of Christianity in a hostile environment.

the author.[245] Yet the view of blood is obviously congruent with his general thought: it is here the medium of resurrection. Αἷμα as direct, lively potency could not be better illustrated than this.

As we review these passages outside Hebrews 9–10, it is apparent that the religious conception of blood which we noticed there is strongly confirmed. In every case, αἷμα is used in a positive sense: it is the medium of benefit, of blessing, of life. Further, it seems evident that this motif of blood was one which was never far from the forefront in the author's thinking, so that a curious reference like Genesis 4 brings it immediately into the limelight and so that he inevitably reverts to its use when he wishes to make his strongest affirmations.

The language of defilement, in contrast to αἷμα, is hardly to be found outside Hebrews 9–10. In fact, κοινοῦν does not occur at all, and there are but three instances where μιαίνειν (to stain, to defile)[246] is to be found. The first of these is in 7.26: Christ as high priest is ἀμίαντος, and hence does not need to offer a sacrifice for his own sins, as do the Levitical priests. At 12.15, the author warns against the springing up of a ῥίζα πικρίας ("a root of bitterness") which will lead to the defilement of οἱ πολλοί ("the many," or "the community"). In its original setting in the LXX,[247] the ῥίζα πικριάς has to do with turning away from Yahweh; there is no mention of defilement. That the *auctor ad Hebraeos* should introduce the idea of μιαίνειν here is interesting: it is clearly a breaking-through of a cultic view of humanity's "problem" into a non-cultic setting. But the presentation of that defilement is even more significant: it leads to the corruption of the whole community. This idea of the contagious nature of defilement accords exactly with the general phenomenological data.[248] Again in 13.4 the author casually injects the language of defilement into a non-cultic setting: let the marriage bed be ἀμίαντος. Here it is not a question of sexual intercourse per se leading to defilement, as in some cultures, but of illicit sexual intercourse defiling the marriage bed. Once again, the contagious sense of defilement is in view: the πορνοί (immoral) and μορχοί (adulterers) defile the κοίτη (bed) as they bring with them their defilement.

---

245 The material for the thirteenth chapter has been subject to scrutiny as to its authenticity. W. Wrede, *The literarische Rätsel des Hebräerbriefs* (Göttingen: 1906). We may take it with Grässer, "Der Hebräerbrief 1938–1963," 156, and F. V. Filson, *"Yesterday": A Study of Hebrews in Light of Chapter 13* (Alec R. Allenson, Inc., 1967), that these doubts have not been substantiated. This of course does not preclude the possibility that in 13.20–21 the author makes use of liturgical material from the common tradition (cf. Michel, *An der Hebräer*, 534–41).
246 Arndt and Gingrich, *Greek-English Lexicon*, 512.
247 Deut 29.18.
248 *Supra*, Ch. 3, "The Nature of Defilement."

These three references to defilement, brief though they be, are all the more significant for the casual manner in which they are introduced by the author. Not only do they conform to the view of defilement as set out in Hebrews 9–10, but they serve to show that the idea of defilement is not a theologoumenon contrived by the author. If the defilement idea were no more than an accessory of an overriding interest in Jesus as high priest, we would expect to have finished with it after chapter 10.

Turning to the language of purgation, only one reference to καθαρίζειν occurs outside Hebrews 9–10. This is in the pregnant phrase at 1.3b—καθαρισμὸν τῶν ἁμαρτιῶν ποιησάμενος ("after he had made purgation of sins"). Our study of Hebrews 9–10 has shown how those chapters may rightly be considered to be an expansion of 1.3b. In view of that discussion, we may therefore see it as being cosmic in sweep: not only the "subjective" benefits of purification of συνείδησις and the gaining of access to deity, but also the "objective" benefits of purged heavenly things and an inaugurated heavenly cultus.[249] The thrust of 1.3 is precisely that of Hebrews 9–10: the purgation has been made with finality. Thus, Christ is pictured as being *seated* in heaven.

Two words closely related to the idea of καθαιρίζειν are also found: βαπτισμοί (lustrations) and ῥαντίζειν (to sprinkle). The first of these occurs at 6.2, where the author lists "teachings of lustrations" among the ABC's of the faith. It is a purely incidental reference, yet it finds its significance as part of the total view of the author toward ritual: obviously, he cannot be opposed to ritual per se, as some scholars have endeavored to show. We have already observed the occurrence of ῥαντίζειν in the discussion of the blood of Christ vis-à-vis the blood of Abel.[250]

In our investigation of purgation in Hebrews 9–10, we noticed that the general concept (of purgation) was given specificity by the author's use of two further terms: ἁγιάζειν (to separate, consecrate) and τελειοῦν (to "perfect," incorporate), with the latter standing as the *summum bonum*, as it were. How then are these terms employed elsewhere by the author?

Considering ἁγιάζειν first, we first take notice of 2.11. Here, Christ is the one who separates or consecrates, and his followers are those who are separated or consecrated. Without entering into the debate about the ἐξ ἑνὸς πάντες ("all of one"),[251] there is no question that the author in this context is

---

249 Héring, who is alert to the idea of an actual purgation of "heavenly things" in 9.23, also sees 1.3 as having a cosmic sense: "So we can straightaway underline that 'purification' is a much more radical and mysterious operation than the simple forgiveness of sins, which God could freely grant.... Are we to think not only of the sins of humanity but of those also of the angels?" (*Epistle to the Hebrews*, 6).

250 12.24.

251 That is, concerning the Gnostic origin of the ideas of Hebrews—one of the major concerns of Käsemann's *Das wandernde Gottesvolk*.

concerned to show a fundamental unity of Jesus and his people. It is in such a setting that the two uses of ἁγιάζειν become meaningful: they sharply indicate the idea of *cultic separation*, the idea of a community that seems oblivious to the rest of the world, which characterizes the whole document. This very idea is the point of the ἁγιασμός mentioned at 12.14: it is to be religiously pursued, for without it no one shall see God. The final occurrence of ἁγιάζειν is in 13.12, where, as we saw above, Christ's blood avails to consecrate, separate (that is, gain entree to the cult) the people (collective sense).

Τελειοῦν and cognates occurs ten times outside Hebrews 9–10. Four of these instances are manifestly to be understood as parallel to the understanding of τελειοῦν which was brought out in Hebrews 9–10. Indeed, these four occurrences are inextricably tied to those chapters, both as anticipation and response. The first two are from chapter 7[252] and argue that the old cultus could not bring τελειοῦν, a point that is fully demonstrated in the contrasts of Hebrews 9–10. The other two, however, have to do with the response to this argument: what then of the heroes of old? The reply is given: they could not attain to τελείωσις without us, but now the heavenly cultus does include them.[253] Four other references link τελειοῦν directly to Jesus. The author is concerned to establish the idea of progress, maturing, or preparation for the office of high priest in the life of the person of Jesus. In 2.10 and 5.9, this "perfecting" of Jesus is linked to his suffering.[254] Clearly, the use of τελειοῦν with reference to Christ is not precisely parallel to the way in which it denotes his benefits to the believers. For him, it indicates the attainment of the office of high priest of the heavenly cultus;[255] for them, the incorporation into that cultus. Thus, we may only bring these together if we give to τελειοῦν the general significance of "consummation." Such a general sense must be understood in 12.2 where Christ is called the τὸν τῆς πίστεως ἀρχηγὸν καὶ τελειωτήν—the pioneer and consummator of faith, since the accent in this context is on the *future* rather than the present. This is almost certainly true of the other two references to τελειοῦν. When the author says, "Solid food is for the τελείων,"[256] there is patently no concern with the heavenly cultus in view, and the τελείων are

---

252 7.11, 18.
253 11.40; 12.18–24.
254 Just as a bland equation of "blood" and "death" fails to catch the author's meaning, so we should beware of regarding πάσχειν in Hebrews as a euphemism for death—even though at 2.9 (explicitly) and 9.26; 13.12 (implicitly) the sufferings of Jesus are linked to his death. The remarks of W. Michaelis concerning πάσχειν in Hebrews (*TDNT*, V, 916–18) require modification—he makes πάσχειν equal death.
255 A point clearly made in the summation of the argument of Hebrews 7: Jesus as high priest is εἰς τὸν αἰῶνα τετελειωμένον.
256 5.14.

apparently the "spiritually mature." Likewise, the τελειότητα which they are to consider are, in contrast to the ABC's, the things for those who are mature.[257]

We may now summarize our findings concerning blood, defilement, and purgation in portions of Hebrews apart from the ninth and tenth chapters. First, while these motifs do not occur prominently and nowhere dominate the course of the argument as they do in Hebrews 9–10, yet they are not entirely absent and sometimes are introduced most unexpectedly in non-cultic settings. That is, the data suggest that these motifs are deeply rooted in the author's understanding of religion. Of the three, it is indisputably blood which is most in evidence. Second, there is a very close conformity of the views of blood, defilement, and purgation to those in Hebrews 9–10. Blood again appears as a positive, powerful, medium of life, with the view from Hebrews 9–10 being heightened by showing blood as apotropaic, as "speaking," and as raising Christ from the dead. Defilement again appears as a blot or stain which contaminates the community. With regard to purgation, the author's definitive vocabulary of ἁγιάζειν and τελειοῦν likewise is used to indicate respectively entry into the cult and the full incorporation into the heavenly cultus. Τελειοῦν, however, is shown to be a term of much wider application by the *auctor ad Hebraeos*. Its general thrust is that of consummation, maturity, or fulness: thus, it designates Christ's attaining to his heavenly office as well as the attaining of the believers to the heavenly cultus (incorporation) which is its sense in Hebrews 9–10.

Conclusion

Our discussion of the ideas of blood, defilement, and purgation in Hebrews, especially as these have entered in the argumentation of the ninth and tenth chapters, has led to the following general conclusions.

First, while blood, defilement, and purgation form the very undergirding of Hebrews 9–10, they are by no means confined to these chapters. Elsewhere they come to expression in such an unreflective manner as to suggest that these ideas were deeply rooted in the religious consciousness of the author.

Second, the patterns of blood, defilement, and purgation in Hebrews show remarkably close agreement with those already noticed from religion in general. Indeed, the study of the "structures" from phenomenology of religion alerts the student of Hebrews to similar ideas in his letter. By this means, the cultic argumentation of Hebrews 9–10, which long has been obscure, is considerably illumined. It becomes apparent that the *auctor ad Hebraeos*,

---

257 6.1.

at least in this passage, conceives of humanity's basic "problem" as defilement—a problem to which the only satisfactory "solution" is purgation. It is blood which appears as the medium to effect the passage from the one state to the other. Furthermore, the argument of Hebrews in these chapters points to an anthropology in which humanity finds itself inseparably bound up with the life of the community and the cultus, and in which cultus and cosmos are interdependent—a view which also conforms to the general "structures" previously noticed.

Third, while the general "structures" thus illumine the argument of Hebrews 9–10 by showing the points of indubitable correspondence, at the same time they indicate the particularity of Hebrews by the points of divergence. The most striking of these is in the affirmation of Hebrews that the cycle defilement-purgation-defilement may be broken. The author of Hebrews is vividly aware of this oscillatory pattern in the religious experience of humanity, but the theme to which he constantly returns is that the means for its cessation are available. This leads to the second point of divergence: the author puts forward a particular blood, once applied, as the medium par excellence—the blood of Christ. Finally, whereas in the general "structures" blood is an ambivalent agent which may bring about either purgation or defilement, in Hebrews blood—with one possible exception—is set forth as *the* positive life-imparting potency.

Fourth, these considerations shed considerable light on the cultic axioms which underlie the argumentation of Hebrews 9–10. Of these, 9.22b is to be considered the foundation, and is to be understood in terms of the application of blood to bring about decisive purgation. Likewise, the statements of 9.13–14 and 10.4 are to be seen as setting forth the relative efficacy of two means of purgation: animal blood and Christ's blood. Again, the "necessity" of the purgation of the "heavenly things" at 9.23 derives from the understanding of defilement as "contagious" and the view of an interlocking of the earthly and the heavenly cultus; however, the full treatment of this problem calls for a study of the cosmology of Hebrews beyond the scope of this study.

Fifth, we cannot here review all the insights concerning particular verses in the argumentation of Hebrews 9–10. We may state, however, our finding that our methodology has enabled us to discern a masterly, coherent development of thought whose internal logic plays upon the religious ideas of defilement, blood, and purgation. While in some statements it may be possible to discern evidence of chiastic structure, the overall plan is not to be subsumed under such "external" types of structuring. Rather, the plan is developed on the basis of the internal logic springing from the cultic presuppositions. It should be added that in one place (the discussion of διαθήκη and death), the author appears to have momentarily turned aside from the mainstream of his argument: at least to this extent is his development flawed.

Finally, it is now possible to state our position concerning the fundamental issues of interpretation of Hebrews 9–10 as they were brought to light in the second chapter above. These issues, we are convinced, can only be rightly dealt with if the language of Hebrews 9–10 is discerned in its full force as *religious*. Thus, the balancing of continuity/discontinuity is at the level of cultic axioms: these axioms, especially the "blood rule," provide the underlying base for comparison, while the new thing come in Christ (his blood) furnishes the factor of discontinuity within the underlying continuity. Again, to talk of "literal" or "spiritualized" blood is to introduce categories which are foreign to the religious understanding that is operative. Thus, Hebrews 9–10 is seen as a continuous piece of developing argument, entirely comprehensible from its own point of view. That is, no fundamental tension between the manner of argumentation of the two chapters is to be posited, even as we would be altogether in error in suggesting dichotomies such as cultic/moral, body/spirit, or external/internal. Finally, the understanding of the argument of the passage cannot be advanced further by means of the *religionsgeschichtliche* approach; only as the exegete learns from phenomenology of religion to come to the cultic language with the appropriate preparation is progress in discerning the author's reasoning possible.

A case could be made for concluding our study at this point. We have been able to suggest a methodology which has, we feel, proved itself by greatly illuminating an extremely obscure portion of the New Testament. Yet to stop here would be to leave many questions unanswered. While we have succeeded in opening up two chapters of Hebrews, this very elucidation has itself disclosed new problems as to the relation of these chapters to the overall book. These problems are primarily anthropological and can be comprehended under the following question: Why does Hebrews 9.1–10.18 set forth its anthropology only in terms of defilement-purgation? We noticed above that there are occasional suggestions of such an anthropology elsewhere in Hebrews, but it must be acknowledged that it nowhere comes to prominence as in the ninth and tenth chapters. Indeed, the "problem" elsewhere seems to be clearly in terms of unfaithfulness, with endurance as the appropriate solution. Is there then a basic tension in the anthropology of Hebrews? Or is it possible to show a manner by which the two anthropologies form a consistent whole? This must be our concern in the next chapter of this study.

CHAPTER 5

CULTUS AND PARENESES—DEFILEMENT
AND PURGATION IN RELATION TO THE
TOTAL ARGUMENT OF HEBREWS

In this chapter we attempt to stand back, as it were, and see the book of Hebrews as a whole. The immediate grounds for such an undertaking became apparent in the work of the previous chapter: here we found that the ideas of defilement and purgation were almost wholly confined to the ninth and tenth chapters of Hebrews. In this they were in sharp contrast to the parenetic sections of the letter, where unfaithfulness is the great threat; thus, there is obvious need to attempt to account for this apparent tension in anthropology. Beyond this specific and immediate problem, however, our efforts here must ultimately be directed toward a larger purpose—the relating of defilement and purgation to the total argument of Hebrews. We have been able to demonstrate the deep significance of these motifs for one section of the writing, but how is the integration of this set of results into the whole—so that the argument stands out *in toto*—to be achieved? This, we hope, will be the final thrust of our investigation in this study.

It is unnecessary for us to deal at length with humanity's "problem" and its "solution" in the pareneses of Hebrews. A series of Protestant scholars, among which Käsemann[1] and Grässer[2] are the most significant, have devoted careful study to these matters. It will suffice to lay out briefly the chief textual data.

In the first parenetic passage (2.1–4), the danger facing the readers is specified by the verbs παραρρεῖν and ἀμελεῖν. The former is a nautical metaphor meaning "to flow by, slip away, be washed away, drift away";[3] the latter signifies "to neglect, be unconcerned about, disregard."[4] It is obvious that

---
[1] *Das wandernde Gottesvolk.*
[2] *Der Glaube in Hebräerbrief.*
[3] Arndt and Gingrich, *Greek-English Lexicon,* 627.
[4] Ibid., 44.

the "problem" to be avoided appears in this passage as a *gradual* falling away rather than a deliberate act of severance from the community. The second parenetic section (3.1–4.11) both underlines and modifies this idea. On the one hand, the *auctor ad Hebraeos* repeatedly warns against the danger of σκληρύνειν[5]—the "hardening" of the heart due to the ἀπάτη (deceitfulness, or pleasures) of sin.[6] Such a heart—an evil, unfaithful heart—leads to the ἀποστῆναι, falling away from the community, just as the wilderness generation perished in the desert. On the other hand, a more "active" type of danger is presented, one that comes to focus in ἀπειθεῖν (to disobey)[7] and παραπικραίνειν (to rebel).[8] That is, we see here that the danger threatening the community is that they may fall away from the realization of the promised inheritance under the influence of an unbelieving, unfaithful heart which may or may not be manifested in overt disobedience. A third parenesis (5.11–6.20) maintains this distinction. The readers are rebuked for having become "dull of hearing" and are reminded that the blessings of God turn to curse if no "fruit" is forthcoming. Yet at the same time we have presented a vivid picture of open rejection of the religious values of the community: the apostates (παραπίπτειν)[9] crucify on their own account the Son of God (ἀνασταυροῦν)[10] and expose him to contempt (παραδειγματίζειν).[11] We find the same sort of divide in the fourth section (10.19–39), which we already have noticed: first, the danger of "wavering," of neglecting the assembly, of forgetting the "former days" of Christian steadfastness, of "casting away" (ἀποβάλλειν) confidence, of lacking ὑπομονή (endurance), of ὑποστολή (shrinking back); second, the possibility of sin done ἑκουσίως (deliberately), when the Son of God is spurned, the covenant blood profaned, the Spirit outraged. In the final two chapters of the letter we may again discern this differentiation of "gradual" and "radical" unfaithfulness. Thus, the danger is that the Christians will grow "weary" (κάμνειν)[12] or "lose heart" (ἐκλύεσθαι),[13] that under the hardships of Christian life they may drop out, that they may neglect to show hospitality or to remember their fellows, that they may fall into idolatry, immorality, the love of money, or the snare of false teachings. But at the same time, the ex-

---

5 Ibid., 763.
6 Ibid., 81.
7 Ibid., 82.
8 Ibid., 626.
9 Ibid.
10 Ibid., 60.
11 Ibid., 619.
12 Ibid., 403 (12.3).
13 Ibid., 242 (12.3, 5).

ample of Esau is introduced: he was βέβηλος (profane, godless, irreligious),[14] so that at length he found no way to recover the inheritance; in the same way, the peril of παραιτεῖσθαι (to reject, refuse)[15] is always a fearsome possibility for Christians.

These data lead us to two observations. The first concerns the shift in temporal focus (over that of chapters 9–10) which is evident. Whereas the schema of defilement/purgation is concerned with the "now" time as it has been made vibrant by the work of Christ in the past (that is, past → now), the pareneses are principally concerned with the "now" time as it may come to expression in the *future* (now → future). The very fact of *now* belonging to the community which is destined to inherit the promises is no *guarantee* of actually attaining to that inheritance. The second observation has to do with the ways in which the inheritance may be lost. The general problem is unfaithfulness, a falling away from the community. It is the community that is to receive the promise, so he who leaves it is without hope. Such apostasy, however, may come about in one of two ways: either a "weariness" may lead to a gradual drifting away from the community, or the inroads of sin in the heart may result in deliberate, overt rejection of the religious values of the group.

We find these observations confirmed if we examine the "solution" which is held out by the author in the above passages. The great need is for προσέχειν (to pay attention, give head to, be alert),[16] κατέχειν (holding fast),[17] κρατεῖν (grasp, hold fast),[18] σπουδή (earnestness),[19] κατανοεῖν (to consider),[20] παρακαλεῖν (to exhort),[21] ἀναμιμνήσκειν (to recall),[22] and ὑπομονή (endurance, patience).[23] The great word, however, is πίστις: faithfulness. It was πίστις which characterized the life of Jesus, as of Moses; it was lack of πίστις which led to the failure of the promise to the wilderness generation.[24] The famous eleventh chapter is built around this word: by their πίστις the heroes of old overcame all physical hardships and conquered all temptations. Even so will the readers of the letter attain to the goal: instead of being νωθροί ("sluggish"),[25]

---

14 Ibid., 138 (12.16).
15 Ibid., 621–22 (12.19, 25).
16 Ibid., 721 (2.1).
17 Ibid., 423–24 (3.6, 14; 10.23).
18 Ibid., 449–50 (4.14; 6.18).
19 Ibid., 77 (6.11; 4.11).
20 Ibid., 416 (3.1).
21 Ibid., 622–23 (3.13; 10.15; 13.19, 22).
22 Ibid., 57 (10.32).
23 Ibid., 854 (10.36; 12.1).
24 3.2; 4.12.
25 Arndt and Gingrich, *Greek-English Lexicon*, 549.

they are to be "imitators of those who through faith (πίστις) and patience (μακροθυμία) inherit the promises."[26]

But what part do the ideas of defilement and purgation have in this? And what of αἷμα, so dominant in the argument and so powerful a medium as it came to expression in Hebrews 9–10? Our investigations in the previous chapter showed that all these motifs sink into relative insignificance in the pareneses. Purgation per se is not found; defilement occurs sporadically and unreflectively; only αἷμα retains any degree of force. Yet the usage of αἷμα itself is striking: it occurs in the past ⟶ now framework rather than in the now ⟶ future schema of which humanity's "problem" in the pareneses forms part.[27] That is, outside chapters 9–10, "blood" is pointed to as that which has effected the incorporation *into* the community (as in chapters 9–10), but not as that which is to prevent the possibility of apostasy.

As we attempt to see Hebrews holistically, then, we see as it were two "sets":

Set One: defilement/purgation; blood; past ⟶ Now
Set Two: apostasy/faithfulness; now ⟶ Future

The first "set" seems to come into play in the so-called "cultic" argumentation, and the second in the "parenetic" sections. Obviously, we must grapple with this complex picture to see whether the work as a whole carries its own internal logic wherein these two "sets" find satisfactory integration.

So far as we are aware, this difficulty of comprehension of Hebrews has not so far been tackled in the secondary literature—understandably, since before now the ideas of defilement and purgation have not been given their due place in the book.[28] We shall attempt a resolution of the problem by setting forth a series of possible explanations which might be suggested in the light of previous scholarly reflection on the letter as a whole. In each case, we shall point to the weaknesses of such "explanations." Finally, we shall offer our own way to a solution.

An Unconscious Tension in the Writer's Anthropology. According to this explanation, whenever the author thinks in cultic categories, he immediately has in view the defilement/purgation anthropology, whereas when he de-

---

26 6.12.
27 Cf. 11.28; 12.24; 13.11–12, 20.
28 Since the famous study by Käsemann, the danger of *unfaithfulness* has been seen as the leading "problem" addressed by the writer. Where the defilement-purgation syndrome has been sighted, it has not been taken seriously or integrated with the "unfaithfulness" motif (cf. Spicq, *L'Épître aux Hébreux*, I, 284–87).

parts from cultic categories he unconsciously moves to an apostasy/faithfulness schema.

Manifestly, such an explanation must always be given as a distinct possibility. But its very strength is also its weakness: just as we have no way of proving it to be false, so we have no way of showing it to be correct. Certainly, we are not about to embark upon the psychoanalysis of our long-departed author! Indeed, this solution can only commend itself if all other efforts come to a *cul-de-sac*.

It seems to us, furthermore, that the explanation itself is open to searching strictures. For a start, an absolute separation of anthropologies cannot be maintained: we noticed in the last chapter that the defilement motif does occur (admittedly, in very fragmentary and unreflective fashion) outside strictly cultic passages.[29] More significantly, the whole endeavor of dividing material as to "cultic" or "non-cultic" is to be called into serious question. The people are not merely a "wandering" community—they are the new *people of* God, as Oepke[30] has demonstrated. That is, as Spicq[31] recognized, the community is throughout a cultic community. It is the cult that constitutes the community: it has no identity apart from it. So, the so-called "parenetic" sections of Hebrews must always be seen as admonitions to the cultic people. In this light, the "explanation" as we set it out above is patently inadequate; however, the possibility of an unconscious tension in the writer's anthropology, connected in some way as to whether his purpose is argumentative or hortatory, must still be granted.

The Defilement/Purgation Anthropology is Not to be Taken Seriously. Thus, the anthropological tension is dissolved. This explanation, in fact, is the one taken by almost all students of Hebrews. For most of them, the step was an unknowing one: we noticed in the second chapter of our study how often the language of defilement and purgation is assimilated to extraneous categories such as "atonement," "forgiveness," and "righteousness." Occasionally, however, the step is explicitly acknowledged. Here it is held that the defilement/purgation categories are merely dictated by the author's employment of the motifs of temple and high priest, the implication being that defilement and purgation are not in themselves of any consequence to the author.[32]

If the work of this study in the first four chapters is to be accorded any weight, it will be obvious that this explanation cannot be allowed. We have

---

29 *Supra*, p. 166.
30 Albrecht Oepke, *Das neue Gottesvolk in Schriftum, Schauspiel, bildender Kunst und Weltgestaltung* (C. Bertelesmann, 1950), 57–73.
31 *L'Épître aux Hébreux*.
32 E.g., *Wenschkewitz, Der Spiritualisierung der Kultusbegriffe*, 131–49.

shown that it is only as these ideas are given their due place that some of the most difficult argumentation of the letter reveals its internal logic. Indeed, we would hold that the programmatic statement of 1.3b *demands* that we afford full valence to the categories of defilement and purgation. The readiness of exegetes to pass off these ideas is understandable: they appear remote, non-theological; yet, as we have seen, the phenomenology of religion opens them to us as tapping primordial springs in human experience.

We shall take up later the question of the interaction of christology and anthropology. Here we need only to note our response to the suggestion that the high-priestly christology has dictated the anthropology. Even if we grant this, it must be understood that anthropology is amenable to the writer's purpose. His purpose, as is commonly held, is pastoral:[33] he is not so much concerned to give a disquisition on christology as he is to counteract certain tendencies of which he is aware in the life of his readers. That is, we cannot be justified in lightly dismissing any portion of his anthropology.

And finally, we would pose this question: what if, in fact, the relation between christology and anthropology is just the reverse of the above premise—that is, that the view of man as defiled and in need of purgation has given rise to the high-priestly christology? It seems to me that the case is at least as good for this possibility, although a final answer is probably impossible to attain. In any event, it has become clear that the glib setting aside of the defilement/purgation anthropology as unessential in the writer's purpose is a grave error.

Anthropological Tension Corresponds to Religious/Theological Tension. That is, the defilement/purgation anthropology derives from viewing humanity phenomenologically, but the apostasy/faithfulness anthropology comes from a specifically theological viewpoint.

We introduce this explanation, not because we feel it has much to commend it, but because it may be suggested from the methodology we have adopted in this study. It may be useful, however, for bringing to full clarity the relation of phenomenology of religion to theology—a clarity now possible in view of our exegesis of Hebrews 9–10.

We have employed phenomenology of religion as another useful methodology alongside established historical-critical methods. It has enabled us to see the statement "Humanity is defiled" as first of all *religious* in character. It has taught us to attempt to "enter in" to the existential depths of the "experience" to which the statement points—not to dismiss it out of hand. It has shown us that such experience of defilement in fact is not a strange thing in

---

33 E.g., Grässer, "Der Hebräerbrief 1938–1963," 197–204.

the religious life of people, but rather is primordial in character and follows well-defined "patterns" or "structures." Thus, when the *auctor ad Hebraeos* begins to speak of Christ's work as a purgation of sins, when he belabors the failure of the old cultus to deal decisively with defilement, we are ready to "hear" his argument.

But it would be a misunderstanding to oppose phenomenology of religion to theology. The relationship between the two disciplines is not one of tension but of cooperation, as Tillich has suggested: phenomenology of religion enables the theologian to see his work in a particular tradition against the backdrop of universal religious experience.[34] Thus, we hold that our exegesis of Hebrews 9-10, employing insights from phenomenology of religion, enabled us to *understand* the faith there expressed—that is, phenomenology of religion aided the theological task.

What then of the distinction between "religious" and "theological" language which was made at the beginning of this study—does this resolve the anthropological tension? It cannot. Even if we were to take the extremely dubious step of labeling the pareneses as "theological" in contrast to the cultus as "religious," and thereby suggest that the anthropology of the pareneses manifests more advanced reflection on the human condition than the cultus, the tension remains. Defilement and unfaithfulness do not vary in *degree*: they are different categories.

It is obvious, then, that the tension in anthropology in Hebrews is not something "artificial"—that is, it is not the byproduct of a particular methodology. Our approach has merely served to highlight a tension already there.

Anthropological Tension Follows Christological Tension. It is possible to argue that Hebrews lays out its christology in terms of two distinct categories. On the one hand, there is the high-priestly christology, in which Jesus is set forth as the high priest and sacrifice of the heavenly sanctuary. His work in this frame of reference is to inaugurate the real temple by providing purgation for sins. On the other, there is the not infrequent motif of Jesus as the pioneer or trailblazer, whose work is to provide an example in faithfulness for his "brothers."[35] This is a motif which comes to expression in the words ἀρχηγός (leader, ruler, originator, founder)[36] and πρόδρομος (forerunner).[37] Thus, the anthropological tension would be a direct correlate of this christological

---

34 Paul Tillich, "The Significance of the History of Religions for the Systematic Theologian," *The History of Religions: Essays on the Problem of Understanding*, ed. Joseph M. Kitagawa, Mircea Eliade, and Charles H. Long (University of Chicago Press, 1967), 241-55.
35 2.9-16; 3.1-6; 4.14-16; 5.7-9; 6.20 10.19-20; 12.1-3, 13.12-13.
36 Arndt and Gingrich, *Greek-English Lexicon*, 112 (2.10; 12.2).
37 Ibid., 711 (6.20).

cleft: where the high-priestly work is in view, humanity's "problem" is seen as defilement; where the ἀρχηγός christology is to the fore, the danger is unfaithfulness.

Such an explanation is altogether superficial. It would merely attempt a solution by raising a further problem. In fact, the supposed christological tension cannot be maintained. The ἀρχηγός christology functions as *a part* of the high-priestly christology, since the way which Jesus opens is the way into the heavenly sanctuary. That is, it is *as* ἀρχιερεύς that Jesus is ἀρχηγός.[38] The argument of the ninth and tenth chapters of Hebrews, with its stress on access, clearly establishes this point. Thus, as high priest Jesus can both bring cleansing of sin and provide an example to his followers.

We conclude, therefore, that the christology of Hebrews cannot supply us with satisfactory grounds for the anthropological tension which the work manifests. The christology is indeed presented in two strands, but the author has succeeded in making the high-priestly motif the unifying idea. But that this priestly motif is able to reconcile the tension between defilement/purgation and unfaithfulness/faithfulness is not at all obvious.

Anthropological Tension Corresponds to Eschatological Tension. The eschatology of Hebrews has long been a matter of scholarly studies, among which that of Barrett[39] must be accorded most prominence.[40] Barrett demonstrated the affinities of that eschatology with apocalyptic and showed how the "now-not yet" tension so characteristic of earliest Christianity is subtly modified by the *auctor ad Hebraeos* by his intersection of temporal with spatial categories. Thus, the "not yet," once rooted in the certainty of the παρουσία, becomes grounded in the assurance of a heavenly sanctuary and liturgy. But this by no means signifies the rejection of the Parousia; rather, as Barrett argues, the contrary: the future is now guaranteed by the existence of the "real," invisible world.[41]

It is obvious that this conception of eschatology closely parallels the anthropological ideas of Hebrews. As we saw earlier, the defilement/purgation anthropology focuses on the "now" time (past ⟶ now), while the apos-

---

38 Shown especially in 2.5–18, where the two ideas are merged. The point we make here (the integration of the ἀρχηγος christology in the high-priestly christology) is not at all new; cf. Spicq, *L'Épître aux Hébreux*, I, 300–1, for instance.

39 C.K. Barrett, "The Eschatology of the Epistle to the Hebrews," *The Background of the New Testament and Its Eschatology*, ed. W. D. Davies and D. Daube (Cambridge University Press, 1956), 363–93.

40 Klappert's *Die Eschatologie des Hebräerbriefs* is useful in placing Barrett's treatment alongside alternative views of the eschatology of the letter; the force of Barrett's work remains, however, in our view.

41 Barrett, "The Eschatology of the Epistle to the Hebrews," 373–86.

tasy/faithfulness anthropology focuses on the "not yet" (now ⟶ FUTURE). The *now* is the time of purgation realized, of access to the heavenly cultus attained, of the decisive answer to the previously unending problem of defilement. But the "now" is also the time of the *not yet*—the best, called σωτηρία by the author[42]—is yet to be: when humanity shall see God.[43] Since the "now" is at once the "not yet," the danger looms of failing to attain to that beatific vision, as one grows weary in the way or is beguiled by sin to a radical break with the people of God.

True, the "not yet" lacks specificity in the author's treatment. On the one hand, there is the strongly underlined motif of journeying, of progress toward the "city," the "better country."[44] We wonder whether that goal is to be attained by death or by the παρουσία. For, on the other hand, the writer clearly holds to the near prospect of the Parousia.[45] Yet nowhere does he explicitly link that Parousia with the wandering motif, so we are left in doubt and it would be unwarranted to strain for his intent. His point concerning the "not yet," however, is quite clear: though there is a waiting time, the future is absolutely certain.

Clearly, then, the eschatological viewpoint of Hebrews serves to illumine its anthropological tension. But just as clearly it fails to give a wholly satisfactory explanation of the problem. Why is it, we ask, that only here in the New Testament do we find such an anthropological cleft? After all, the "now-not yet" eschatology occurs in other writings: why has it not issued elsewhere in terms of defilement/purgation and apostasy/faithfulness? And within the book of Hebrews itself, we have not really shown the integration of these two anthropologies when we have been able to show that they reflect the tension in eschatology. Why, for instance, is blood all important in one but absent in the other? And how is it that ideas of defilement do show up, albeit sporadically, in terms of the "not yet?"

We must press beyond eschatology in an endeavor to find an answer to these questions. But it seems apparent that any final answer will rest at least in part on the perspectives which the eschatological framework has supplied.

The explanations suggested above in terms of christology and eschatology point the way to what we consider to be a convincing resolution of the anthropological tension of Hebrews. The attempt to relate that tension to a christological tension was patently inadequate, while the juxtaposing with the eschatological "now-not yet" also left many questions unanswered. But

---

42 1.14; 2.3, 10; 5.9; 6.9; 9.28. "Salvation" as future is clearly indicated by 1.14 ("those who are to obtain salvation") and 9.28 (Christ appears the second time for salvation).

43 12.14: without holiness, no one will "see God."

44 3.1–4.11 (journeying to "Canaan"); 11.10, 13, 16; 13.14 (the city); 11.14–16 (country).

45 9.28; 10.37–38—"yet a little while."

with both these efforts it was apparent that some measure of correspondence could be discerned. When we recall that Hebrews is such a tightly woven piece of work that christology, soteriology, eschatology, and ecclesiology inexorably flow together and interact, we realize that we must attempt a holistic approach, an overview of the book, if we are to resolve the problem of its anthropology. By concentrating upon only the christology, eschatology, or ecclesiology, we cannot find the integrative principle that we seek.

We are in this manner led to seek out, if possible, the dominant conception of the book in which all other aspects find their focus. And, as we found that the ninth and tenth chapters of Hebrews could be made to yield splendid sense when viewed as functioning as a *religious* text, so we look first of all to the ruling *religious* conception of the book. Immediately we encounter an idea long since worked over by scholars, but one that comes with startling newness when seen in its full force as religious—the motif of pilgrimage. Thus, we come to our final "explanation."

Anthropological Tension in View of Pilgrimage as a Religious "Structure." Since Käsemann's classic study of the wandering motif of Hebrews, it has not been uncommon for writers to refer to the language of pilgrimage in discussion of the letter.[46] "Pilgrimage," however, has been used uncritically: no one has endeavored to probe it in its religious depths. We shall see that this motif, often so lightly taken up, in fact may be opened to reveal great richness when we bring to the task the insights of phenomenology of religion.

In our discussion of pilgrimage, we intend to use the term in the specific sense designated by phenomenology of religion. The work of Partin[47] is of great help in this regard. His careful study of the Muslim *hajj* issued in a full-blown exposition of pilgrimage as a religious "structure." He found four essential elements in this "structure": (1) Pilgrimage entails a separation, a leaving home. Thus, it is not uncommon for the departure for pilgrimage to resemble funerary rites. In any event, it is clear that one does not merely begin his pilgrimage without the appropriate ceremony which designates his separation from home and usual activity. (2) Pilgrimage involves a journey to a sacred *place*. That is, we cannot designate the mere act of religious wandering, such as that of the *bhikkus* in the ear-

---

46 E.g., Spicq, *L'Epître aux Hébreux*, I, 243–46, and "L'Epître aux Hébreux. Apollos, Jean-Baptiste, les Hellénistes et Qumrân," *RQ*, I (1959), 365–90. Spicq argues that "to the Hebrews" means "to the pilgrims." F. F. Bruce, *Epistle to the Hebrews*, likewise makes several references to "pilgrimage" (pp. 295, 304–6, 375). Cf. also H. Reissner, "'Wir haben heir keine bleibende Stadt, sondern die zukünftige suchen wir' (Heb 13.14). Erwägungen über das Wallfahren," *GL*, XXXV (1962), 96–103; and R. Obermüller, "Una mística del camino. El tema de la peregrinación en la carta a los Hebreos," *Rev B*, XXXIII (1971), 55–66.

47 Harry B. Partin, "The Muslim Pilgrimage: Journey to the Center" (unpublished Ph.D. dissertation, University of Chicago, 1967).

Cultus and Pareneses 183

ly Buddhist *sangha*, as pilgrimage. No; the pilgrim always has in mind a definite place to which his journeying is to lead. (3) Pilgrimage is made for a fixed *purpose*, such as purification or forgiveness of sins. The attainment of this purpose is linked to arrival at a sacred place. (4) Pilgrimage involves *hardship*. Physical difficulty and religious trial loom large; the threat of failure is always present.[48]

In view of Partin's account of pilgrimage, it becomes apparent that the generalized understandings of terms such as travel in distant lands, journey through life, and visits to historic sites[49] must be rigorously excluded. We are dealing with something that involves deep religious feelings, and which touches a primordial spring *in* humanity's being. Thus, going to church or making a visit to Canterbury could not be encompassed under the rubric of "pilgrimage" as a religious "structure."[50]

Furthermore, it becomes apparent that those writers who have referred to "pilgrimage" with regard to the book of Hebrews expressed far more than they intended. In fact, the ruling idea of the letter shows remarkable, point-for-point correspondence with the "structure" which Partin has disclosed—although Partin himself makes no mention of Hebrews. Let us quickly elaborate this correspondence.

The idea of having left home, of separation, of journeying is unquestionably strong throughout Hebrews. The author seems oblivious to what is going on outside the community: all that he has to say about the world is that it is *not* that of the people of God—the πατρίς they seek is a heavenly one.[51] That they have separated from what once they considered home is everywhere assumed and only occasionally referred to: they have been "washed" (baptized),[52] they *were* "enlightened,"[53] they endured a "hard struggle" after their joining the community.[54] Like the patriarchs of old, they have no place here which is really "home": they are strangers and exiles.[55]

But their journeying is not an aimless wandering—it will lead to a "city which has foundations, whose builder and maker is God."[56] That is, not a *Wan-*

---

48 Ibid., 145–52.
49 Cf. Gove, ed., *Webster's Third New International Dictionary*: "pilgrimage" includes "a trip taken to visit a place of historic or sentimental interest or to participate in a specific event for a definite purpose ... the course of life on earth ... a particular part of the life course of an individual ... a search for mental and spiritual values."
50 Going to church does not entail a separation or hardship, while a visit to Canterbury lacks the deep religious purpose as well as hardship.
51 11.16.
52 10.22 (cf. 6.2).
53 6.4.
54 10.32.
55 11.13.
56 11.10.

dern but a *Pilgerfahrt*. This is the "real" city, for it is invisible. It *is*, so it is therefore "to come." We have already noticed the difficulty in trying to decide when that "coming" will be (death? the Parousia?) but this problem cannot hide the force of the city as something *yet to be attained* in the writer's conception.

And it is not merely a city: it is *God's* city. It is worth pausing here to notice what Partin has said concerning the idea of a sacred place in pilgrimage. The place to which the pilgrims strive is *the* place: it is the center of the cosmos, the navel of the earth, the place which gives orientation to all other space; it is the point nearest to deity; it is thus *qualitatively* different from all other space.[57] While we have deliberately bypassed speculation concerning the cosmology of Hebrews in this study, the resemblances in Partin's description to the "sacred place" of the pilgrims of Hebrews cannot be overlooked. The city to which the Christians aspire is God's city: it is the city of the heavenly sanctuary where Jesus Christ is high priest at the right hand of the μεγαλωσύνη ἐν ὑψηλοῖς and where innumerable angels assemble in festal gathering.[58] It is, if we may be allowed the expression, the "*really* real," for the world in which Christians now journey has only temporary reality, being transient.

Likewise does the Christians' pilgrimage have a clear-cut purpose in view. The very fact of journeying signifies a dissatisfaction with that which is "home" to others; it points to a translation of values in which the "real"—the supreme value—is to be found only beyond the world. That is, the Christian pilgrims seek to attain to the real world where all is sacred. No matter that already they have been purged decisively by the blood of Christ, no matter that already they participate proleptically in the cultus of heaven—it is only by arrival at the sacred place par excellence that they will find "rest." And for the Christian, as for the Muslim, that "rest" finds its high point in the ultimate blessing—the beatific vision.[59]

But the way is a difficult one. Like the heroes of old, they face perils physical and spiritual. Sin beckons with its pleasures and is of deceitful power to erode faith and faithfulness. The way at times is a struggle; even martyrdom may mark its ascent.[60] So they may find themselves growing weary, being led astray by false teachings, or gradually falling back from the group in its onward progress. Worse yet, they may decide that the pilgrim way is not for them and by a deliberate act sever their connection with the pilgrim band.

---

57 Partin, "Pilgrimage," 166–75.

58 11.10, 16; 13.14; 1.3; 10.12; 12.22.

59 Partin, "Pilgrimage," 193–94, observes that the Muslim who has completed the *hajj* has the hope of seeing the face of God on the morning of the Resurrection. Cf. Heb 12.14.

60 3.12–18; 5.11–6.12; 10.23–26; 12.4.

For such a person there can be no hope. This difficulty of the way is not to cause surprise: indeed, it is *characteristic* of the way.

That the leading religious conception of Hebrews conforms precisely to pilgrimage as a religious "structure" seems to us incontestable. But we feel that, going beyond Partin's four characteristics, we may even further illumine this conception of Hebrews. In Partin's discussion of the *hajj*, two other points designating pilgrimage came clearly into focus: the ideas of imitation and community. He did not include these in his "structure" of pilgrimage, which inevitably must be quite general in form, because exceptions might quickly be raised. But these two characteristics of the *hajj* and certainly of pilgrimage in some other religions are to be discerned in Hebrews.

For the Muslim, the *hajj* is founded in the example of two prototypes—Abraham and Mohammed. In theory, the attempt is made to associate each station and act on the pilgrim's route with Abraham; in practice, it is the personal *hajj* of Mohammed in the last year of his life which has laid the pattern for subsequent generations of his followers.[61] Even so does Jesus Christ function as the pilgrim's prototype in Hebrews. He too endured great "hostility against himself," was tempted in every respect as the Christians and even came to the point of praying "with loud cries and tears."[62] But he was πιστός[63]— this was the key to his ultimate triumph, as he journeyed the path to the very presence of God. Thus, he is the true ἀρχηγός—the Pathfinder; and Christians who now desire to attain to that same place of reality to which he attained must follow in the way he has opened for them.

There is likewise a strong sense of *participation*, of *community*, associated with the *hajji*. The Muslim may leave his home as an individual, but the very pressure of religious ceremony cannot but dilute that individuality in favor of corporate religious devotion. This one goes, like scores of generations before him, at a prescribed time and place; dons the prescribed garment; unites with hundreds of thousands of likeminded devotees; performs the prescribed ceremonies; when they return, they have a new name—they are *hajji*.[64] I have witnessed a similar phenomenon in India. Partin was no doubt loathe to stress the community aspect of pilgrimage since in India it has often been the individual in his private search for God that has been stressed—such a person's path to Brahma is like that of a fish in the sea.[65] But we ought not

---

61 Partin, "Pilgrimage," 118, 129–39.
62 12.3; 4.15; 5.7.
63 3.2, 6.
64 Partin, "Pilgrimage," 40.
65 That is, it leaves no trace: "As the birds fly in the air, as the fish swim in the sea, leaving no traces behind, even so is the pathway to God traversed by the seeker of spirit." Quoted by S.

to forget the great Hindu *melas* which draw the thousands and the millions for the cleansing plunge at the sacred place and sacred time. Creaking and groaning, torsos bursting from open windows, the pilgrim buses creep up the mountain; belching black smoke, jammed with sweating bodies, the pilgrim trains crawl across the landscape; and, at the holy moment, the rush to the water! Even so does the individual per se not come into view in the book of Hebrews. Only one individual, Jesus Christ, has opened the way; it is now as a *community* of pilgrims that his followers are to reach that holy place which he has first attained.

In his concluding discussion of pilgrimage as a religious phenomenon, Partin argues that the practice *in toto* is to be viewed as a *rite de passage*—that is, a religious transition from the profane to the sacred.[66] He shows that the three stages made famous by van Gennep[67]—separation, transition, and incorporation—may be applied to pilgrimage: the first indicates those rites of leave-taking, of cutting oneself off from what once was home, to which we have already referred; the second, those rites along the way, obligatory for the pilgrim community; the third, those rites at the sacred place itself.

So too is the ruling idea of pilgrimage in the book of Hebrews to be understood in view of these three states. We feel that they clearly parallel the eschatological pattern of the work. Let us set out the plan diagrammatically:

THEN (past)   separation (baptism, persecution)
NOW (present)   transition (journeying, proleptic incorporation)
NOT YET (future)   incorporation (attainment of the city; see God)

The past comes into view as the time when Jesus made his ἐφάπαξ offering, which gave rise to the community: those who chose to separate from this world as their home and to follow his path to the real, invisible world. The "now" time is the time of purgation realized, of proleptic incorporation into the heavenly cultus; but still the time of waiting, of journeying, of continued progress along the path laid down by the prototype. The "not yet" points to that moment, assured by the existence of the heavenly order, when the pilgrims will arrive at the new Jerusalem, take their place among the heavenly hosts, and see God.

In these ideas of Jesus as prototype, of community, and of the three stages of a *rite de passage*, we are now able to see how the one ruling religious idea

---

Radhakrishnan, *The Hindu View of Life* (George Allen & Unwin Ltd., 1961), 58.
  66 Partin, "Pilgrimage," 155–66.
  67 See his *Rites of Passage, passim.*

of pilgrimage in Hebrews embraces christology, ecclesiology, and eschatology. And with that it has become apparent why an attempt to resolve the anthropological tension by focusing on merely one of these aspects of the ruling idea could not be successful.

We now see how the *auctor ad Hebraeos* is able to hold together the defilement/purgation anthropology with the apostasy/faithfulness anthropology. The first derives from his view of Christianity as a cultic community, the second from the fact that this cultic community is *on the march*, that is, a pilgrim community. The latter embraces the former—pilgrim community at once signifies cultic community; but cultic community would not necessarily signify pilgrim community. It will be helpful to elaborate these two aspects deriving from pilgrimage: *cultic* community and *moving* cultic community.

Because the Christian group is on a pilgrimage, it is a *separated* community. In a profane world, it is "holy," so that this world can no longer be considered its home. It has taken its leave of the profane by the washing of baptism and started out on the journey to the "real" world where all is holy. Precisely because of this dichotomy of sacred and profane, the anthropology which comes to focus in this act of separation, of transition from the world to the sacred community is that of defilement/purgation. Humanity is defiled: this is the basic anthropology, reducible to no other category, as perceived by the author of our document. *How* or *when* humanity became defiled does not concern him; his focus is on humanity as they *are*. Or rather, as they *were* before they joined the community of the separated ones. The world is the world of κοινοῦν: "defiled" signifying both its state of disorder, death, and negative power as well as its absolute disjunction from the state of the "holy." This is the world to which the pilgrims once belonged. It is a world in which humanity is conscious of their defilement through a numinous unease which continually reminds them that what they *are* is in some way not what they *might* be and indeed *ought* to be; thus, they are drawn to the primal time when the "ought" was the "is" or to future time when the primal bliss will again be realized. In that world, all their efforts toward purgation are at best fragmentary and ephemeral. But, for the pilgrim, that is the world of the "then," a world from which they are now utterly separated religiously. The blood of Christ has availed to purge away with thoroughness and finality their "problem" of defilement. Through this act of Christ they belong to the community of the purged, separated from the world.

This community of the separated ones belongs to the new order introduced by the blood of Christ. Just as humanity's defilement on earth was cosmic in its effects, so that even the heavenly things themselves must be purged by the work of Christ, so the participation of the separated ones reaches beyond the confines of the world in which they still physically stand to the very heavenly cultus itself. Since they are a separated, a "holy" people, they no longer "belong" to the profane world but to the sacred order. The actual attainment of that order is yet to be; but already they participate proleptically in its worship.

This is why the defilement/purgation anthropology comes to focus in the past (in the blood of Christ which brought about purgation and enabled the crossing of the threshold into the community) and in the present (in the proleptic participation in the heavenly cultus which is the privilege of the purified ones).

What then of the author's occasional references to the possibility of defilement for the members of the community? These unreflective remarks seem to us to accord splendidly with the nature of defilement as our focus in this study has revealed it. Defilement appears as a contagion, a blot which comes *upon* humanity, rather than something which is deliberately chosen. To update the language, it is a "fall-out": before the clean person is aware of it, they have become dirty. And that is an ever-present possibility for the pilgrims: they may "belong" religiously to the heavenly order, but physically they are in the worldly order. We may take up again the illustration of disease: as we noticed, defilement not only may bring about physical sickness but is itself like an infection. Even so, one may *become* infected, since we live in a world where infections abound. But normally we would not expect someone to deliberately *choose* to be infected. Even so may the infection of defilement come upon the members of the pilgrim community of Hebrews. If it does, it is likely to spread quickly. But presumably (the author does not tell us specifically) the blood of Christ which first availed to bring about their transition from the profane to the separated ones will still be efficacious to purge this partial defilement *within* the community.

Very different, however, is the author's thinking in terms of apostasy and faithfulness. The apostate is one who, as it were, has *chosen* to be reinfected by the defilement of the old way. They have given up on the pilgrimage, lapsed into the realm of the profane. They no longer "belong" to the heavenly order because they have, through neglect or through rejection of the religious values of the community, become part of the order of the κοινοῦν. We may say that they have sought to deny their being as a religious person: they have collapsed the sacred into the profane. For such a person, the blood of Christ, which once had separated them from the world, is itself κοινός;[68] thus, they

---

[68] Cf. 10.29.

crucify Christ to themselves, holding him up to contempt by their fellows in the worldly order.

To speak of such a one merely as "defiled" would fail to bring out the radical nature of their offence as viewed by the author in terms of the pilgrim community. True, they are defiled—but so are the rest of the people in the profane world. Theirs is the case of the ultimate degree of defilement, the permanent "non-person" who must remain forever cut off from the cultus.[69]

The "separation" by which the defiled person of the world becomes a member of the pilgrim community of Hebrews is not like the "initiation" rites of the mystery religions. These, of course, could be often repeated; that is, one could be "initiated" over and over again. Rather, the Christian *rite de passage* is similar to many examples given by Eliade in his classic study of initiation[70] as a religious phenomenon where the rite cannot be repeated for the individual. The one, therefore, who, having once been inducted into the community with its "experience" of purgation and proleptic participation in the heavenly cultus, deliberately turns their back on the community in its forward journey and takes their place squarely in the profane world, is like Esau—there is no way for them to rejoin the pilgrims.[71] That is to say, the πόσῳ μᾶλλον of privilege is balanced by the πόσῳ χείρονος of peril.[72]

What then of the people of God of the Old Testament? The author is not interested in them per se—they function as no more than as propaedeutic and foil in his argument. The old cultus was no more than a shadow, a parable of the new order: it pointed to humanity's "problem" of defilement but could affect no decisive purgation. True, the use of animal blood was of limited power to cleanse and to set apart the people as God's separated ones. But there was no finality in humanity's efforts to gain access to deity or in its search for thoroughgoing purification. The old people of God were likewise a

---

69 *Supra*, p. 61.

70 *Rites and Symbols of Initiation*. Eliade distinguishes three categories of initiation: (1) tribal initiations, such as puberty rites (these are obligatory); (2) initiations for entering a secret society; and (3) initiations to a mystical vocation (p. 2). In each case, initiation is of such a nature that it is a "once-for-all" matter. Eliade gives the following definition of initiation: "The term initiation in the most general sense denotes a body of rites and oral teachings whose purpose is to produce a decisive alteration in the religious and social status of the person to be initiated. In philosophical terms, initiation is equivalent to a basic change in existential condition; the novice emerges from his ordeal endowed with a totally different being from that which he possessed before his initiation; he has become another" (p. x). While this definition and most of Eliade's examples point to a "once-for-all" (i.e., unrepeatable) experience, Eliade does note that some initiatory experiences are repeatable (e.g., the diksha, pp. 54–55).

71 12.16–17.

72 9.14; 10.29.

pilgrim people. The "wilderness wanderings"[73] showed this aspect clearly and furnish the author with an effective illustration of the dangers which beset the pilgrim in the way. Yet the writer cannot admit that the old people of God ever attained to the true sacred place, the goal of the pilgrimage: the "rest" could only become a possibility through the way opened by Christ, the ἀρχηγός.[74] Thus, in a larger sense, the history of the old people was an unfinished pilgrimage. But the author nowhere develops this pilgrimage motif with regard to the Jews, for his interest is with Christian existence as pilgrimage.

In concluding this final "explanation" of the anthropological tension in Hebrews, we may find it instructive of the ideas we have suggested to notice again a particularly arresting passage of Hebrews—12.18–29. The writer here bounces his discussion off the story of the children of Israel standing before God at the foot of Sinai, as recorded in Exodus 19. Instead of Sinai, the Christians have come to Mt. Zion; instead of the voice from heaven, it is the blood of Jesus that speaks; instead of a tribal horde, they are part of a vast throng that includes angels and perfected heroes of old worshipping in the "real" world. Now it is significant that the scene of Exodus 19 has a close counterpart in the *hajj*. Partin has pointed out how the *wuqūf* ("standing") at 'Arafa precisely parallels the Israelite experience: consecration, wearing of holy clothes, refraining from sexual relations, and standing before God at the foot of a holy mountain.[75] The similarities in the three accounts—Exodus 19, Hebrews 12, and Islam—should not surprise us. What we have coming to view are outworkings of the "structure" of pilgrimage, ingrained in humankind as a religious being. Each of the three accounts comes to understanding in the light of the phenomenology of religion: each is describing a station on the pilgrim's way. In this light we see more clearly the principal features of the passage of Hebrews: a cultic people, purged by the blood of Jesus, on the way to the city, now experiencing proleptically the joys of worship amid the cultus

---

73 We have taken over the common expression for Israel's journeyings. In fact, that experience meets Partin's four characteristics of pilgrimage as a *technicus terminus*: a separation (from Egypt—3.16), a journey toward a definite place, a religious purpose, and hardship. We find these same specifications met in the examples of Hebrews 11.

74 The argument of 3.11–4.11, of course, focuses in the idea of "rest." There is a tension in the author's presentation: on the one hand, he seems to argue that the "rest" was available from creation (4.3) and so was held out to the wandering people of God in the Old Testament (but they failed to "enter" it because of lack of πίστις). On the other, it is Jesus who as ἀρχηγός opens the way to that "rest" which is his principal emphasis. The old people of God then merely are introduced to provide the warning of failure—obviously, they could not serve as a negative example unless the *possibility* of attainment could be shown. The author seeks to blunt this basic tension in his argumentation by using "rest" ambiguously.

75 Partin, "Pilgrimage," 58–59. The "standing" before God at Muzdalifa re-enacts the sacred thunder also (ibid., 62).

of heaven. And even so does the anthropology of the passage come to clarity: while the applied blood of Jesus is powerful to purge sins, beware of refusing the voice from heaven![76] That is, the present benefits and future rewards for the pilgrim people are matched only by the perils of falling out along the way.

We see, therefore, that it is as the defilement/purgation anthropology finds its place within the ruling conception of Hebrews of the Christian life as community pilgrimage that the "tension" in anthropology becomes understandable. There is, in fact, no such tension. The author's emphasis shifts from defilement/purgation to apostasy/faithfulness depending on the *time* which is in view: whereas the former refers to the "now" time in the light of the past, the latter is concerned with the future which may grow out of the "now."

If we focus our attention upon the defilement/purgation anthropology, it seems indisputable that it is the idea of Christianity as a cultic community, vividly conscious of a radical disjunction from the profane world "without," which is determinative. One might well argue that this anthropology therefore is rooted in ecclesiology rather than in the christology or eschatology of Hebrews. Such an approach, while having much to commend it, is not in our opinion the correct one, however. We have noticed the interweaving of christology, soteriology, ecclesiology, and eschatology with anthropology. It seems to us preferable rather to begin with religious categories, that is, to take one's point of departure from humanity as defiled/ humanity as part of cultus (the cultic community itself being on the march—a pilgrim group). Out of such conceptions one may proceed to take up christology, soteriology, ecclesiology, eschatology, or anthropology.

The apostasy/faithfulness anthropology of Hebrews has long attracted the attention of scholars. Some have wondered whether its strong note of uncertainty—so striking in its contrast to the "full assurance" of the defilement/purgation anthropology—indicates a deficient view of the Gospel on the part of the author of the letter.[77] This is not a question which we have sought to adjudicate in this study however, it seems to us likely that the overall view of cultus which we have noticed in our study—its sense of separateness, the privileges of participation in it, and especially the "initiation" into it as a *rite de passage*—must speak in favor of the author. Certainly, he seems

---

76 12.25.
77 Cf. Purdy, *Epistle to the Hebrews*, on 10.26–31: "At this point, it may be said, the author did not catch the full import of the gospel. His words reveal his passionate eagerness to save his readers from catastrophe, but his analogy from the old to the new covenant turns out to impose a limitation on the new rather than a liberation from the old. Can he have known of the record that Peter, who denied his Lord at a moment of crisis, became a leader in the church?" (p. 715).

to be consistent in his differentiation of "sins of ignorance" from acts of deliberate apostasy.[78] Of course, his ruling view of Christianity as cultus might still be challenged. We cannot here go further into such questions. Our concern throughout has been with the defilement/purgation anthropology of the work. We hold to have shown that this anthropology supplies the primary and essential view of man, that it carries its own internal logic in the argumentation of the work, and that it is made comprehensible by reference to the "structures" revealed by the phenomenology of religion.

We have now been able to see the place of defilement and purgation, not only in Hebrews 9–10, but in the total schema of the letter as a whole. It remains for us only to draw together the lines of thought which have run throughout this study: we are ready to state overall conclusions of the study and to point beyond the immediate task for its implications for continued research. These will be the concerns of the final chapter of this study.

---

78 Cf. 5.1–2; 9.7; 6.4–6; 10.26–29; 12.16–17, 25.

Chapter 6

Conclusions and Implications

The study of defilement and purgation in the book of Hebrews—especially as these motifs come to expression in the ninth and tenth chapters of the letter—points to the following overarching conclusions:

1. The insights of phenomenology of religion have been shown to provide the exegete with a fruitful methodology in their attempt to grasp the cultic argumentation of the text. These insights have been of two kinds: (a) attitudinal, in that the reader has been directed to discern the language of the cult as first of all *religious*, and to approach it accordingly. That is to say, they have been alerted to the necessity of a deliberate bracketing out of all questions of "truth" or "value" as they endeavor to allow the text to reveal its own religious "value" and internal logic; and (b) conceptual, in that the data furnished by phenomenology of religion from "religious experience" manifested apart from the book of Hebrews point to primordial "patterns" or "structures" of defilement and purgation in the experience of humanity *qua homo religiosus*. These "structures" have proved to be most helpful in illuminating the text: they have revealed at once the essential conformity of the author's understanding of defilement and purgation to the basic patterns as well as the particularity with which these patterns have come to expression in his work.

This study, then, has shown—at least in this one case—the *need* and the *possibility* of an enlarged scope for established methodology in the exegesis of a biblical text. The need arises from the failure of conventional, historical-critical oriented approaches to address the problems of the text as brought to focus in its cultic presuppositions and argumentation. The religious symbols of defilement and purgation are essentially timeless; therefore, a diachronic approach, such as long furnished the exegete in their task of grappling with the biblical literature, falls short. Herein we find the reason for the common complaint of exegetes of Hebrews that the ideas of the letter are "primitive," "foreign," "archaic." But for this need pointed to by a diachronic approach we have shown the possibilities opened up by a supplementation of traditional methodology with a *synchronic* approach to the text as indicated via phenomenology of religion. The juxtaposing of the schema of defilement-purgation as set out in Hebrews against the essentially timeless "structures" for defilement and purgation which come into view from the universal experience of *homo religiosus* reveals an indubitable correspondence. By this means the ideas of Hebrews cease to be "primitive" "foreign," or "archaic" for the exegete.

2. Our studies thus inexorably lead to an enlarged view of *genre*. Historical-critical methodology has endeavored to group biblical materials according to form and *Sitz im Leben*; this established sense of genre will continue to aid the biblical scholar. But this study has indicated that, at least in terms of the motifs of defilement, blood, and purgation, biblical materials belong to a much larger category. This expanded view of "genre" has to do with *universal* religious experience: it cuts across cultures and religions and is not historically focused. In harmony with our previous discussion of the "religious," we might term this category "religious genre."

3. The study of defilement and purgation likewise has served to confirm the underlying assumptions of this study. These assumptions are two: (a) that, because humankind by nature is a religious being, there are basic "patterns" or "structures" in which their religion comes to expression and which may be made understandable; (b) the cultic argumentation of the *auctor ad Hebraeos*, at first sight so remote to the modern mind, can be discerned to proceed by its own internal logic if the exegete is able to find the appropriate approach. The first assumption is one which appears less and less open to dispute under the impact of ever-increasing data from the religions of the world. Nevertheless, in the field of biblical scholarship there appears to have been a reluctance to allow it full sway for the interpretation of the text. This is mainly because—at least since the time of F. C. Baur—historical considerations have directed the exegete's approach. This study is clearly a departure; and, just as it has sought to give full rein to the first assumption, so have the results obtained (the congruence of the schema of defilement-purgation in Hebrews to the general "structures" apart from Hebrews) served to confirm that assumption. Likewise has the second assumption been established. The ninth and tenth chapters of Hebrews have long presented a problem to scholars, not only in traditional *crux interpretum* such as 9.23 and 10.20, but in

terms of following the overall drift of the argument. We have shown that it is the cultic presuppositions and the author's reliance on religious terminology which have caused the chief difficulties. But we have been able to show also that, when the text is given its full value as religious and viewed in the light of universal religious "structures," it is seen to present a tightly knit, coherent argument.

4. Certain negative conclusions follow as corollaries of the above results. First, it is manifest that the view that the cultic language of the author is not significant for his purpose and so may quickly be passed over is found to be in error. Again, the suggestion that this language in fact is employed in the service of a denigration of cultus per se—that is, that the letter to the Hebrews in effect is an anti-cultic polemic—has completely missed the mark: it turns the author's argument on its head. But the taking seriously of the cultic language by no means points to an allegorizing or typologizing wherein each article of furniture or detail of ritual is held to have a "spiritual" counterpart. No; as we have seen throughout this study, terms such as "defilement," "purgation," and "blood" are to be understood only by reference to the deep primordial springs of religious experience which they tap.

Our attempt to show the religious value of the cultic terminology of Hebrews may appear to be a recrudescence of the "guilt and gore" theology of the pietism of an earlier generation. We admit to points of contact in only one respect: to the extent that the language of pietism, particularly in its hymnody, has evoked the primordial "structures" of defilement, blood, and purgation, it belongs to the same religious genre as that of Hebrews in its cultic argumentation.

5. The author of Hebrews views the basic "problem" of humanity as defilement. This is a contagious state which issues in negative concomitants for the cultus and the community, as well as in subjective feelings of dread. The writer's focus is on humanity, yet he takes for granted that, because of the very nature of defilement, its manifestation among people carries a sense of cosmic defilement. The "solution" to defilement—purgation—while it is expressed with primary reference to people, must likewise be cosmic in its sweep.

We can press the author no further than his description of humanity as they *are*: humanity is defiled. That is, there is no attempt to account for the *fact* of defilement as to how and when it came about. Defilement is simply *there*: it is the stain, the blot, the contagion which separates from deity and community and calls for cleansing.

6. The change from defilement to purgation is therefore a religious passage. It is explicable only in view of the religious idea of *power* which comes

to expression in the terms "defilement," "blood," and "purgation." As defilement is a state of negative power, so purgation is that of positive power, with blood coming to view as the medium extraordinary between the two. We may express this change as that from death to life, or from disorder to order, so that blood is viewed also as potent life-power and ordering means.

The argument of Hebrews thus revolves around the idea of *relative powers*. It is in such light that the leitmotif "better blood" is explicable. What the author is arguing for is the power of Christ's blood vis-à-vis the blood of animals. To introduce ideas of a ritual/moral dichotomy completely misses the internal logic of the discursion. Further, it is on this axis (relative powers) that the balance of continuity and discontinuity of the old cultus with the new is to be struck.

7. The "structures" of defilement-purgation brought to light by phenomenology of religion from outside Hebrews illuminate the author's argument by showing its congruence with the structures and also its individuality. In his idea of the nature of defilement, in the effects of defilement, in the type of "solution" called forth by defilement, in the interdependence of community and cosmos—in all these aspects the points of similarity are remarkable. But even more do they highlight the particularity of the writer's schema: not many means of purgation, but one par excellence (blood); not many applications of blood, but *one* application of *one* blood (Christ's); not inevitable oscillation from defilement to purgation and back again to defilement, but a once-for-all breaking of the cycle. These concerns led him to a detailed treatment of purgation in which ἁγιάζειν and τελειοῦν are the key terms.

8. The anthropology of Hebrews cannot be separated from its ecclesiology. The individual per se is never in view in the letter: it is always an individual as a member of the cultic community with which we have to do. This is a community of the purged into which one has entered by a *rite de passage* (ἁγιάζειν) and which carries with it extraordinary benefits—present realization of decisive purgation (that is, even of the very consciousness) and proleptic participation in the cultus of heaven (both encompassed by τελειοῦν). It is only in view of the radical nature of the transition from the defiled world to membership in the community and the extraordinary blessings of such membership that the author's strictures against those who choose to cut themselves off from the community become understandable—for them there can be no hope.

9. If defilement is the basic "problem" of humanity, as a member of the cultic community it is the danger of apostasy which is to be strenuously resisted. True, the author allows for a defilement which may come upon the

members of the community, but this seems to be viewed as involuntary. Unfaithfulness, on the other hand, is an act of studied neglect or rejection of the religious values of the community. The defilement-purgation anthropology and the apostasy-faithfulness anthropology are held together by this overriding conception of the letter: the cultic community is *on the march*. While it has already experienced the privileges and benefits of purgation, the best is yet to be—when participation in the heavenly cultus is actual and no longer proleptic.

We have shown that this ruling idea of a cultic community on the march accords exactly with the "structure" of pilgrimage as a religious phenomenon. It is in this idea that the anthropology of the letter not only finds its tension resolved but is integrated with christology, eschatology, soteriology, and ecclesiology.

10. The study we have concluded may justifiably be seen as the culmination of two earlier investigations of Hebrews. It is a remarkable fact that one must go back as far as 1889 to the work of Westcott to find the methodological antecedent of this study. Westcott had but limited data at this disposal and confined his very brief attempts at structuring to the ideas of priesthood and sacrifice. His efforts today appear crude and sketchy, yet methodologically they are clearly an anticipation of the full-blown integration of the "structures" of defilement and purgation as revealed by phenomenology of religion in the exegetical task. For Westcott, the methodology is no more than vague and implicit, as indeed it had to be given the yet-nascent state of phenomenology of religion in his day; our task has been to make the methodology explicit and to carry it through with rigorous consistency.

The second investigation to which we refer is that of Käsemann. His epochal work served to establish the motif of the wandering people of God as constitutive of the book. His work is suggestive and convincing, yet curiously one-sided: it fails to give account of the cultic argumentation, because it cannot, given the categories with which Käsemann has to work. But in detecting the idea of pilgrimage Käsemann had discovered more than he was immediately aware of. We have been able to show conclusively that the motif of the wandering people of God in Hebrews conforms precisely with "pilgrimage" as a *technicus terminus* of phenomenology of religion. It is in this specialized sense of pilgrimage that the problem left so blatantly unanswered in Käsemann's work—that is, the integration of the parenesis and cultus—finds its resolution. In that resolution the anthropology of Hebrews likewise emerges as a self-consistent whole: the basic pattern of defilement-purgation encompasses the pattern of unfaithfulness-faithfulness peculiar to the pilgrim community.

Implications of the Study

While this study is complete and carries its own value in itself, it also seems suggestive for further study. We shall briefly indicate the possibilities which it appears to open up in terms of methodology and the historical situation of the book of Hebrews.

Methodological

The most significant implications of the study appear to come under this category. We have confined ourselves to but one set of religious ideas (the defilement-blood-purgation complex) and one book of the New Testament, but it is obvious that, if the approach employed has been considered sound and fruitful, it is applicable for many other parts of the biblical text.

So far as the book of Hebrews itself is concerned, it would seem to us that further motifs related to the cultus may be explored by the same methodology. We refer especially to the ideas of priesthood and temple (holy place). The former has attracted considerable attention in the past, but again from a historical perspective. Perhaps it is time for a new investigation of Christ's high-priestly office in the light of the "structures" of priesthood brought to view by phenomenology of religion. Very little attention has been given to the temple (tabernacle) motif by students of Hebrews, but the idea is one which is exceedingly rich in terms of phenomenology of religion. It is possible that such an approach would be helpful in grasping the obscure cosmology of the book and so would provide a needed supplementation of the anthropological focus of our study.

It is obvious that the method may be helpful wherever one finds cultic language in the New Testament. Such documents as 1 Peter and the Apocalypse would therefore appear to provide fruitful soil for experimentation along the lines of this study.

One always faces the danger of claiming too much for a method: there is no *one* method which is the master key to unlock every passage of the New Testament. Nor will the methodology we have proposed in this study provide that key. Certainly, it is not to be seen as a substitute for established methodology. But it does seem to us that it may be helpful across a wider span than purely cultic passages, and further, that it may be used to reopen some old matters of dispute. We shall confine ourselves to two examples.

The birth stories of Jesus have been a continuing source of scholarly interest. With the recovery of the Buddhist texts in the nineteenth century, this interest was heightened: the birth stories of Gautama seemed to present remarkable similarities. The question took on a historical focus: which scriptures had influenced the others?[1] Eventually, however, the search for origins proved to be a *cul-de-sac*: dependency of one tradition on the other could not be established. The differences in the accounts were emphasized. But it seems necessary to pose the question whether the historical issue is the only one in this matter: what about the indubitable similarities in the accounts (prediction of the birth, miraculous character of the event, and so on)? These similarities demand renewed consideration when one comes to realize that the problem is far broader than cross-influences of Christianity and Buddhism: other religions also display related birth stories in connection with salvific figures (for example, the stories of Krishna).[2] Surely the student of the New Testament, in his grappling with the Matthean and Lukan accounts, must take this material into consideration, even though direct historical links are not established. For such a task it would seem to us that the methodology followed in this study would be well suited. We must protest the effort to dismiss lightly the Gospel stories under the rubric of "legend," even as we have throughout this study shown the error of a superficial dismissal of the cultic language of Hebrews as "primitive" or "archaic."

We turn for the second example to the long-discussed topic of the relation of the Christian sacraments to the pagan "mysteries." This was a field which called forth some of the strongest efforts of the advocates of *Religionsgeschichte*.[3] Yet, with all their labors, the historical link could not be conclusively established. From A. Schweitzer[4] to G. Wagner,[5] opponents of the thesis could point to ways in which the Christian rites varied from the pagan ones: these

---

1 A good overview of previous discussion of this topic is provided in Edward J. Thomas, *The Life of Buddha as Legend and History* (Kegan Paul, Trench, Trubner & Co. Ltd., 1931), 25–50, 237–48. The classical studies are by R. Seydel, *Das Evangelium von Jesu in seinen Verhältnissen zu Buddha: Saga and Buddha-Lehre mit fortlaufender Rücksicht auf andere Religionskreise untersucht* (Leipzig, 1882), and G. A. van den Bergh van Eysinga, *Indische Einflüsse auf evangelische Erzählungen* (Göttingen, 1904).

2 Book Ten of the Bhagavata Purana. Cf. the summary account in W. G. Archer, *The Loves of Krishna in Indian Painting and Poetry* (Macmillan Co., n.d.), 26ff. Egyptian parallels are evinced by E. Brunner-Traut, "Die Geburtsgeschichte der Evangelien im Lichte ägyptologischer Forschungen," ZRGG, XII (1960), 97–111.

3 E.g., Richard Reitzenstein, *Die hellenistischen Mysterienreligionen, nach ihren Grundgedanken und Wirkungen: Vortrag ursprünglich gehalten in dem wissenschaftlichen Predigerverein für Elsass-Lothringen den 11. November 1909* (3. umgearb. aufl.; B. G. Teubner, 1927); Wilhelm Heitmüller, *Taufe und Abendmahl im Urchristentum* (J. C. B. Mohr, 1911).

4 Albert Schweitzer, *Paul and His Interpreters: A Critical History*, trans. W. Montgomery (Adam & Charles Black, 1956), 179–236.

5 Günter Wagner, *Pauline Baptism and the Pagan Mysteries: The Problem of the Pauline Doctrine of Baptism in Romans VI. 1–11, in the Light of its Religio-Historical "Parallels*," trans. J. P. Smith (Oliver & Boyd, 1967).

differences have proved insuperable. The historical question was important, but again we must ask whether the issue should have been, or should be, confined to this. For instance, granted that Paul's account of baptism in Romans 6 can be shown to be specifically Christian, is there not much more to be said concerning the *religious* dimension that underlies the motifs of death, burial, and rebirth? Is not his language to be studied in the light of rites of passage? These surely are not unimportant questions, the more so when we reflect upon the vastly greater significance of baptism for Christian experience in the first century over our own generation. Again, we would expect that the methodology followed in our study might be fruitful in opening up new insights on this much disputed topic.

Finally, it seems to us that the methodology of this study is significant for the current debate concerning structural exegesis.[6] The commonly used historical methods (diachronic) stand confronted by methods borrowed from the social sciences (synchronic), notably from linguistics, sociology, and anthropology. At issue is the relation between the two approaches: is the new to *replace* the old? If not, then how are the two types of methods to be integrated? We have endeavored to suggest an answer by our study: structural exegesis, at least insofar as it works out of the "structures" drawn from phenomenology of religion, is to *supplement* historically oriented methodology. It provides the basis for the appropriate approach to the text as a *religious* document: before dialogue, there must be religious "hearing." That is, the exegete is enabled to enter the thought-world of the text, to grasp its inner logic and to discern the rationale of its presuppositions. If the exegete is first able to "hear" the text in its own right, they may then truly enter into dialogue, as they proceed along established historical-critical lines.

Two examples from our exegesis of Hebrews 9–10 illustrate the manner in which a synchronic approach to the text may be integrated into traditional methodology. In 9.13–14, conventional methodology leads to an impasse: we establish only that the argument differs from Philo and rests upon obscure Old Testament sacrifices. Phenomenology of religion, however, shows how the impasse may be overcome: it illumines the internal logic of the text by reference to universal religious "structures." Here, the synchronic approach *complements* the diachronic. In 9.22, however, the relationship is one of *reinforcement*. *Religionsgeschichte* suggests that αἱματεκχυσία means "application" rather than "shedding" of blood, an interpretation which is also indicated by consideration of the argument of the text in terms of the religious "structure" of blood.

---

6 *Supra*, pp. 50ff.

The Historical Situation of Hebrews

While this study has not concentrated upon historical questions, the results of the study nevertheless appear to carry implications for the problems of introduction which have long engaged students of Hebrews. It appears to us that at least some light is shed on the author and the community.

Certainly, we do not intend to raise again the futile question as to the writer's identity. But this restriction does not prevent us from mentioning insights into his personality. First, we should characterize the *auctor ad Hebraeos* as a deeply *religious* man. For him, Christianity is a cult. It seems that cultic categories are ingrained in his subconscious mind, so that he argues spontaneously from cultic presuppositions and underlines his most powerful protestations by reverting to religiously emotive terms such as "blood."

Does this signify that the writer had a priestly background? Does it point to at least a Jewish antecedent? We do not think that either thesis is necessitated by the evidence. The author is steeped in the LXX; he lived in a world in which cults and cult sacrifices were common; above all, as we have seen, "structures" such as those of defilement, blood, and purgation are primordial, the common property of *homo religiosus*—all these factors eliminate the necessity of either thesis. The data of Hebrews *prima facie* make unlikely the first idea: for instance, he does not, as in 1 Peter,[7] refer to Christians as "priests." As to the second idea, it must be admitted that the writer's sustained references to the Jewish cult, with corresponding omission of any reference to pagan sacrifices, are in favor of his having a Jewish background. But the point cannot be affirmed with certainty.

Nor can it be concluded that his readers were ex-priests or even Jewish Christians. We may take it for granted that his argumentation, so obscure to the modern mind, presented no insuperable difficulties to them. That being so, they shared the cultic thought-world with the overarching view of Christianity as a cultic community. But this no more signifies a Jewish background than it does for the author. Indeed, for the readers the thrust of the letter points away from this conclusion: the danger which threatens (apostasy) is not a return to Judaism but a dropping-out from the community. That is, the reasoning is set in the framework of cultic community (separate)/profane world (outside) rather than in terms of Christian cult/Jewish cult. When once the student of Hebrews has caught the author's balancing of old cultus against new cultus, in which there is a clear basis of *continuity* as well as discontinuity, he is enabled to see that endeavors to find in his severe warnings

---

[7] 1 Pet 2.5.

a danger of a relapse to Judaism are utterly inadequate. It is only in an understanding of the Christian group as a cultic community, radically separated from the profane world outside, that his language is comprehensible.

This type of thinking clearly points to a Qumran style community. From what we have observed above, it does not follow that the readers were ex-Qumranites.[8] Nor are we to envisage a *physically* isolated community: their separation is religious (that is, conceptual), and they are clearly in midst of a threatening, profane environment. It would seem to me hazardous to suggest that such a self-view represented that of a conventicle, a Christian backwater, as it were.

We have not been able to point to any liturgical acts (with the exception of oblique references to baptism)[9] of the community corresponding to designated points in the text, along the lines of the proponents of the Old Testament myth-ritual school. Indeed, this has not been our quest. Granted a new emphasis on Hebrews as a cultic document, such an approach would have merit. We would suggest, however, that an attempt to use the insights of the interplay of myth and ritual as revealed by the recent studies in phenomenology of religion may prove to be a more significant endeavor.

What of the significance of the defilement-purgation anthropology for modern man? Does not the congruence of these ideas in Hebrews to universal religious patterns suggest the possibility of restating Christianity in terms of a modern purification myth? Intriguing as these questions are, they cannot be followed in this study. We must leave the motifs of defilement, blood, and purgation with our anonymous author and his equally unknown readers. But the end is not like the beginning. If the writer and his friends remain incognito, they have nevertheless revealed much of themselves as *religious* people. Nor are these motifs and the cultic argumentation into which they enter so prominently now so "foreign" to our ears. At last we can appreciate in some measure the religious force of the climactic affirmation of the letter:

> So now, my friends, the blood of Jesus makes us free to enter boldly into the sanctuary by the new, living way which he has opened for us through the curtain, the way of his flesh. We have, moreover, a great priest set over the household of God: so let us make our approach in sincerity of heart and full assurance of faith, our guilty hearts sprinkled clean, our bodies washed with pure water.[10]

---

8 As suggested by Hans Kosmala, *Hebräer-Essener-Christen* (E. J. Brill, 1959).
9 6.2, 4; 10.22.
10 Heb 10.19–22 (NEB).

Bibliography

Books and Reference Works

Anderson, Charles Pattillo. "The Setting of the Epistle to the Hebrews." Unpublished Ph.D. Dissertation, Columbia University, 1969.

Anderson, Robert. *The Hebrews Epistle in the Light of the Types.* J. Nisbet & Co., 1911.

Arndt, William F. and Gingrich, F. Wilbur. *A Greek-English Lexicon of the New Testament and Other Early Christian Literature.* University of Chicago Press, 1969.

Banton, Michael, ed. *Anthropological Approaches to the Study of Religion.* Frederick A. Praeger, 1966.

Barclay, William. *Epistle to the Hebrews.* Lutterworth Press, 1965.

Barr, James. *The Semantics of Biblical Language.* Oxford University Press, 1961.

——. *Biblical Words for Time.* 2nd rev. ed. Alec R. Allenson, Inc. 1969.

Barrett, Charles Kingsley, ed. *The New Testament Background: Selected Documents.* Rev. ed. SPCK, 1958.

Barthes, Roland, et al. *Exégèse et herméneutique.* Editions du Seuil, 1971.

Baur, Ferdinand Christian. *The Church History of the First Three Centuries.* Translated by Allan Menzies. 2 vols. 3rd ed. Williams and Norgate, 1878–79.

——. *Vorlesungen über neutestamentliche Theologie.* 2. Teil. Gotha: Friedrich Andreas Berthes, 1892.

Black, J. S. and G. W. Chrystal. *The Life of William Robertson Smith.* A. & C. Black, 1919.

Blass, F., and Debrunner, A. *A Greek Grammar of the New Testament and Other Early Christian Literature.* Translated and revised by Robert W. Funk. University of Chicago Press, 1961.

Bonsirven, P. Joseph. *Saint Paul: Épître aux Hébreux.* Verbum Salutis. 2e edit. Paris: Beauchesne et ses Fils, 1953.

Bousset, Wilhelm. *Kyrios Christos.* Translated by John E. Steely. Abingdon Press, 1970.

Bruce, Alexander Balmain. *The Epistle to the Hebrews: The First Apology for Christianity.* Charles Scribner's Sons, 1899.

Bruce, F. F. *The Epistle to the Hebrews.* New International Commentary on the New Testament. Eerdmans, 1964.

Bultmann, Rudolf. *Theology of the New Testament.* Translated by Kendrick Grobel. 2 vols. Charles Scribner's Sons, 1954–55.

Campbell, Joseph, ed. *Myths, Dreams, and Religion.* E. P. Dutton and Co., Inc., 1970.

Cody, Aelred. *Heavenly Sanctuary and Liturgy in the Epistle to the Hebrews: The Achievement of Salvation in the Epistle's Perspectives.* Grail Publications, 1960.

Colpe, Carsten. *Die religionsgeschichtliche Schule: Darstellung und Kritik ihres Bildes vom gnostischen Erlösermythus.* Forschungen zur Religion und Literatur des Alten und Neuen Testamentes. Vandenhoeck and Ruprecht, 1961.

Congar, Yves, M-J. *The Mystery of the Temple.* Translated by Reginald F. Trevett. Newman Press, 1962.

Culley, Robert C. "Studies in the Structure of Biblical Narrative." Paper presented at the International Congress of Learned Societies in the Field of Religion, Los Angeles, September 1–5, 1972.

Davidson, A. B. *The Epistle to the Hebrews*. Handbooks for Bible Classes and Private Students. T&T Clark, n.d.

Davies, John H. *A Letter to Hebrews*. Cambridge: University Press, 1967.

Deissmann, G. Adolf. *Bible Studies: Contributions, Chiefly from Papyri and Inscriptions, to the History of the Language, the Literature, and the Religion of Hellenistic Judaism and Primitive Christianity*. Translated by Alexander Grieve. T&T Clark, 1923.

_____. *Paul: A Study in Social and Religious History*. Translated by William E. Wilson. 2nd ed. George H. Doran Co., 1926.

Delitzsch, Franz. *Commentary on the Epistle to the Hebrews*. Translated by Thomas L. Kingsbury. 2 vols. T&T Clark, 1862–72.

Douglas, Mary. *Purity and Danger: An Analysis of Concepts of Pollution and Taboo*. Penguin Books, 1970.

DuBose, William Porcher. *High Priesthood and Sacrifice: An Exposition of the Epistle to the Hebrews*. Longmans, Green, and Co., 1908.

Durkheim, Emile. *The Elementary Forms of the Religious Life*. Translated by J. W. Swain. Free Press, 1954.

Edwards, Thomas Charles. *The Epistle to the Hebrews*. Hodder and Stoughton, 1888.

Eliade, Mircea. *From Primitives to Zen: A Thematic Sourcebook of the History of Religions*. Harper and Row, 1967.

_____. *Patterns in Comparative Religion*. Translated by Rosemary Sheed. Meridian Books. World Publishing Co., 1970.

_____. *Rites and Symbols of Initiation*. Translated by Willard R. Trask. Harper and Row, 1965.

_____. *The Sacred and the Profane*. Translated by Willard R. Trask. Harvest Books. Harcourt, Brace and World, Inc., 1959.

_____. *Shamanism: Archaic Techniques of Ecstasy*. Translated by Willard R. Trask. Pantheon Books for the Bollingen Foundation, 1964.

Eliade, Mircea, and Kitagawa, Joseph M., eds. *The History of Religions: Essays in Methodology*. University of Chicago Press, 1959.

Farrar, F. W. *The Epistle of Paul the Apostle to the Hebrews*. University Press, 1894.

Feldman, Emanuel. "Law and Theology in Biblical and Post-Biblical Defilement and Mourning Rites." Unpublished Ph.D. Dissertation, Emory University, 1971.

Feuerbach, L. A. *Lectures on the Essence of Religion*, trans. by Ralph Manheim. 1851. Reprint, Harper & Row, 1967.

Filson, Floyd V. *"Yesterday": A Study of Hebrews in the Light of Chapter 13*. Alec R. Allenson, Inc., 1967.

Fujita, Shozo. "The Temple Theology of the Qumran Sect and the Book of Ezekiel: Their Relationship to Jewish Literature of the Last Two Centuries B.C." Unpublished Th.D. Dissertation, Princeton University, 1970.

Gaboury, Antonio. "The Christological Implication of 'Structurgeschichte.'" Paper presented at the International Congress of Learned Societies in the Field of Religion, Los Angeles, September 1–5, 1972.
Gärtner, Bertil. *The Temple and the Community in Qumran and the New Testament*. University Press, 1965.
Gennep, Arnold van. *Rites of Passage*. Translated by Monika B. Vizedom and Gabrielle L. Caffee. University of Chicago Press, 1960.
Gossett, Earl Fowler. "The Doctrine of Justification in the Theology of John Calvin, Albrecht Ritschl, and Reinhold Niebuhr." Unpublished Ph.D. Dissertation, Vanderbilt University, 1961.
Govett, Robert. *Christ Superior to Angels, Moses and Aaron: A Comment on the Epistle to the Hebrews*. J. Nisbet & Co., 1884.
Grässer, Erich. *Der Glaube im Hebräerbrief*. N. G. Elwert, 1965.
Herbert, Jean. *Shinto: At the Fountain-head of Japan*. Stein and Day, 1967.
Héring, Jean. *The Epistle to the Hebrews*. Translated by A. W. Heathcote and P. J. Allcock. Epworth Press, 1970.
Hewitt, Thomas. *The Epistle to the Hebrews*. Tyndale New Testament Commentaries. Eerdmans, 1960.
Hofius Otfried. *Katapausis: Die Vorstellung vom endzeitlichen Ruheort im Hebräerbrief*. Wissenschaftliche Untersuchungen zum Neuen Testament. J. C. B. Mohr, 1970.
Hollmann, Georg. *Der Hebraerbrief*. Vol. III of *Die Schriften des Neuen Testaments*. Edited by Wilhelm Bousset and Wilhelm Heitmuller. 3 Aufl. Vandenhoeck and Ruprecht, 1917.
Hubert, H. and Mauss, M. *Sacrifice: Its Nature and Function*. Translated by W. D. Halls. University of Chicago Press, 1964.
Hurd, John C., Jr. "The Structure and Function of First Thessalonians." Paper presented at the International Congress of Learned Societies in the Field of Religion, Los Angeles, September 1–5, 1972.
James, E. O. *Sacrifice and Sacrament*. Thames and Hudson, 1962.
Jensen, Adolf E. *Myth and Cult among Primitive Peoples*. Translated by Marianna T. Choldin and Wolfgang Weissleder. University of Chicago Press, 1951.
Johnson, F. Ernest, ed. *Religious Symbolism*. Religion and Civilization Series. Kennikat Press, 1969.
Käsemann, Ernst. *Das wandernde Gottesvolk*. 4 Aufl. Vandenhoeck and Ruprecht, 1961.
Kelly, William. *An Exposition of the Epistle to the Hebrews*. T. Weston, 1905.
Kendrick, A. C. *Commentary on the Epistle to the Hebrews*. American Baptist Publication Society, 1889.
Ketter, Peter. *Hebräerbrief*. Herders Bibelkommentar. Freiburg: Herder, 1950.
Kistemaker, Simon. *The Psalm Citations in the Epistle to the Hebrews*. Amsterdam: Wed. G. van Soest, 1961.
Kitagawa, Joseph M., Eliade, Mircea, and Long, Charles H., eds. *The History of Religions: Essays on the Problem of Understanding*. University of Chicago Press, 1967.

Kittel, Rudolf, et al. *Biblica Hebraica*. 7th ed. Württembergische Bibelanstalt, 1966.

Klappert, Bertold. *Die Eschatologie des Hebräerbriefs*. C. Kaiser, 1969.

Klatt, Werner. *Hermann Gunkel: Zu seiner Theologie der Religionsgeschichte and zur Entstehung der formgeschichtlichen Methode*. FRLANT. Vandenhoeck and Ruprecht, 1969.

Kosmala, Hans. *Hebräer-Essener-Christen: Studien zur Vorgeschichte der frdhchristlichen Verkündigung*. E. J. Brill, 1959.

Kuss, Otto. *Der Brief an die Hebräer*. Regensburger Neues Testament. 2 Aufl. Friedrick Pustet, 1966.

Lampe, G. W. H., ed. *A Patristic Greek Lexicon*. 5 vols. Clarendon Press, 1961–68.

Lane, Michael, ed. *Introduction to Structuralism*. Basic Books, Inc., 1970.

Leeuw, G. van der. *Religion in Essence and Manifestation*. Translated by J. E. Turner. 2nd ed. George Allen and Unwin Ltd., 1964.

Lewis, Thomas Wiley, III. "The Theological Logic in Hebrews 10.19–12.29 and the Appropriation of the Old Testament." Unpublished Ph.D. Dissertation, Drew University, 1965.

Liddell, Henry George and Scott, Robert. *A Greek-English Lexicon*. 2 vols. 9th ed. Clarendon Press, 1948.

Lohse, Eduard, et al. *Der Ruf Jesu and die Antwort der Germeinde*. Vandenhoeck and Ruprecht, 1970.

Lünemann, Göttlieb. *The Epistle to the Hebrews*. Translated by Maurice J. Evans. Funk and Wagnalls, 1885.

Manson, William. *The Epistle to the Hebrews: An Historical and Theological Reconsideration*. Hodder and Stoughton Ltd., 1951.

Macneill, H. R. *The Christology of the Epistle to the Hebrews, Including its Relation to the Developing Christology of the Primitive Church*. University of Chicago Press, 1914.

May, Rollo, ed. *Symbolism in Religion and Literature*. George Braziller, 1960.

Maxwell, Kenneth LeRoy. "Doctrine and Parenesis in the Epistle to the Hebrews, with Special Reference to Pre-Christian Gnosticism." Unpublished Ph.D. Dissertation, Yale University, 1953.

Ménégoz, Eugène. *La théologie de l'Épître aux Hébreux*. Librairie Fischbacher, 1894.

Meyer, F. B. *The Way Into the Holiest*. Fleming H. Revell, 1893.

Michel, Otto. *Der Brief an die Hebräer*. Meyer Kommentar. 13 Aufl. Vandenhoeck and Ruprecht, 1966.

Milligan, George. *The Theology of the Epistle to the Hebrews*. T&T Clark, 1899.

Mishnayoth. Pointed Hebrew Text, Introductions, Translation, and Notes by Philip Blackman. 7 vols. Mishna Press Ltd., 1951–56.

Moffatt, James. *A Critical and Exegetical Commentary on the Epistle to the Hebrews*. International Critical Commentary. Charles Scribner's Sons, 1924.

Montefiore, Hugh. *A Commentary on the Epistle to the Hebrews*. Harper New Testament Commentaries. Harper and Row, 1964.

Moulton, James Hope and Milligan, George. *The Vocabulary of the Greek Testament Illustrated from the Papyri and Other Non-Literary Sources*. Hodder and Stoughton, 1930.

Nairne, Alexander. *The Epistle of Priesthood*. 2nd ed. T&T Clark, 1915.
_____. *The Epistle to the Hebrews*. Rev. ed. University Press, 1957.
Neil, William. *The Epistle to the Hebrews*. S.C.M. Press, 1955.
Nestle, Eberhard, and Aland, Kurt. *Novum Testamentum Graece*. 25th ed. Württembergische Bibelanstalt, 1962.
The New English Bible. 2nd ed. Oxford University Press, 1970.
Nilsson, Martin P. *Greek Folk Religion*. Harper Torchbooks, 1961.
_____. *Greek Piety*. Translated by Herbert J. Rose. Clarendon Press, 1951.
_____. *A History of Greek Religion*. Translated by F. J. Fielden. Preface by Sir James G. Frazer. Clarendon Press, 1925.
_____. *Religion as Man's Protest against the Meaninglessness of Events*. C. W. K. Gleerup, 1954.
Ninck, Martin. *Die Bedeutung des Wassers im Kult und Leben der Alten: Eine symbolgeschichtliche Untersuchung*. Wissenschaftliche Buchgesellschaft, 1960.
Oepke, Albrecht. *Das neue Gottesvolk in Schriftum, Schauspiel, bildender Kunst und Weltgestaltung*. C. Bertelsmann, 1950.
Otto, Rudolf. *The Idea of the Holy: An Inquiry into the Non-Rational Factor in the Idea of the Divine and Its Relation to the Rational*. Translated by John W. Harvey. 2nd ed. Oxford University Press, 1950.
Parsons, Ernest William. *The Religion of the New Testament*. Harper and Brothers, 1939.
Partin, Harry B. "The Muslim Pilgrimage: Journey to the Center." Unpublished Ph.D. Dissertation, University of Chicago, 1967.
Paton, Herbert James. *The Modern Predicament: A Study in the Philosophy of Religion*. George Allen and Unwin Ltd., 1955.
Patte, Daniel. "The New Exegesis: An Evaluation of the Diversification in Exegetical Methods." Unpublished paper, Vanderbilt University, 1972.
Pierce, C. A. *Conscience in the New Testament: A Study of "Syneidesis" in the New Testament; in the Light of Its Sources, and with Particular Reference to St. Paul: with Some Observations Regarding Its Pastoral Relevance Today*. Studies in Biblical Theology. Alec R. Allenson, Inc., 1955.
Plessis, Paul Johannes du. *ΤΕΛΕΙΟΣ: the Idea of Perfection in the New Testament*. Uitgave J. H. Kok, 1959.
Purdy, Alexander C. *The Epistle to the Hebrews*. Vol. XI. *The Interpreter's Bible*. Edited by George Arthur Buttrick. Abingdon Press, 1955.
Rahlfs, Alfred, ed. *Septuaginta*. 2 vols. Privilegierte Württembergische Bibelanstalt, 1962.
Rendall, Frederic. *The Epistle to the Hebrews*. Macmillan and Co., 1888.
Renner, Frumentius. *"An die Hebräer"—ein pseudepigraphischer Brief*. Münsterschwarzacher Studien. Winsterschwarzach: Vier-Turme, 1970.
Revised Standard Version of the Bible. Thomas Nelson and Sons, 1952.
Richardson, Peter. "Social and Theological Tensions in Luke/Acts." Paper presented at the International Congress of Learned Societies in the Field of Religion, Los Angeles, September 1–5, 1972.

Ricoeur, Paul. *The Symbolism of Evil*. Translated by Emerson Buchanan. Beacon Press, 1969.
Ritschl, Albrecht. *The Christian Doctrine of Justification and Reconciliation*. Translated by H. R. Mackintosh and A. B. Macaulay. T. & T. Clark, 1900.
_____. *Die christliche Lehre von der Rechtfertigung and Versöhnung*. Vol. II: *Der biblische Stoff der Lehre*. 2 Aufl. Bonn: Adolph Marcus, 1882.
_____. *A Critical History of the Christian Doctrine of Justification and Reconciliation*. Translated by John S. Black. Edmonston and Douglas, 1872.
_____. *Instruction in the Christian Religion*. Translated by Alice Mead Swing. Longmans, Green, and Co., 1901.
Robertson, A. T. *A Grammar of the Greek New Testament in the Light of Historical Research*. Hodder and Stoughton, 1914.
Robinson, Theodore H. *The Epistle to the Hebrews*. Moffatt Commentary. Harper, 1933.
Saphir, Adolph. *The Epistle to the Hebrews*. Gospel Publishing House, 1902.
Schierse, F. J. *The Epistle to the Hebrews*. Translated by Benen Fahy. Burns and Oates, 1969.
_____. *Verheissung and Heilsvollendung: Zur theologischen Grundfrage des Hebräerbriefes*. Münchener theologische Studien. K. Zink, 1955.
Schmoller, Alfred. *Handkonkordanz zum griechischen Neuen Testament*. 7 vermehrte Aufl. Privilegierte Württembergische Bibelanstalt.
Schneider, H. W. and Proosdij, B. A. van, eds. *Proceedings of the XIth Congress of the International Association for the History of Religions*. Vol. II: *Guilt or Pollution and Rites of Purification*. E. J. Brill, 1968.
Schröger, Friedrich. *Der Verfasser des Hebräerbriefes als Schriftausleger*. Friedrich Pustet, 1968.
Scott, E. F. *The Epistle to the Hebrews: Its Doctrine and Significance*. T&T Clark, 1922.
Smith, Jerome. *A Priest for Ever: A Study of Typology and Eschatology in Hebrews*. Sheed and Ward, 1969.
Smith, William Robertson. *Lectures on the Religion of the Semites: The Fundamental Institutions*. 3rd ed. A. & C. Black Ltd., 1927.
Strathmann, Hermann. *Der Brief an die Hëbraer*. Das Neue Testament Deutsch. Vandenhoeck and Ruprecht, 1963.
Swing, Albert Temple. *The Theology of Albrecht Ritschl*. Longmans, Green, and Co., 1901.
Theissen, Gerd. *Untersuchungen zum Hebräerbrief*. Studien zum Neuen Testament. Gütersloher Verlagshaus Gerd Mohn, 1969.
Tillich, Paul. *Theology of Culture*. Ed. Robert C. Kimball. Oxford University Press, 1959.
Turner, Victor Witter. *The Forest of Symbols: Aspects of Ndembu Ritual*. Cornell University Press, 1967.
Vanhoye, Albert. *A Structured Translation of the Epistle to the Hebrews*. Translated by James Swetnam. Pontifical Biblical Institute, 1964.
_____. *La structure littéraire de l'Épître aux Hébreux*. Descleé de Brouwer, 1963.
Vaughan, C. J. *Πρὸς Ἑβραίους: The Epistle to the Hebrews*. Macmillan and Co., 1890.

Wach, Joachim. *The Comparative Study of Religions.* Edited by Joseph M. Kitagawa. Columbia University Press, 1958.

———. *Religionswissenschaft: Prolegomena zu ihrer wissenschaftstheoretischen Grundlegung.* J. C. Hinrichs, 1924.

———. *Types of Religious Experience, Christian and Non-Christian.* University of Chicago Press, 1951.

Watts, Alan W. *Myth and Ritual in Christianity.* Vanguard Press, 1953.

Weiss, D. Bernhard. *A Commentary on the New Testament.* Translated by George H. Schodde and Epiphanius Wilson. Funk and Wagnalls Co., 1906.

Wellhausen, Julius. *Prolegomena zur Geschichte Israels.* 5 Aufl. George Reimer, 1899.

———. *Der Hebräerbrief in zeitgeschichtlicher Beleuchtung.* J. C. Hinrichs, 1910.

Wenschkewitz, Hans. *Die Spiritualisierung der Kultusbegriffe.* Eduard Pfeiffer, 1932.

Westcott, Brooke Foss. *The Epistle to the Hebrews.* Reprint of the 2nd ed. Eerdmans, 1950.

Wickham, E. C. *The Epistle to the Hebrews.* Westminster Commentaries. Methuen and Co., Ltd., 1910.

Williamson, Ronald. *Philo and the Epistle to the Hebrews.* Arbeiten zur Literatur und Geschichte des hellenistischen Judentums. E. J. Brill, 1970.

Windisch, Hans. *Der Hebräerbrief.* Handbuch zum Neuen Testament. 2 Aufl. J. C. B. Mohr, 1931.

Yerkes, Royden Keith. *Sacrifice in Greek and Roman Religions and Early Judaism.* Adam and Charles Black, 1953.

Articles

Abe, Masao. "The Idea of Purity in Mahayana Buddhism." *Numen*, XIII (1966), 183–89.

Andriessen, P. "L'Eucharistie dans l'Épître aux Hébreux." *Nouvelle revue théologique*, XCIV (1972), 269–77.

———. "Das grössere und volikommenere Zelt (Hebr 9, 11)." *Biblische Zeitschrift*, XV (1971), 76–92.

——— and Lenglet, A. "Quelques passages difficiles de l'Épître aux Hébreux (5.7. 11; 10.20; 12.2)." *Biblica*, LI (1970), 207–20.

Aner, Karl. "Sin and Guilt in the History of Doctrine." *Twentieth Century Theology in the Making*, II, 185–98. Edited by Jaroslav Pelikan. Translated by R. A. Wilson. William Collins Sons and Co., 1970.

Baaren, Th. P. van. "Theoretical Speculations on Sacrifice." *Numen*, XI (1964), 1–12.

Baeck, Leo. "Sin and Guilt in Judaism." *Twentieth Century Theology in the Making*, II, 174–77. Edited by Jaroslav Pelikan. Translated by R. A. Wilson. William Collins Sons and Co., 1970.

Barrett, C. K. "The Eschatology of the Epistle to the Hebrews." *The Background of the New Testament and Its Eschatology.* Edited by W. D. Davies and D. Daube. Cambridge University Press, 1956, 363–93.

Behm, Johannes. "Αἱματεκχυσία." *Theological Dictionary of the New Testament.* Vol. I.

Bertholet, Alfred. "Sin and Guilt in Comparative Religion." *Twentieth Century Theology in the Making*, II, 161–68. Edited by Jaroslav Pelikan. 'Translated by R. A. Wilson. William Collins Sons and Co., 1970.

Betz, Hans Dieter. "Schöpfung und Erlösung im hermetischen Fragment, 'Kore Kosmu.'" *Zeitschrift für Theologie und Kirche*, LXIII (1966), 160–87.

———. "Zum Problem des religionsgeschichtlichen Verständnisses der Apokalyptik." *Zeitschrift für Theologie und Kirche*, LXIII (1966), 391–409.

Bharati, Agehananda. "Pilgrimage in the Indian Tradition." *History of Religions*, III (1963), 135–67.

Blau, Joseph L. "The Red Heifer: A Biblical Purification Rite in Rabbinic Literature." *Numen*, XIV (1967), 70–80.

Bleeker, C. J. "Comparing the Religio-Historical and the Theological Method." *Numen*, XVIII (1971), 9–29.

———. "Guilt and Purity in Ancient Egypt." *Numen*, XIII (1966), 81–87.

———. "The Relation of the History of Religions to Kindred Religious Sciences, Particularly Theology, Sociology of Religion, Psychology of Religion and Phenomenology of Religion." *Numen*, I (1954), 142–52.

Bloom, Alfred. "The Sense of Sin and Guilt in the Last Age (Mappo) in Chinese and Japanese Buddhism." *Numen*, XIV (1967), 144–49.

Bode, Framrose A. "Rites of Purification in the Zoroastrian Religion." *Guilt or Pollution and Rites of Purification*. Edited by H. W. Schneider and B. A. van Proosdij. E. G. Brill, 1968, 54–56.

Bolle, Kees W. "History of Religions with a Hermeneutic Oriented Toward Christian Theology?" *The History of Religions: Essays on the Problem of Understanding*. Edited by Joseph M. Kitagawa et al. University of Chicago Press, 1967, 89–118.

Bouquet, A. C. "Numinous Uneasiness." *Guilt or Pollution and Rites of Purification*. Edited by H. W. Schneider and B. A. van Proosdif. E. J. Brill, 1968, 1–8.

Bouttier, M. "Deux problèmes de l'Épître aux Hébreux en suspens." *Foi et vie*, LXII (1963), 313–23.

Bover, Jose M. "Las variantes μελλόντων y γενομένων en Hebr. 9, 11." *Biblica*, XXXII (1951), 232–36.

Brooks, W. E. "The Perpetuity of Christ's Sacrifice in the Epistle to the Hebrews." *Journal of Biblical Literature*, LXXXIX (1970), 205–14.

Bruce, F. F. "The Kerygma of Hebrews." *Interpretation*, XXIII (1969), 3–19.

———. "Recent Contributions to the Understanding of Hebrews." *Expository Times*, LXXX (1969), 260–64.

Bultmann, Rudolf. "'Άφεσις.'" *Theological Dictionary of the New Testament*. Vol. I.

Caird, G. B. "Underestimated Theological Books: Alexander Nairne's 'Epistle of Priesthood.'" *Expository Times*, LXXII (1961), 204–06.

Carlston, Charles Edwin. "Eschatology and Repentance in the Epistle to the Hebrews." *Journal of Biblical Literature*, LXXVIII (1959), 296–302.

Chang, Chung-Yuan. "Purification and Taoism." *Guilt or Pollution and Rites of Purification*. Edited by H. W. Schneider and B. A. van Proosdij. E. J. Brill, 1968, 139–40.

Clavier H. "Resurgences d'un problème de méthode in histoire des religions." *Numen*, XV (1968), 94–118.

Dahl, N. A. "A New and Living Way: The Approach to God according to Hebrews 10.19–25." *Interpretation*, V (1951), 401–12.

Dibelius, Martin. "Der himmlische Kultus nach dem Hebräerbrief." *Theologische Blätter*, XVI (1942), 1–11.

Douglas, Ian K. "Guilt and Purification in Modern Urdu Quranic Commentary." *Guilt or Pollution and Rites of Purification*. Edited by H. W. Schneider and B. A. van Proosdij. E. J. Brill, 1968, 113–14.

Dumoulin, Heinrich. "Consciousness of Guilt and the Practice of Confession in Japanese Buddhism." *Guilt or Pollution and Rites of Purification*. Edited by H. W. Schneider and B. A. van Proosdij. E. J. Brill, 1968, 165–66.

Dupont-Sommer, André. "Culpabilité et rites de purification dans la sect Juive de Qoumrân." *Guilt or Pollution and Rites of Purification*. Edited by H. W. Schneider and B. A. van Proosdij. E. J. Brill, 1968, 78–80.

Earhart, H. Byron. "Ishikozume—Ritual Execution in Japanese Religion, especially in Shugendo." *Numen*, XIII (1966), 116–27.

Eliade, Mircea. "Crisis and Renewal in History of Religions." *History of Religions*, V (1965), 1–17.

_____. "Methodological Remarks on the Study of Religious Symbolism." *The History of Religions: Essays in Methodology*. Edited by Mircea Eliade and Joseph M. Kitagawa. University of Chicago Press, 1959, 86–107.

Fallaize, E. N. "Purification (Introductory and Primitive)." *Encyclopedia of Religion and Ethics*. Vol. X.

Fitzer, G. "Auch der Hebräerbrief legitimiert nicht eine Opfertodchristologie: Zur Frage der Intention des Hebräerbriefes und seiner Bedeutung für die Theologie." *Keryma und Dogma*, XV (1969), 264–319.

Friedrich G. "Das Lied vom Hohenpriester im Zusammenhang von Hebr. 4.14–5.10." *Theologische Zeitschrift*, XVIII (1962), 95–115.

Fuhrmann, Paul T. "Adam's Guilt and Man's Need for Innocence, according to Zwingli." *Guilt or Pollution and Rites of Purification*. Edited by H. W. Schneider and B. A. van Proosdij. E. J. Brill, 1968, pp. 95–97.

Geertz, Clifford. "Religion as a Cultural System." *Anthropological Approaches to the Study of Religion*. Edited by Michael Banton. New York: Frederick A. Praeger, 1966, pp. 1–46.

Gerlitz, Peter. "Fasten als Reinigungsritus." *Zeitschrift für Religions-und Geistesgeschichte*, XX (1968), 212–22.

Gispen, W. H. "The Distinction between Clean and Unclean." *Oudtestamentische Studien*, Vol. V. Edited by P. A. H. De Boer. E. J. Brill, 1948, 190–96.

Glombitza, O. "Erwägungen zum kunstvollen Ansatz der Paraenese im Brief an die Hebräer—x 19–25." *Novum Testamentum*, IX (1967), 132–50.

Grasser, Erich. "Der Hebraerbrief 1938–1963." *Theologische Rundschau*, XXX (1964), 138–236.

_____. "Der historische Jesus in Hebräerbrief." *Zeitschrift furr die neutestamentliche Wissenschaft*, LVI (1965), 63–91.

Gunkel, Hermann. "Sin and Guilt in the Old Testament." *Twentieth Century Theology in the Making*, II, 168–74. Edited by Jaroslav Pelikan. Translated by R. A. Wilson. William Collins Sons and Co., 1970.

Gyllenberg, Rafael. "Die Komposition des Hebräerbriefs." *Svensk exegetisk årsbok*, XXII-XXIII (1957–58), 137–47.

Harper, Edward B. "Ritual Pollution as an Integrator of Caste and Religion." *Journal of Asian Studies*, XXIII (1964), 151–97.

Harrelson, Walter. "Guilt and Rites of Purification Related to the Fall of Jerusalem in 587 BC." *Numen*, XV (1968), 218–21.

Havens, T. R. "Dynamics of Confession in the Early Sangha." *Guilt or Pollution and Rites of Purification*. Edited by H. W. Schneider and B. A. van Proosdij. E. J. Brill, 1968, p. 133.

Hermanns, M. "Schuld und Reinigungsriten unter den Primitiven Indiens." *Kairos*, VIII (1966), 107–13.

Hidding, K. A. H. "Schuld und Reinigungsriten im Javanischen Islam." *Guilt or Pollution and Rites of Purification*. Edited by H. W. Schneider and B. A. van Proosdij. E. J. Brill, 1968, pp. 111–12.

Higgins, A. J. B. "The Priestly Messiah." *New Testament Studies*, XIII (1967), 211–39.

Hink, R. "Rein und Unrein—religionsgeschichtlich." *Die Religion in Geschichte und Gegenwart*. 3 Aufl., Vol. V.

Hirai, Naofusa. "Shinto Purification and Concept of Man." *Guilt or Pollution and Rites of Purification*. Edited by H. W. Schneider and B. A. van Proosdij. E. J. Brill, 1968, pp. 185–87.

Hoenig, Sidney B. "Qumran Rules of Impurities." *Revue de Qumran*, VI (1969), 559–67.

Hofius, O. "Das 'erste' und des 'zweite' Zelt. Ein Beitrag zur Auslegung von Hbr 9–10." *Zeitschrift für die neutestamentliche Wissenschaft*, LXI (1970), 271–77.

_____. "Inkarnation und Opfertod Jesu nach Hebr 10.19f." *Der Ruf Jesu und die Antwort der Gemeinde*. Edited by E. Lohse, et al. Vandenhoeck and Ruprecht, 1970, 132–41.

Honko, Lauri. "Breach of Taboo as a Primitive Concept of Disease." *Guilt or Pollution and Rites of Purification*. Edited by H. W. Schneider and B. A. van Proosdij. E. J. Brill, 1968, 31–32.

Hori, Ishiro. "Rites of Purification and Orgy in Japanese Folk Religion." *Guilt or Pollution and Rites of Purification*. Edited by H. W. Schneider and B. A. van Proosdij. E. J. Brill, 1968, 192–93.

Hsiao, Paul S. V. "Schuld als Spaltung vom Tao." *Kairos*, VIII (1966), 117–24.

Jeremias, J. "Hebraer 10.20: τοῦτ' ἔστιν τῆς σαρκὸς αὐτοῦ. *Zeitschrift für die neutestamentliche Wissenschaft*, LXII (1971), 131.

Kamata, Jun-Ichi. "Pollution and Sin in Shinto." *Guilt or Pollution and Rites of Purification*. Edited by H. W. Schneider and B. A. van Proosdij. E. J. Brill, 1968, pp. 183–84.

Kerr, Hugh T. "The Christ-Life as Mythic and Psychic Symbol." *Numen*, IX (1962), 143–58.
Kitagawa, Joseph M. "Ainu Bear Festival." *History of Religions*, I (1961), 95–151.
_____. "Gohei Hasami—ein Ritus der 'Läuterung der Zeit' auf dem Berg Koya." *Kairos*, VIII (1966), 114–17.
Klimkeit, Hans J. "Guilt, Pollution, and Purification Rites in Vajrayana Buddhism." *Guilt or Pollution and Rites of Purification*. Edited by H. W. Schneider and B. A. van Proosdij. E. J. Brill, 1968, pp. 154–56.
Koester, H. "'Outside the Camp': Hebrews 13.9–14." *Harvard Theological Review*, LV (1962), 299–315.
Kornfeld, Walter. "Reine and unreine Tiere im Alten Testament." *Kairos*, VII (1965), 134–47.
Kuss, Otto. "Der theologische Grundgedanke des Hebräerbriefes: zur Deutung des Todes Jesu im Neuen Testament." *Münchener theologische Zeitschrift*, VII (1956), 233–71.
Lapointe, R. "Hermeneutics Today." *Biblical Theology Bulletin*, II (1972), 120–27.
Leach, Edmund R. "The Legitimacy of Solomon." *Introduction to Structuralism*. Edited by Michael Lane.
Basic Books, Inc., 1970, 248–92.
_____. "Levi-Strauss in the Garden of Eden: An Examination of Some Recent Developments in the Analysis of Myth." *Transactions of the New York Academy of Sciences*, XXIII (1961), 386–96.
Leclant, Jean. "Les rites de purification dans le cérémonial pharaonique du couronnement." *Guilt or Pollution and Rites of Purification*. Edited by H. W. Schneider and B. A. van Proosdij. E. J. Brill, 1968, 48–51.
Lesur, Yolotl G. de. "The Concept of Pollution, of Guilt, and the Rites of Purification among the Aztecs." *Guilt or Pollution and Rites of Purification*. Edited by H. W. Schneider and B. A. van Proosdij. E. J. Brill, 1968, pp. 39–43.
Linss, W. C. "Logical Terminology in the Epistle to the Hebrews." *Concordia Theological Monthly*, XXXVII (1966), 365–69.
Loewinich, W. von. "Zum Verständnis des Opfergedankens im Hebräerbrief." *Theologische Blätter*, XII (1933), 162–72.
Lohse, E. "Rein und Unrein im NT." *Die Religion in Geschichte und Gegenwart*. 3. Autl., Vol. V.
Long, Charles H. "Prolegomenon to a Religious Hermeneutic." *History of Religions*, VI (1967), 254–64.
Luck, U. "Himmlisches und irdisches Geschehen im Hebraerbrief: ein Beitrag zum Problem des 'historischen Jesus' im Urchristentum." *Novum Testamentum*, VI (1963), 192–215.
Maag, Victor. "Nicht sühnbare Schuld." *Kairos*, VIII (1966), 90–106.
Matsumoto, Koichi. "Soto Zen's Idea of Purification." *Guilt or Pollution and Rites of Purification*. Edited by H. W. Schneider and B. A. van Proosdij. E. J. Brill, 1968, pp. 171–72.
Michel, O. "Zur Auslegung des Hebräerbriefes." *Novum Testamentum*, VI (1963), 189–91.

_____. "Die Lehre von der christlichen Vollkommenheit nach der Anschauung des Hebräerbriefes." *Theologische Studien und Kritiken*, CVI (1934–36), 333–35.

Moe, Olaf. "Der Gedanke des allgemeinen Priestertum im Hebräerbrief." *Theologische Zeitschrift*, V (1949), 161-69.

Morris, L. "The Biblical Use of the Term 'Blood.'" *Journal of Theological Studies*, III (1952), 216–227.

Nakajima, Hideo. "The Basic Structure of the Idea of Salvation and Purification in Tenrikyo." *Guilt or Pollution and Rites and Purification*. Edited by H. W. Schneider and B. A. van Proosdij. E. J. Brill, 1968, 196–97.

Nida, Eugene A. "Implications of Contemporary Linguistics for Biblical Scholarship." *Journal of Biblical Literature*, XCI (1972), 73–89.

Nieda, Rokusaburo. "The Significance of Pollution and Purification in Japanese Religious Consciousness: A Comparative Study." *Guilt or Pollution and Rites of Purification*. Edited by H. W. Schneider and B. A. van Proosdij. E. J. Brill, 1968, pp. 181–82.

Nomoto, S. " Herkunft und Struktur der Hohepriester-vorstellung im Hebräerbrief." *Novum Testamentum*, X (1968), 10–25.

Norbeck, Edward. "Pollution and Taboo in Contemporary Japan." *Southwestern Journal of Anthropology*, VIII (1952), 269–85.

Obermuller, R. "Una mística del camino. El tema de la peregrinacíon en la carta a los Hebreos." *Revista Biblica*, XXXIII (1971), 55–56.

Oepke, Albrecht. "'Ev." *Theological Dictionary of the New Testament*, Vol. II.

Ono, Sokyo. "The Way of Purification: The Shinto Case." *Guilt or Pollution and Rites of Purification*. Edited by H. W. Schneider and B. A. van Proosdij. E. J. Brill, 1968, pp. 188–89.

Ort, L. J. R. "Guilt or Purification in Manichaeism." *Guilt or Pollution and Rites of Purification*. Edited by H. W. Schneider and B. A. van Proosdij. E. J. Brill, 1968, p. 69.

Patte, Daniel. "Proclamer la joyeuse nouvelle de la Résurrection." *Communion verbum caro*, XXV (1972), 51–66.

Pezzali, Amalia. "Santideva's Statement about Confession." *Guilt or Pollution and Rites of Purification*. Edited by H. W. Schneider and B. A. van Proosdij. E. J. Brill, 1968, pp. 134–35.

Pfleiderer, Otto. "Die Theologie Ritschl's nach ihrer biblischen Grundlage." *Jahrbücher für protestantische Theologie*, XVI (1890), 42–83.

Randall, E. L. "The Altar of Hebrews 13.10." *Australasian Catholic Record*, XLVI (1969), 197–200.

Rasjidi, Mohammad. "Guilt, Pollution, and Rites of Purification in Islam." *Guilt or Pollution and Rites of Purification*. Edited by H. W. Schneider and B. A. van Proosdij. E. J. Brill, 1968, pp. 108–10.

Reissner, H. "'Wir haben hier keine bleibende Stadt, sondern die zukünftige suchen wir' (Hebr. 13, 14). Erwägungen über das Wallfahren." *Geist und Leben*, XXXV (1962), 96–103.

Rendtorff, R. "Rein und Unrein im AT." *Die Religion in Geschichte und Gegenwart*. 3 Aufl., Vol. V.

Ricoeur Paul. "Guilt, Ethics and Religion." *Moral Evil Under Challenge*. Edited by Johannes B. Metz. Herder and Herder, 1970, 11–27.

———. "The Hermeneutics of Symbols and Philosophical Reflection." *International Philosophical Quarterly*, II (1962), 191–218.

Ringgren, Helmer. "Sin and Forgiveness in the Koran." *Guilt or Pollution and Rites of Purification*. Edited by H. W. Schneider and B. A. van Proosdij E. J. Brill, 1968, p. 103.

Rusche, H. "Glauben und Leben nach dem Hebräerbrief." *Bibel und Leben*, XII (1971), 94–104.

Sabourin, L. "'Liturgie du sanctuaire et de la tente veritable' (Heb. viii. 2)." *New Testament Studies*, XVIII (1971), 87–90.

———. "Sacrificium ut liturgia in Epistula ad Hebraeos." *Verbum domini*, XLVI (1968), 235–58.

Salom, A. P. "Ta Hagia in the Epistle to the Hebrews." *Andrews University Seminary Studies*, V (1967), 59–70.

Schilling, Werner. "Die psychologischen Zusammenhänge von religiösem Urerlebnis, Sühngedanken und ethischem Handeln." *Guilt or Pollution and Rites of Purification*. Edited by H. W. Schneider and B. A. van Proosdij. E. J. Brill, 1968, 17–18.

Schmitt, J. "La pureté sadocite d'apres 1QS III, 4–9." *Revue des sciences religieuses*, XLIV (1970), 214–24.

Schmitz, Otto. "Sin and Guilt in the New Testament." *Twentieth Century Theology in the Making*, II, 177–185. Edited by Jaroslav Pelikan. Translated by R. A. Wilson. William Collins Sons and Co., 1970.

Schneider, Johannes. "Προσέρχομαι." *Theological Dictionary of the New Testament*. Vol. II.

Schrag, Calvin O. "Towards a Phenomenology of Guilt." *Journal of Existential Psychiatry*, III (1963), 333–42.

Schrager, F. "Der Gottesdienst der Hebräerbriefgemeinde." *Münchener theologische Zeitschrift*, XIX (1968), 161–81.

Schweizer, Eduard. "Σάρξ." *Theological Dictionary of the New Testament*. Vol. XII.

Scott, W. M. F. "Priesthood in the New Testament." *Scottish Journal of Theology*, X (1957), 399–415.

Simon, Marcel. "Souillure morale et souillure rituelle dans le Christianisme primitif." *Guilt or Pollution and Rites of Purification*. Edited by H. W. Schneider and B. A. van Proosdij. E. J. Brill, 1968, pp. 87–88.

Slater, Robert Lawson. "Buddhist Serenity and the Denial of Guilt." *Guilt or Pollution and Rites of Purification*. Edited by H. W. Schneider and B. A. van Proosdij. E. J. Brill, 1968, p. 145.

Snell, A. "We Have an Altar." *Reformed Theological Review*, XXIII (1964), 16–23.

Spicq, C. " L'Épître aux Hébreux: Apollos, Jean-Baptiste, les Hellénistes et Qumrân." *Revue de Qumran*, I (1959), 365–90.

Stendahl, Krister. "Biblical Theology, Contemporary." *The Interpreter's Dictionary of the Bible*, Vol. I.

Stewart, R. A. "The Sinless High-Priest." *New Testament Studies*, XIV (1967), 126–35.
Stott, W. "The Conception of 'Offering' in the Epistle to the Hebrews." *New Testament Studies*, I (1962), 62–67.
Streng, Frederick J. "The Problem of Symbolic Structures in Religious Apprehension." *History of Religions*, IV (1964), 126–53.
_____. "Purification through Non-Discrimination, according to Nāgārjuna." *Guilt or Pollution and Rites of Purification*. Edited by H. W. Schneider and B. A. van Proosdij. E. J. Brill, 1968, pp. 119–20.
Swetnam, J. "'The Greater and More Perfect Tent': A Contribution to the Discussion of Hebrews 9.11." *Biblica*, XLVII (1966), 91–106.
_____. "Hebrews 9.2 and the Uses of Consistency." *Catholic Biblical Quarterly*, XXXII (1970), 205–21.
_____. "On the Imagery and Significance of Hebrews 9.9–11." *Catholic Biblical Quarterly*, XXVIII (1966), 155–73.
_____. "Sacrifice and Revelation in the Epistle to the Hebrews: Observations and Surmises on Hebrews 9.26." *Catholic Biblical Quarterly*, XXX (1968), 227–34.
Takenaka, Shinjo. "The Significance of the Rite of Purification in Buddhism." *Guilt or Pollution and Rites of Purification*. Edited by H. W. Schneider and B. A. van Proosdij. E. J. Brill, 1968, pp. 167–68.
Tani, Seigo. "The Meaning of 'Harae' in Shintoism." *Guilt or Pollution and Rites of Purification*. Edited by H. W. Schneider and B. A. van Proosdij. E. J. Brill, 1968, pp. 190–91.
Tatia, Nathmal. "Purification in Jainism." *Guilt or Pollution and Rites of Purification*. Edited by H. W. Schneider and B. A. van Proosdij. E. J. Brill, 1968, pp. 130–32.
Thornton, T. C. G. "The Meaning of αἱματεκχυσία in Heb. 9.22." *Journal of Theological Studies*, XV (1964), 63–65.
Thüsing, W. "‚Lasst uns hinzutreten....' (Hebr 10.22). Zur Frage nach dem Sinn der Kulttheologie im Hebräerbrief." *Biblische Zeitschrift*, IX (1965), 1–17.
Tillich, Paul. "The Nature of Religious Language." *Theology of Culture*. Edited by Robert C. Kimball. Oxford University Press, 1959, pp. 53–67.
_____. "The Problem of Theological Method." *Journal of Religion*, XXVII (1947), 16–26.
_____. "The Religious Symbol." *Symbolism in Religion and Literature*. Edited by Rollo May. George Braziller, 1960, pp. 75–98.
_____. "The Significance of the History of Religions for the Systematic Theologian." *The History of Religions: Essays on the Problem of Understanding*. Edited by Joseph M. Kitagawa, Mircea Eliade, and Charles H. Long. University of Chicago Press, 1967, 241–55.
_____. "Theology and Symbolism." *Religious Symbolism*. Edited by F. Ernest Johnson. Kennikat Press, 1969, 107–16.
Torm, Frederik. "Om τελειοῦν i Hebraeerbrevet." *Svensk exegetisk orsbok*, V (1940), 116–25.
Vanhoye, A. "De 'aspectu' oblationis Christi secundum Epistolam ad Hebraeos." *Verbum domini*, XXXVII (1959), 32–38.

———. "De instauratione novae Dispositionis (Heb 9.15-23)." *Verbum domini*, XLIV (1966), 113-30.

———. "Longue marche ou accès tout proche? Le contexte biblique de Hébreux 3.7-4, 11." *Biblica*, XLIX (1968), 9-26.

———. "Mundatio per sanguinem (Heb 9.22-23)." *Verbum domini*, XLIV (1966), 177-91.

———. "Par la tente plus grande et plus parfaite ... (Heb 9.11)." *Biblica*, XLVI (1965), 1-28.

———. "La structure centrale de l'Épître aux Hébreux (Heb. 8.1-9.28)." *Recherches de science religieuse*, XLVII (1959), 44-60.

———. "De structura litteraria Epistolae ad Hebraeos." *Verbum domini*, XL (1962), 73-80.

———. "Thema sacerdotii praeparatur in Heb. 1.1-2, 18." *Verbum domini*, XLVII, (1969), 284-97.

Vereno, Matthias. "Ritual und Bewusstseinswandlung als zwei Aspekte von Sühne und Versöhnung." *Kairos*, VIII (1966), 125-29.

Villapadierna, C. de. "La alianza en la Epistola a los Hebreos: Ensayo de nueva interpretacion a Hebrews 9.15-20." *Estudios Biblicos*, XXI (1962), 273-96.

Wach, Joachim. "The Place of the History of Religions in the Study of Theology." *Journal of Religion*, XXVII (1947), 157-77.

Wallace, Anthony F. C. "Rituals: Sacred and Profane." *Zygon*, I (1966), 60-81.

Weckman, George. "Understanding Initiation." *History of Religions*, X (1970), 62-79.

Wheelwright, Philip. "Hamartia and Its Resolution in Three Religious Perspectives." *Guilt or Pollution and Rites of Purification*. Edited by H. W. Schneider and B. A. van Proosdij. E. J. Brill, 1968, pp. 15-16.

Wikgren, Allen. "Patterns of Perfection in the Epistle to the Hebrews." *New Testament Studies*, VI (1960), 159-67.

Wilder, Amos N. "The Cross: Social Trauma or Redemption." *Symbolism in Religion and Literature*. Edited by Rollo May. George Braziller, 1960, pp. 99-117.

Williamson, R. "Hebrews and Doctrine." *Expository Times*, LXXI (1970), 371-76.

———. "Platonism and Hebrews." *Scottish Journal of Theology*, XVI (1963), 415-24.

www.ingramcontent.com/pod-product-compliance
Lightning Source LLC
Chambersburg PA
CBHW071334110526
44591CB00010B/1140